I0187792

The Intelligence War in Afghanistan

The Intelligence War in Afghanistan

Regional and International Intelligence
Agencies Play the Tom & Jerry Endless
Game on the Local Chessboard

Musa Khan Jalalzai

Vij Books India Pvt Ltd

New Delhi (India)

Published by

Vij Books India Pvt Ltd
(Publishers, Distributors & Importers)
2/19, Ansari Road
Delhi – 110 002
Phones: 91-11-43596460, 91-11-47340674
Fax: 91-11-47340674
e-mail: vijbooks@rediffmail.com
www.vijbooks.com

Copyright © 2019, *Author*

ISBN: 978-93-88161-49-7 (Hardback)
ISBN: 978-93-88161-50-3 (ebook)

All rights reserved.

No part of this book may be reproduced, stored in a retrieval system, transmitted or utilised in any form or by any means, electronic, mechanical, photocopying, recording or otherwise, without the prior permission of the copyright owner. Application for such permission should be addressed to the publisher.

Contents

Introduction

Blood can't wash Blood or revenge can't repair the damage......howsoever, strong your armies may be, you will always need the favour of the inhabitants to the possession of a province. If a forest catches fire, both the dry and the wet will burn. (Afghan Persian Proverbs)

Afghanistan today looks aloof. The US spun out war has now stretched out. As 2018 gave way to 2019, the war mellowed into a terror-stricken shape-pushing the panic button. The American civil society lives under Cimmerian-Shade about the war strategy Pentagon has adopted. Majority of security experts have got the real picture of the CIA and Pentagon failure to bring home Gallus-Gallus chicken. Coalition casualties are rapidly pullulating, while Afghanistan has become the trauma state. The US civilian and military leadership were routinely issuing inflated assessments of progress that contradicted what was actually happening in major provinces of Afghanistan since 2001. They were unable to explain their yearning and hankering. The real failure of the American army in Afghanistan is much broader than the internal cold war in the White House. Disastrously, the entire national security infrastructure of the country failed to recognize or acknowledge the actual misalliance. More worrisome is the inability of CIA, MI6, and Pentagon to address the need of regional players for peace in Afghanistan.

The US outstretched war kept the ball rolling to devastate lives in Afghanistan.[1] The war cracked resources and strategic focus, while the US army remained cemented to strategic nothingness in the country.[2] For all that, how many states deployed their regular troops and private militias, the road ahead was full of slipperiness and precariousness.[3] Direct talks (2018) with the Taliban symbolized to find out an easy escape, but this war has become President Trump's increasingly bloody worriment.[4] It is time to declare defeat as there is no shame in defeat, but there is shame in covering up the truth.[5] "The United States "cannot win militarily in Afghanistan", General Austin Scott Miller, (2018) the top US commander in the country conceded in an interview with NBC News.[6] On 21 August 2017, in his Port Myer speech, President Trump also advocated the idea:

> "I share the American people's frustration. I also share their frustration over a foreign policy that has spent too much time, energy, money, and most importantly lives, trying to rebuild countries in our own image, instead of pursuing our security interests above all other considerations. That is why, shortly after my inauguration, I directed Secretary of Defence Mattis and my national security team to undertake a comprehensive review of all strategic options in Afghanistan and South Asia"[7]

President Trump's abrupt announcement of troop withdrawal from Afghanistan, and all at once, White House rubbished media reports (Dawn-2018) in an emailed statement: "The President has not made a determination to draw down United States military presence in Afghanistan and he has not directed the Department of Defence to begin the process of withdrawing US personnel from Afghanistan". These contradictory and antithetical statements of the President clearly stipulated his frustration, and exasperation, and exposed the increasingly undependable position of his government.

Analyst Sara flounders (2018) viewed the decision of President Trump as a complete failure of the US military establishment: "The announcement has opened a chasm within U.S. ruling circles. Resignations from the Trump administration and ensuing denunciations are calling the attention of the masses to the heated conflict. Mattis' resignation reflects how the announced withdrawal is a dramatic break with countries that have collaborated with the U.S. in Syria, such as France, Germany, Belgium and Britain. All of them are former colonial powers that destroyed Indigenous cultures and looted the Americas, Africa and Asia".[8]

Non-observance and weariness of the US and NATO commanders in Afghanistan is comparatively perceptible from their untraditional anger against Children and women they killed with impunity. The war brought instability, hatred, disparities and destruction[8,] and the US army shamelessly uses an eye for eye strategies - kills civilians and destroys national critical infrastructure. Due to the rivalries of different regional powers, peace became far away dream in Afghanistan, while the United States and its allies also comprehended the disputed point.[9]

The longest war that impacted liberal societies in the West unfathomably in many ways; has now entered a crucial phase.[10] Russia and China have joined the theatre of war as the strongest stakeholders and dancing in the combat zones. After a dishonourable and discreditable defeat in Syria at the hands of the Russian army and President Asad's forces, the US President Donald Trump prepared a strategy to pull thousands of US troops out of Syria, but faced irritability in White House and Pentagon.[11] The allies also got out of joint and felt sore due to their whitewashing and embarrassment. They have now dog-tired to stand or act professionally.[12]

The US and NATO forces used all means of viciousness, including unwarrantable dog-rape, and dropped the most powerful Nonnuclear-Mother-of-Bombs which caused incurable disease, death and suffering.[13] They bombed houses, killed children and women with impunity, destroyed the Kunduz hospital and MSF's fully functioning trauma centre, but never succeeded in winning the loyalty of the Afghan nation.[14] Resentful by their kill and burn tactics, Afghan army turned its guns on their officers and soldiers killed hundreds inside forts and battlefield.[15] Throughout its three decades of war in Afghanistan, Washington's military operations have never been helpful to stabilize the country. Its strongest intelligence infrastructure failed (Fixing Intel, General Flynn 2010) to understand the mental outlook of the people of Afghanistan.[16]

The US war crimes are more irksome and heartbreaking. In 2012, a group of women were killed by US air strike in Laghman province. On 30 November 2018, a UN report noted the killing of 23 civilians by US forces. On 20 July 2018, air strike of US army killed fourteen members of a family, including three small children, in northern Afghanistan. On 15 December 2018, more than 20 women and children were killed intentionally by US army in Kunar Province. However, on 26 July 2010, Telegraph reported the killing of Afghan civilians by the British army. According to the Ministry of Defence report, (Mirror Online, 3 January 2015) British soldiers killed 186 innocent civilians in Afghanistan.

In 2010, an American soldier deliberately killed Afghan citizens for sport.[17] Global Research, on 25 November 2018, published revelations of Afghan writer, analyst, and representative of Revolutionary Association of the Women of Afghanistan (RAWA) on the intentional killings of US and NATO forces in Afghanistan. Mrs. Friba spotlighted the US-Taliban-ISIS's Tom & Jerry endless game on the local chessboard: "The ISIS and Taliban serve a dual purpose for the US in Afghanistan. While the UN's shameful past is one of a pro-US body, the ICC has yet to earn this unpopular status. The present wars in Afghanistan, Iraq, Libya and Syria are also testing grounds for the ICC to establish whether it is an impartial body that will go after all war criminals, or just be a pro-US body that ignores the crimes committed by the US and its allies and its puppets, like the UN... The majority of the attacks by the US are carried out without accurate intelligence and regard to civilian lives, resulting in bloody massacres through airstrikes, drone strikes, night raids, and shootings across Afghanistan".[18]

On 14 November 2013, Global Research in its report documented some aspects of US and NATO forces war crimes in Afghanistan: "The US war criminals remain unpunished. Accountability is denied. Conflict persists. Trillions of dollars go mass slaughter and destruction. They're spent for unchallenged global dominance. Children were massacred while they slept. Women were raped before soldiers killed them. Pentagon officials and mainstream media whitewashed what happened. Seventeen Afghan men were detained. They disappeared. Residents found 10 buried in shallow graves. They were several hundred meters from where US forces are based".[19]

What happened in Bagram prison was heartbreaking, and it can be seen in the CIA torture report prepared by Senator Diane Feinstein (D-CA).[20] With the materialization of that report, (Emran Feroze 2014) the world was reeling in shock at the level of brutality revealed in the documents: "Afghan prisoners were tied face down on small chairs. Then fighting dogs entered the torture chamber. If the prisoners did not say anything useful, each dog got to take a turn on them. After a procedure like these, they confessed everything. They would have even said that they killed Kennedy without even knowing who he was."[21]

On 11 September 2018, Voice of America (VOA) reported the United States discountenance to cooperate with the International Criminal Court.[22] National Security Adviser Mr. John Bolton told conservative Federalist Society in Washington that the court should not have jurisdiction over Americans or people from other nations that never ratified the treaty that created the court in 2002.[23] The VOA reported Bolton's statement on the ICC investigation that warned; "if it carried out the investigation of U.S. military actions in Afghanistan, the U.S. would ban its judges and prosecutors from entering the country, freeze any funds they have in U.S. financial institutions, and attempt to prosecute them in U.S. courts".[24]

The killing of innocent children in Kunar province in 2013 and 2018, and the MSF hospital strike of 2015 in Kunduz province that killed 42 and injured more than 30, were only a few incidents of the bloodshed caused by US actions in Afghanistan.[25] Notwithstanding all these atrocities of the US army, Security Advisor of President Trump warned (September 2018) that if ICC tried to investigate the War Crimes in Afghanistan its judges would be arrested.[26] The Prosecutor of the International Criminal Court, Mrs. Fatou Bensouda, issued her annual Report on Preliminary Examination Activities (2016). The Bensouda report spotlighted the US army torture and physical abuse of detainees:

"The information available suggests that victims were deliberately subjected to physical and psychological violence, and that crimes were allegedly committed with particular cruelty and in a manner that debased the basic human dignity of the victims. The infliction of "enhanced interrogation techniques," applied cumulatively and in combination with each other over a prolonged period of time, would have caused serious physical and psychological injury to the victims. Some victims reportedly exhibited psychological and behavioural issues, including hallucinations, paranoia, insomnia, and attempts at self-harm and self-mutilation".[27]

In spite of their sweat and continuous combat since the invasion of October 2001, the CIA, MI6, and Eye-5 Intelligence Alliance failed to put the Taliban insurgency in nutshell.[28] With the US forces demoralised faces, and the Taliban aggressive fighters-equipped with night-vision and sophisticated weapons, airstrikes became the last tenuous line of defence.[29] The failure of America's intervention in Afghanistan offered broader insight into the limits to its global power. President Trump, instead of the promised fundamentally different approach, repeated President Obama's go off in smoke and miss and boat strategy-to cut a deal with the Afghan Taliban, for which the U.S. needed the full backing of Pakistan's military establishment.[30]

Failure of Afghan intelligence agencies to defeat the Taliban in Afghanistan has deeply gloomed international community that consequences of wrongly designed counterinsurgency and counterterrorism strategies are consistently substandard.[31] Disorder and complications the United States and its allies created in Afghanistan are more evident than ever before.[32] Through its appalling and unsuccessfully engineered strategies and military adventures, the CIA, MI6, the NATO spy agencies, and Pentagon facilitated the rise of a new terrorist group (ISIS) that never existed prior to the war on terrorism in Afghanistan.[33] The US civilian and military intelligence fashioned a strategic mistake-reasoning that military action can put the state back in order, but unfortunately failed.[34] The British MI6 came to nothing to collect high-quality intelligence information from Helmand, while the EU intelligence agencies were also running wrong horses to meet security challenges in Afghanistan.[35]

During the last 18 years so-called war on terrorism in Afghanistan, we haven't read or seen any successful narrative from the National Directorate of Security (NDS) and Pentagon about their achievement and operational mechanism.[36] They were teetering on the brink, and all their technologies and billions of dollar-worth computers failed to lead policymakers on right direction.[37] The fall of Kunduz and Ghazni provinces, suicide attacks across the country, and the abrupt appearance of ISIS terrorist group in 2014, raised important questions about the failure and incompetence of the US and NATO intelligence to stabilize Afghanistan.[37]

Before the Taliban attack on Kunduz, Afghan intelligence operatives safely left the city without informing the government in Kabul,[38] while Pentagon and CIA reasoned that their five-billion dollar worth computer system had failed.[39] Intelligence war in Afghanistan has intensified since China and Russia sought a bigger role by supporting Taliban insurgents, and Pakistan. They received Taliban delegations in 2017 and 2018.[40] India was also in trouble and became adamant to tolerate Pakistan's presence in Afghanistan.[41] Notwithstanding its reluctant ties with Washington, India concerned that U.S. direct talks with the Taliban could lend respectability to a fanatical terrorist organization.[42]

Deploying under-trained and inexperienced intelligence officers-with limited knowledge of technical tools or key operational skills, resulted in the collection of low-quality disinformation, which led military commander on wrong direction.[43] The main objective of intelligence information gathering is to maintain a swift flow of information, but Afghan intelligence agents are not well-versed in this task.[44] In fact, writing on intelligence mechanism and operations of the NDS is an industrious task as there is limited information available to analysts and researchers in libraries and market, but I will try to touch all sources highlighting NDS and its operations in detail. The NDS is a remnant of the Khidmat-e-Etlaat-e-Dulat (KHAD), established in the 1980s, and trained by KGB experts, but after the US invasion in Afghanistan, its way of intelligence information collection changed and followed the CIA and Pentagon streaks in the war against terrorism in Afghanistan.[45]

After the fall of the Taliban regime in 2001, the CIA and Pentagon reinvented Afghan intelligence and trained it on controversial streaks.[46] The CIA, and Pentagon armed, trained and used NDS for their own operational purposes.[47] Afghan intelligence units needed more advanced technology, intercept capabilities and cross-communication between the National Directorate of Security (NDS) and security forces in the field, but the US and NATO forces failed to meet their requirements.[48] The National Directorate of Security (NDS) continued to suffer key intelligence capabilities, especially in gathering intelligence information from remote areas in order to prevent neighbouring states from interfering in the internal affairs of Afghanistan.[49]

The NDS officers collect unreliable, ethnicized, sectarianized and politicized intelligence information from illiterate sources in towns and cities, which could not occur beneficial to all stakeholders.[50] Many NDS personnel maintained loyalty to their ethnic and sectarian leaders, external and internal stakeholders, rather than the agency, and tended to act more like political leaders than spies.[51] Indian analyst, Manish Rai, has criticized ethnic composition and incompetency of the Afghan intelligence (NDS) in his article, and argued that this type of composition poses challenges to the ability of the agency:

> "The Afghan government has weak intelligence. Afghan forces require a robust intelligence collection and targeting capability if they want to turn back the tide of a reinvigorated Taliban insurgency. Afghanistan intelligence agency i.e. National Directorate of Security (NDS) not only suffers from an inability to share and disseminate actionable intelligence, but also is plagued by accusations of favouritism and nepotism. While its ethnic composition is dominated by Panjshiris Tajiks from Panjshir; a group affiliated with the former Northern Alliance. The NDS ethnic composition poses challenges to the intelligence agency's ability to infiltrate the Pashtun groups most likely affiliated with the continued insurgency in Afghanistan. There is also urgent need to increase more advanced voice intercept capabilities and cross-communication between the National Directorate of Security (NDS) and security forces in the field".[52]

The agency chief in 2018 warned that Russian and Iranian intelligence agencies provided assistance to Taliban under the pretext of fighting the Islamic State.[53] In 2017, NDS also alleged that Iran and Russia had teamed up to undermine the US-led stabilization mission in Afghanistan.[54] In fact, the presence of Russian and Chinese intelligence in Northern Afghanistan, and Southern parts of the country created fear, and complicated the process of intelligence information collection.[55] The secret war between Russian, Chinese and US strategic clandestine intelligence in Afghanistan raised serious question on the credibility of MI6, CIA and Afghan intelligence while they failed to counter rival intelligence agencies.[56]

The exponentially spreading web of foreign espionage in the region and recruitment of Afghans agents poorly caused fear and anxiety among policymakers that the country once again becoming the battlefield of new cold war.[57] Dr Abdullah in his statement raised concern about the existence of foreign spies within the state institutions: "Double agents are more dangerous than insurgents," he said.[58] The fall of Kunduz, Pakistan's re-engagement in the peace process and policy differences between the President and Intelligence Chief Rahmatullah Nabil, prompted his resignation.[59] He was, in fact, unprofessional, and an incompetent chief who knew nothing about the way intelligence operated. He was acting like a politician. His precursors were also street children who made the agency ethnicised, sectarianised and regionalised.[60] The yesteryears' news stories showed that former Afghan intelligence chiefs also acted like politicians and interfered in the decision making process in the country. Distrust between the government and intelligence chiefs affected friendly relations between Afghanistan and its neighbours. They openly issued statements on television channels and criticised government.[61]

They opposed Pakistan's role in the peace process and branded the country as an enemy of the Afghans. The way the NDS operated was mere an immature business.[62] Government and CIA tried to reform NDS to make it effective and its countrywide networks, which might lead the fight against ISIS and the Taliban in the right direction, but all decisions and proposals remained on paper. No single proposal was implemented.[63] The fact is Afghan leadership needed to depoliticise the agency, replace the old infrastructure with the new one, and expel illiterate elements from the agency appointed on ethnic and sectarian lines.[64]

The Mujahedeen and Taliban supporters within the intelligence agency were making things worse. The roots of the NDS needed to be re-established in the south and east, and the influence of drug smugglers and war criminals needed to be undermined, but resistance within the NDS agency forced the government to retreat.[65] The NDS' leaders were making money, purchasing properties in Pakistan, US, UK and Dubai, and plundering secret funds.[66]

When we read the role of NATO intelligence agencies, the CIA, Russian and Chinese intelligence, Defence and Strategic Clandestine Intelligence (DSCI) and the Pentagon, we come across several stories of intelligence failures in the country, because they were unable to stabilise the country or counter regional intelligence agencies effectively.[67] For the US and NATO intelligence agencies, the information needed by their military commanders to conduct a population-centric counter-insurgency operation was very important, but they could not retrieve it from remote districts, towns and villages.[68] When intelligence is ignored or then twisted to produce the desired result, it is truly a failure. The US and NATO allies approach to cooperation on civilian and military levels with regional intelligence agencies has never been satisfactory.[69]

Mistrust between CIA, NDS, ISI, and NATO intelligence agencies caused complete failure in the war against the Taliban, and rival intelligence agencies. Every intelligence agency of the alliance acted individually and never tried to share its secrets with others. The ISI remained weak and unprofessional in its actions and mechanism in Baluchistan and FATA. While failing to reinvent its networks and contacts in these two provinces, the ISI started the business of forced disappearance and killed thousands Pashtuns and Baluchs extra-judicially.[70] The development of foreign intelligence networks in these two provinces overnight was the worse failure of ISI and IB to professionalize intelligence mechanism.[71] Having failed to collect all intelligence information from remote areas of Khyber Pakhtunkhwa and Baluchistan, the ISI started recruiting children for suicide bombing inside Afghanistan. (Musharaf interview-2015) This dirty business of Pakistani agencies caused deep resentment among Afghans and Pakistan's civil society.[72]

For a professional intelligence network to be relevant in counter-insurgency operations, it needs to supply wide-ranging military information from the war zone to commanders and policymakers. In January 2010, a US commander in Afghanistan, Mike Flynn, prepared an intelligence report that uncovered some of the worst US intelligence failures in Afghanistan. General Flynn complained that intelligence was working hard but it was doing the wrong job. Later on, he suggested the separation of counterinsurgency strategy (COIN) from intelligence operations.[73]

In his Fixing Intel paper, General Flynn sought to drive home the concept that the US intelligence needed to collect information about the population of Afghanistan.[74] The US military commanders admitted to having very little knowledge of Afghan culture and Taliban insurgents. They showed a predilection for military-led approaches to problems, including those that were essentially political.[75] Research scholar Matt Waldman described the flawed policies of the US and its allies in a recent article: "In the eyes of US officials and informed observers, high-level US policy-making on Afghanistan was severely impaired by fundamental, structural flaws, many of which are interrelated and reinforcing."[76] Another US commander, General Eikenberry, criticised the counterinsurgency strategy promoted by General Petraeus.[77] A new intelligence report from the US army also highlighted the failure of intelligence in Afghanistan. The US National Intelligence Estimate (NIE) warned that the country would quickly fall into chaos if former President Hamid Karzai refused to sign a security deal with the US.[78]

The NIE, which includes input from 16 intelligence agencies in the US, predicted that the Taliban would become more influential as US forces drawdown at the end of 2014.[79] Moreover, in response to these allegations, former Afghan President Hamid Karzai expressed concern that his country was the victim of a war that only served the interests of the US and its western allies:

"Afghans died in a war that is not ours," President Karzai said in an interview with The Washington Post on 02 March 2014.[80] President Karzai said he was in trouble for war casualties, including those in US military operations, and felt betrayed by what he described as insufficient US focus on going after Taliban sanctuaries inside Pakistan.[81]

The US and its allies should know that Chinese and Russian agencies seek influence in the country as a means of securing their borders. In reality, the presence of US forces in Afghanistan provided China with a sense of stability. Beijing understood that now the US was focusing on terrorist networks in the country, and it was in China's interest to engage NATO and US forces there. With the geographical expansion of the Islamic state terrorist network, and the emergence of Khurasan terrorist group in Jalalabad province of Afghanistan in 2014, Russia and China comprehended that these development were a direct threat to their national security and territorial integrity.

On 16 October 2017, Tolonews quoted the report of the Times of London, which noted Russian involvement in Afghanistan.[82] The report said that Russia's intelligence services were sending fleets of fuel tankers into Afghanistan through the Hairatan border crossing with Uzbekistan to companies operating on behalf of the Taliban.[83] The Times reported that about $2.5 million USD was raised in cash from the sale of that fuel each month, which was then delivered directly to insurgent paymasters. According to the report, Russia accelerated its support in an apparent attempt to bolster the Taliban against Daesh.[84] "We sell the fuel on and distribute the money directly to our commanders," a Taliban treasurer from Ghazni province told The Times.[85] He had been authorized to speak to a journalist as part of the Taliban's efforts to advertise their relationship with international backers. Russian military sources warned that terrorists retreating from Syria and Iraq by sea to the port of Karachi in Southern Pakistan. After that, they get to Peshawar near the Afghan border and settle in Nangarhar province.[86]

On 02 August 2018, an article of analyst Mr. Nicholas Trickett in Diplomat Magazine explained Russian involvement in Afghanistan: "There are plenty of reasons to seriously examine Russia's role in Afghanistan, but too many articles fail to ask questions fundamental to making sense of Moscow's aims. By refusing to closely scrutinize the facts on the ground, the role of China, and the logic of U.S. policy, the authors of many pieces can claim expertise but never be held accountable for their analysis. Russia is certainly an adversarial power for Washington, but Afghanistan deserves more than talking points from an aerial view".[87]

Warlord Muhammad Gulab Mangal (former governor of Jalalabad) has been the main focus of local and international newspapers in the past. His corruption, land-grabbing business, and his association with the Islamic State terrorist group (ISIS) retarded and enmeshed his personality and loyalty to his motherland. Some tabloid papers interviewed local resident about his illegal business in Jalalabad. Commentators painted an ugly picture of his political and administrative strategies. Mr. Gulab Mangal could not perform as a professional Governor the people of Nangarhar were expecting. But local officials in Nangarhar said he had failed to tackle endemic corruption in the province, which included mismanagement of Torkham border post, the main crossing point into Pakistan for goods and people as well as major smuggling routes.[88] "In Nangarhar, if five Afghanis were going to the smugglers, three of these were received by provincial officials," said Sohrab Qaderi, a member of the local provincial council.[90] Astute News, in its 27 May 2018 report, and Off Guardian News, in its 20 May 2018 commentary explained the role of warlord Gulab Mengal in strengthening the ISIS terrorist group in Jalalabad province:

> "Governor of Nangarhar province, Gulab Mangal, personally oversees militant activities in the region, which plans to expand its influence over other regions of the country at the expense of the radicals. In addition, he actively participates in the financial activities of the Islamic State (ISIS), receiving significant profits.[91] The network informs that any protest actions of the population dissatisfied with the activities of the Islamic State are "severely suppressed by the provincial

authorities, including through punitive operations against whole settlements."[92] Expressing concern on the existence of Daesh terrorist group, Nangarhar lawmakers in the lower house of Parliament said that: "their clients had been fed up with oppression and terror of armed groups and if they are not eliminated these people would have to take refuge or join forceful the terrorists"[93].

The current international confluence of interest to stabilize Afghanistan continues to remain in place, but tranquillity and calmness remained elusive and all endeavours made in this regard came to a stalemate.[94] A bunch of institutions and counsels were formed on the hope of replacing war with a political monologue in Afghanistan, but violence, insurgency and suicide terrorism continue to inflict huge fatalities on the civilian population of the country.[95] Institutions destroyed, and the state has been shattered. Afghan high peace council was established to promote harmony, but failed as the new chapter of the Islamic State (ISIL) was added to the unending conflict of Afghanistan.

Washington, London and Brussels are in dire straits and tumult. Their pain is aggravating by the day when they look at the ungovernable insider attacks against their forces. By Washington's own admission, (Aasim Sajjad Akhtar-2018) "the Taliban still control large parts of the Afghan countryside", but Afghanistan still remains unstable.[96] In Manoj Kumar Mishra (2018) discernment and comprehension, the United States has failed to manage the geographical expansion of the current conflict in Afghanistan: "The complex and volatile nature of intra-state conflicts such as the one that has been unfolding in Afghanistan proved difficult for the US to manage as they fell outside the purview of conventional warfare strategies and professional standing armies, rather than involving civilian concerns and predicaments at each stage".[97]

Musa Khan Jalalzai
February 2019, London

Chapter -1

The Intelligence War in Afghanistan

Regional and International Intelligence Agencies Play the Tom & Jerry Endless Game on the Local Chessboard

The United States and its allies are in a tight spot and pickle. The US and NATO war in Afghanistan has seen pretty much every style of American war-making. None of the strategies of their military establishment could ensure security in the country. The Islamic Terrorist State in Afghanistan (ISKP) controlled major mining sites in Jalalabad province, while Taliban controlled a major portion of the Badakhshan mining industry. On 22 May 2018, Global Witness in its press release warned that the terrorist group (ISIS) in Afghanistan controlled large talc, marble and chromites mines in Achin district. The press release also noted that: "The evidence on how much ISKP have been able to mine and profit from the minerals is mixed, but there has been at least some activity–and the group has fought major battles with the Taliban over neighbouring districts containing even richer deposits. A Taliban commander explicitly linked the ferocity of the conflict to competition over resources, saying: "The fight is over the mines." The Global Witness reported.[1]

As President Ghani recognized the risk of falling victim to the resource curse, in many ways, minerals have become militarized, and are the biggest source of extremists' funding-driving instability across the country. The government, its foreign partners, private criminal militias, Taliban, rogue-governors, war criminals, and the ISIS-all share the biggest slice of the cake, and continue to challenge the authority of the failed state. The Global Witness has made an excellent attempt to investigate the plunder of mineral recourses of Afghanistan that fuel violence. The mines of the rugged North-Eastern province of Badakhshan, the Global Witness report indicated, have been one of the richest assets of the Afghan people. For now, the lapis which supplies much of the world market is, by any reasonable definition, a conflict mineral, GW reported.[2] Global Witness (June 2016) in its report documented important evidence of the involvement of ISIS, Taliban, Central Asian and Pakistan militant groups in stealing natural resourced of Afghanistan; The report focuses on Badakhshan province where these groups have established military training camps:

> Badakhshan's minerals have caused instability and conflict firstly and most directly as a prize to be fought over by strongmen, insurgents, and armed groups, using both political and military means. The abusive competition for the mines has both required conditions of lawlessness, conflict, and a hollowed-out and subverted state, and has provided the means to create them. With or without the façade of government control, one underlying dynamic has been constant: the struggle among armed groups – whether insurgents, militias, or supposedly official forces – for control of a scarce resource. Alongside the Taliban are a smaller number of foreign fighters linked to other militant groups, including the Islamic Movement of Uzbekistan (IMU), Jundullah, Jamaat Ansarullah, Sepahi Sahaba, and the Eastern Turkistan Islamic Movement (ETIM). The IMU's affiliation to the Islamic State in 2015 adds to concerns that Badakhshan is becoming a strategic refuge for militants aiming to take their fight to China, Pakistan, and central Asia (though there are important caveats about the strength of these groups and their operational links to each other and to IS). That concern can only be further increased by evidence from one source that IS has a particular strategic interest in the mines. Foreign militants in the province (along with a substantial number of their women and children), mainly

located in the Khostak valley of Jurm district – an analysis largely supported by other sources. An individual close to the insurgency cited in a more recent report spoke of around 400 IMU militants, operating in Jurm, Yamgan and Warduj districts: between them, the reports mention Uzbeks, Tajiks, Kyrghiz, Kazakhs, Pakistanis, Chechens and Uighurs among the fighters.[3]

The war in Afghanistan has become the war on natural resources. Mineral resources are the bone of contention between the Taliban and the ISIS terrorist groups. The United States established several military bases near the Chinese border to closely watch movements of the Chinese military. Prof Michel Chossudovsky (2018) in his Global Research article has described the consequences of US-Afghan security pact that allowed the Pentagon to establish several military facilities located within proximity of Chinese Western frontiers:

> Under the Afghan-US security pact, established under Obama's Asian pivot, Washington and its NATO partners have established a permanent military presence in Afghanistan, with military facilities located within proximity of China's Western frontier. The pact was intended to allow the US to maintain their nine permanent military bases, strategically located on the borders of China, Pakistan and Iran as well as Turkmenistan, Uzbekistan and Tajikistan. In recent developments, President Trump in his February 28, 2017 address to a joint session of Congress vowed to "demolish and destroy" terrorist groups in Syria and Iraq as well as in Afghanistan under a fake counter-terrorism mandate. According to Foreign Affairs, "there are more U.S. military forces deployed there [Afghanistan] than to any other active combat zone" and their mandate is to go after the Taliban, Al Qaeda and ISIS (which are supported covertly by US intelligence). US military bases in Afghanistan are also intent upon protecting the multibillion narcotics trade. Narcotics at present constitutes the centrepiece of Afghanistan's export economy.[4]

Afghans have been unable to benefit from there mineral assets. Corruption, greediness, and illiteracy caused pillage and plunder of national resources. Unity government and its partner-war criminals have adopted war as a profitable business in their country. Afghanistan Times in its editorial piece described the suffering of Afghans and the plunder of their menial assets:

> Keeping in view the existing circumstances, it is mandatory on the Afghan government to realize its responsibilities of taking steps for making the Afghans united for pulling Afghanistan out of existing crises. And the consensus amongst Afghans always developed through traditional Loya Jirga meetings and assemblies. Almost Afghans are uncertain at this crucial stage as apart from the US and several other global powers, the neighbouring and regional countries are also making a huge investment on militants just to continue war flames and hostilities in Afghanistan.[4]

Now, with the establishment of the ISIS terror group in Afghanistan in 2014, several Western scholars termed it an unwelcome development in the war-torn country, but for Washington, Brussels, and London, it is a welcome development. Russia and China reacted to these abrupt developments in a traditional military means, and started reinventing their old contact in Afghanistan to intercept the ISIS infiltration into their territories.[5] Analyst Anatol Lieven painted a new story of the new cold war between Russia and the United States:

> It is a near consensus among scholars who have devoted their lives to the study of international security that the main drivers of great power competition are trending upwards. An under-analyzed challenge is great powers' propensity to meddle in each others' domestic affairs. Possessing by far the greatest capacity to make and break global orders, great powers belong in a class by themselves. That Russia is in certain respects acting against perceived Western interests is obvious (as in Ukraine), but so too is the fact that in other respects Russia has been aligned with many Western countries, or where it has differed with them, has subsequently

been proved right even from the West's own point of view. Thus Russia sided with Germany and France in opposing the US invasion of Iraq, and they have been proved correct by history. Russia opposed the USA, Britain and France in their campaign to overthrow Gaddafi, and has also been proved correct. Russia is aligned with Britain, France, Germany and the EU in supporting the Iran nuclear deal. Russia is allied with all the Western powers against the Islamic State, Al Qaeda and Islamist terrorism. Russia and the West appear to differ in their attitudes to the Syrian conflict but in fact do so a great deal less than is generally reported, if only because the USA and the West, in general, have no actual plan for how to replace the Baath regime.[6]

On 23 March 2018, the US commander told BBC that Russia was arming Taliban. There were speculations that Russian intelligence established strong networks across Afghanistan, recruits fighters in Spetsnaz Commando camps, train spies, and its old friends. "Russia is supporting and even supplying arms to the Taliban, the head of US forces in Afghanistan told the BBC. In an exclusive interview, Gen John Nicholson said he'd seen "destabilising activity by the Russians."[7] He said Russian weapons were smuggled across the Tajik border to the Taliban, but could not say in what quantity.[4] In his well-written analysis in the National Interest Newspaper, Mr. Arid Raffia unveiled Russian plan of supporting and arming Taliban groups against the US and Afghan forces:

Surprisingly, Afghanistan is emerging as another arena in which Moscow is pointedly working at odds with Washington's interests. Indeed, recent moves by Russia now represent a pivot toward Afghanistan, posing a set of challenges that have been unanticipated by U.S. observers of the region. The incoming Trump Administration ought to be aware of Russia's newfound assertiveness vis-à-vis Afghanistan, both in the threats it poses as well as the potential opportunities it may present. In late December, Moscow hosted a trilateral dialogue with Beijing and Islamabad on the future of Afghanistan. Importantly, left out of the talks were Kabul, Washington and

New Delhi—a historic Russian ally now moving closer to the United States. The joint statement released after the dialogue expressed support for talks with the Afghan Taliban and concern over the spread of Islamic State. The Russo-Sino-Pak trilateral did not emerge out of thin air. It is the latest in a series of Russian efforts to engage both Islamabad and the Afghan Taliban. Together, these moves mark a definitive departure from Moscow's decades-old policy toward the region.....Russian concerns clearly go beyond the Islamic State and the drug trade. It sees the residual U.S. presence in Afghanistan as a latent threat. In a lengthy interview with Turkey's Andale Agency, Ambassador Zamia Kabuli, Russia's top Afghanistan hand, expressed concern over a long-term U.S. military presence in the region, stating that there is no "clear-cut answer" as to why the United States "want[s] land bases in Afghanistan." Kabulov claimed that the present U.S. infrastructure in Afghanistan gives it "two to four weeks to redeploy up to 100,000 soldiers on the same bases.[8]

Pakistan's operation in North Waziristan didn't eliminate terrorists but pushed all outfits into Afghanistan, where their leadership was based.[9] Over the past 18 years, the gap between the Russian and U.S. strategies grown. Russia increasingly believed that the United States' approach wasn't working and that political will in Washington for continued engagement would run out before long.[10] Russian categorically said that it must be prepared to deal with an unstable Afghanistan on its own. Sources in Russian military intelligence agency confirmed that the preparation of a full-scale offensive operation against Russia through Tajikistan and Uzbekistan was in the final phase.[11]

On 06 October 2018, Tolo News reported US Gen. Joseph L. Votel, warned that Russia followed a strategy to compete with the United States around the world, including Afghanistan. Gen Votel said in an interview with VOA that Moscow and Tehran were trying to increase their influence in Afghanistan. The VOA noted that Moscow was posturing to be a "player in the solution" to the decades-long conflict."I think what they [Russia] are doing trying to do is they are pursuing a strategy which is to compete with us by trying to exert their influence wherever they can, whether it is in Afghanistan or Syria or anywhere else," Gen Votel said.[12]

On 02 April, BBC spotlighted some aspects of Russian involvement in Afghanistan. International print and electronic media also published commentaries and opinions on Russia's support to Taliban insurgents in some provinces of Afghanistan: "The US accuses Russia of trying to destabilise Afghanistan by supporting the Taliban. Senior US officials have been saying for years that Moscow even supplied the militants with weapons. Afghan government alleged that Russian intelligence helped the Taliban capture of Kunduz in 2015 and 2016, shortly after Mullah Abdul Salam–one of the insurgents' "shadow governors"–travelled to Tajikistan.[13] According to Afghan and western officials, Russia met several times with Taliban representatives secretly. The Russian involvement in the country can be seen in the context of its support to President Asad regime and its geopolitical ambitions in the greater Middle East. On 21 May 2018, analyst Andrey Afanasyev's commentary on the ISIS operation and Russian fear spotlighted some important aspects of the geographical expansion of the group:

> Sources in the Russian military and intelligence agencies, confirmed that the preparation of a full-scale offensive operation against Russia through Tajikistan and Uzbekistan is in the final phase. Citing data from closed communication channels with defence ministries of China, Pakistan and Afghanistan, they say that Afghanistan is the cornerstone issue in this plan. Similar messages have been received earlier; in particular, this was mentioned at a recent security conference held in Uzbek capital Tashkent.[14]

However, Tajikistan's Foreign Minister Sirodzhddin Aslov, expressed the same concern: "We see the activation of terrorist groups, their advancement to the northern regions of Afghanistan, especially in the territories bordering with Tajikistan, the increase in the number of ISIS supporters, and the participation of a certain number of citizens of the post-Soviet republics in the terrorist groups and movements present in Afghanistan

... this causes our serious concern". Aslov said.[15] The Guardian newspaper, on 22 October 2017 published a news story, in which concerns of the Afghan government were accentuated. After the Russian Taliban carried out successful attacks in Farah province, Afghan government called on Moscow to stop supporting the Taliban.[16] The newspaper underscored the frustration of Afghan commanders and police chiefs about the emergence of Russian Taliban in Afghanistan:

> After weeks of intense battles in the western Farah province–in which Taliban fighters nearly overran the provincial capital for the third time in a year–the commander of the Afghan army's 207th Corps became the latest official to point the finger at Russia. The Guardian reported. "Many large countries are involved in the Afghan war. We can name Russia, who is actively meddling in Farah, and we have seized Russian-made weapons, including night vision sniper scopes," the commander, Brig Gen Mohammad Naser Hedayat, said. Speaking to local television, a local police chief asked the Kabul government to summon the Russian ambassador in protest. The Guardian reported.[17]

On 05 February 2018, analyst Ahmad Majidyar in his paper noted frustration of Afghan intelligence chief about the involvement of Russian intelligence in Afghanistan. Masoom Stanekzai warned that Iranian and Russian intelligence agencies train, arm and financially help Taliban:

> In an interview with the BBC Persian, Mohammad Masoom Stanekzai pointed out that Tehran and Moscow provide assistance to the Taliban under the pretext of fighting the Islamic State, which has gained a foothold in South Asia in recent years. The Afghan intelligence chief, however, cautioned that such a policy is ill-advised as the Taliban and ISIS are two sides of the same coin. He pointed out that the Kabul government has evidence the Taliban are importing foreign fighters, including ISIS militants, into northern Afghanistan and Central Asia. He rejected the allegation that certain Afghan officials support the Taliban. "If we're

spreading rumours for our political ends without analyzing them, we need to assess their impact on the national interest. This provides an excuse to other countries that say the Taliban are better than ISIS and seek their support to eliminate ISIS.[18]

Intelligence sharing and cooperation on law enforcement level remains an important weapon for international actors in any theatre of war whether dealing with covert action or information sharing.[19] This is an effective weapon of the state and law enforcement institutions in dealing with national security challenges as well. Intelligence sharing constitutes an interference with the right to privacy,[20] and also permits states access to data collected through mass surveillance programs.[21] Today, intelligence sharing is not confined to the handover of discrete information, but can encompass direct and unfettered access to "raw" data as it transits the internet or held in databases.[22] The basic task in using intelligence to develop a doctrine and forces for deterrence and defence is to estimate threats posed by adversaries, in terms of both capabilities and intentions, over a period of several years.[23] This risk is particularly acute where intelligence is shared with states with authoritarian governments, weak rule of law and/or a history of systematically violating human rights.[24]

The new scope and scale of intelligence gathering has given rise to a new scope and scale of the sharing of that intelligence between governments, particularly in response to the threats to national security. In these contexts, such intelligence may form the basis for extrajudicial killings or contribute to unlawful arrest or detention or to torture and other cruel, inhuman or degrading treatment.[25] In Afghanistan; intelligence war caused sexual abuses, killing of women and children. A spate of current war crime allegations against Australian and US army is indeed a matter of great concern.[26]

The current international efforts to stabilize Afghanistan continue to remain in place, but tranquillity and calmness remained elusive as all endeavours made in this regard came to a stalemate. On 21 December 2018, AFP reported President Donald Trump's decision to pull out almost 50 per cent of US troops from Afghanistan.[27] This surprise move stunned and dismayed foreign diplomats and officials in Kabul who were involved in an intensifying push to end the 18-year conflict. Defence Secretary Jim Mattis resigned-saying his views were no longer reconcilable with Trump's.[25] The US maintained about 14,000 troops in Afghanistan working either with a NATO mission to support Afghan forces or in separate counter-terrorism operations. The Wall Street Journal reported that more than 7,000 troops would be returning from Afghanistan.[28]

A bunch of institutions and counsels were formed on the hope of replacing war with political monologue in Afghanistan, but violence, insurgency and suicide terrorism continued to inflict huge fatalities on the civilian population of the country. Institutions destroyed, and the state has been shattered. Afghan high peace council was established to promote harmony, but failed as a new chapter of the Islamic State (ISIL) was added to the unending conflict of Afghanistan.[29]

From 2014 to 2016, Afghan intelligence (NDS) outlined several strategies including constancy with the ISIS Khurasan Group that established its networks in more than 20 provinces of Afghanistan. In 2016, the ISIS started carrying out suicide attacks with the help of NDS across the country. On 16 November 2016; Wall Street Journal reported the ISIS suicide attack in Capital Kabul, in which 6 people were killed. The Islamic State of Khurasan, the journal reported killed more than 80 civilians in Kabul in July 2016, but NDS never tried to bring it to justice. Centre for Land Warfare Studies (CLAWS) in one of its reports warned that after 15 years war on terrorism in Afghanistan, scope of optimism is bleak.[30]

The NDS then adopted a strategy of ethnic divide. The agency supported one group against another. In fact, the influx of terrorist groups like ISIS and Taliban in the major province was impossible without the support of NDS, Afghan Parliamentarians, politicians', and military commanders alleged. Control of ISIS and Taliban over many districts, challenged the writ of the administration, where due to the wave of terror reign, thousands of Afghan families left the region for a safe place. International Rescue Committee (2016) in its report spotlighted the causes of insecurity in Afghanistan. However, the United Nation Assistance Mission in Afghanistan (UNAMA) also reported the miseries of internally displaced people in 2016.[31] The UN experts' spotlighted more than 45,000 terrorists fighting against the Afghan army across the country. Propaganda machine of the Islamic State (ISIS) is also causing great concern for parents as their school-going children become a victim of the so-called jihadist culture.

The Afghan secret services were unable to collect true intelligence information, or adapt professional measures in countering Taliban insurgency in the country. The NDS represents several political and religious stakeholders, and operates on wrongly designed ethnic and sectarian strategies. Moreover, NDS works indeed to further American and NATO agendas and, help Daesh (ISIS) in targeting Afghan National Army and civilian population across the country. Analyst Anant Mishra describes incompetency and failing strategies of NDS and its stakeholders:

Intelligence agencies in Afghanistan are failing to collect high-value information that could be beneficial to Afghan's domestic security. Deploying under-trained and inexperienced intelligence officers, with limited knowledge of technical tools or key operational skills, results in the collection of inadequate information [as well as inefficient] flow and management. With amateurish operational skills, these agents are unable to collect vital information for state security; some, even in the best of their experience, collect poor quality intelligence. Information collected from major known terror outfits and key government institutions could force policymakers and military leadership to make wrong decisions. The main objective of intelligence gathering is to maintain a swift flow of information, but the NDS officers are not well versed in this task. For example, the successful capture of Kunduz (a province in northern Afghanistan) by the Taliban did not occur because of their weapons superiority or technical expertise in battlefield; it happened because of massive failure of intelligence cooperation and coordination between the NDS, the National Security Agency of Afghanistan (NSA), the Ministry of Defence (MoD), and the Interior Ministry (MoI)........It is important to note that, right from the initial establishment of the NDS with the assistance from the US Central Intelligence Agency (CIA), collecting and disseminating intelligence, managing information flow and formulating clear operational objectives have all constituted major challenges.[32]

The NDS lacks technical abilities to counter foreign intelligence, while it has also been under resources for years. The NDS ignored relevant and vital information while responding untimely, or withholding certain intelligence vital for other agency operations. Analyst Anant Mishra has noted some flaws in the system and argued that the NDS has repeatedly failed to collect intelligence information from remote areas of Afghanistan:

The command structure of the NDS is independent, which means that it does not come under the architecture of the Ministry of Defence or the Ministry of Interior; however, it does host a close-knit relationship with the Afghan National Security Forces (ANSF) at all levels. Its operations are directed by the National Security Agency of Afghanistan; the head of NDS reports directly to the President. On numerous occasions, the NDS has been blamed for not adequately liaising with regional police commanders or Ministry of Defence (MOD) officials while providing un-timely and inaccurate intelligence when asked by relevant agencies..... Another failure of the NDS is the lack of technical and scientific know-how. Having looked at the previous operational prognosis, the NDS repeatedly failed to assess collected intelligence, which points towards another key issue related to an absent policy framework. NDS intelligence officers face no difficulty in gathering intelligence; however, they appear to be challenged during assessment......In the light of repeated intelligence failures and mistrust with their sister intelligence agencies, the NDS has received acute criticism even for disrespecting and ignoring the orders of their Commander-in-Chief i.e. the President. The frequent inter agency confrontation forced discontented political leadership to initiate numerous debates on open forums acutely criticising the NDS, especially the unruly behaviour of the chiefs who openly criticised actions of the President. This sudden transition of the NDS from an intelligence agency to a political party invited acute criticism from intelligence and military experts throughout the world.[33]

National Directorate of Security (NDS) Taliban, and the Islamic State of Khorasan

"You can fool all the people some of the time, and some of the people all the time, but you cannot fool all the people all the time."

–Abraham Lincoln

The world is in a constant state of instability and precariousness. The emergence of new terror groups, new fronts, alliances, and conflicts cover the globe like pieces from a parti-coloured. Globalization continues to challenge our world at unprecedented speed. Technological innovations, changing geographical developments, regional rivalries, and destruction of national critical infrastructures in several Muslim states due to the US so-called war on terrorism-all transformed the structures and hierarchies of societies. The idea of the development of a nation that sounds on tripods; (food, shelter and security) failed. The Edward Snowden leaks challenged policymakers and the public understanding and perspectives on the role of security intelligence in liberal democratic states.1

The persisting imbalance of power in the United States, its institutional turmoil, intelligence war, and the noticeably tilting power have made the country feel vulnerable and prodded it into military ventures. The calibration of Western allies around Whitehouse as the sole centre of globalization has only brought instability, destruction and loss of human lives. The level of international security has been dramatically used against Russia, and China. This type of globalization, sponsored by Pentagon, CIA and MI6 was conceived and promoted as a way to overcome the Westphalian system. Now, with the emergence of these unexpected developments, the international system is undergoing a dangerously unstable transition.[2]

At an end the past 100 years, globalization generated super-colossal wealth for the Atlantic countries, and during the last three decades, however, Asia managed to capture a majority share of global growth. Thus, global affairs entered an uncertain and volatile era, and the global balance of power is undergoing stop-and-go shift. Since the 9/11, Asia, Africa and the Middle East have been living through a period of progressive abrasion, or state collapse, international orders inherited from the past. Another dwindling system is the bipolar confrontation, even though both Americans and Europeans are eager to renew divisions in Europe, and weaken the continent. The United States wants to advocate new divisions in Western Europe, and control its resources.

The contemporary state of interstate relations is often particularised as a new Cold War. In fact, the higher level of structural tensions, the number of unresolved issues, the proliferation of nuclear weapons, and the emergence of the ISIS terrorist group, mean that Asia is becoming more dangerous in near future. Nuclear and tactical weapons are proliferating across the globe. New development in weapons technology is emerging; nuclear, and conventional. Cyber technology is becoming a strategic weapon, and it prompting comparable damage to weapons of mass destruction. All these developments are taking place at a time when the old system of nuclear arms control and its related structures of dialogue are crumbling.[3]

Elemental geopolitical reposition, hesitancy, and modern technologies not only exacerbate the risk of war, but also thrust international relations back to basics. The innovation and deployment of high-tech strategic weapons, announced by President Putin in his 01 March 2018 address to the nation, and the test of the new chop-chop missile by Russian army means that now the United States is no more the sole superpower. The development of all these trends in international relations, computer technologies, and interstate relations constitute an uninhibited and unmanaged threat to the territorial integrity of Afghanistan. As a weak and fractured state, Afghanistan will remain occupied, dismembered, and war-torn due to its incompetent and illiterate leaders, who loot and plunder it by one way or another.

Afghanistan has long been labelled the graveyard of superpowers. In the past two centuries, Britain and the Soviet Union were defeated. Now, notwithstanding the presence of thousands of foreign troops, Russia and China are again expanding the war to enmesh the United State and Britain in a bloody conflict for a long time. As the United States and NATO allies have deepened their presence in the region, all eyes are on Afghanistan. China is deepening its political and military role in the country by supporting Pakistan and Taliban to humiliate the United State militarily, and crush the Islamic State, and its illegal business of killing, torture and destruction. However, the US war and peace strategy failed to achieve national security interests, said the former Afghan Foreign Minister and security expert, Dr. Rangin Dadfar Spanta. "The government's control of important regions in the country has ended. We can say that the U.S. strategy was defeated," Dr. Spanta said.

Moreover, the picture on the ground is increasingly unclear. Some Afghan military experts are of the view that the US army supports both the Taliban and the ISIS to expand its periphery of war to the borders of Central Asia and China. Pakistan, Russia and China share the same view. The emergence of Russian Taliban in some Province changed the whole storyline. Afghanistan's National Directorate of Security (NDS) also failed to counter foreign intelligence networks and the Taliban. The spy agency has also been ineffective to thwart large scale attacks. Analyst Javed Ahmad has spotlighted some flawed strategies of the NDS in his article:

> Unfortunately, the NDS, enabled by U.S. money and technology, faces crucial gaps in intelligence collection

and analysis, as well as a strong leadership to proactively confront the Taliban's new tactics. The agency's human-intelligence presence across Afghanistan is insufficient and weak, its surveillance and reconnaissance capabilities are deficient, and its sabotage activities are negligible. In fact, the Taliban's network of informants in many provinces is arguably stronger and more credible than that of the NDS, all while the insurgency miraculously manages to maintain its operational security. At the same time, Afghan intelligence and security operations are often not in sync, and tactical operations typically lack intelligence-gathering components that produce information for future operations. Afghan forces have been trained as operators, not intelligence collectors, so they rely on NDS for information.[4]

Afghanistan faces a continuing threat from both Taliban and the ISIS terrorist group. These terror groups constitute a threat to Afghanistan's territorial integrity as well. Revenue from opium trafficking continues to sustain these groups and Afghan criminal networks. Additionally, extortion and kidnappings by low-level criminal networks have increased in some areas of Afghanistan. The trust deficit resulting from Pakistan's support to Afghan-oriented extremists, panniers the bilateral military collaboration required to achieve enduring security. Analyst and security expert, Mohammed Gul Sahibbzada, in his article (01 January 2019) reviewed the appointment of two former intelligence chiefs on important posts:

> After their appointment as Minister of Defence and Minister of Interior, both Ministers Assadullah Khalid and Amrullah Saleh have respectively taken on stage and boasted high profile slogans by issuing new directives and setting up new goals. Mr. Khalid said that 'they will hit the enemy hard and root them out of their positions' and that 'Afghan defence and security forces will no more remain in defensive position and will go on offensive against the enemy'. Mr. Saleh said that 'he would be merciless on criminals and enemy of the country and will serve the people' and issued a number of directives to officials of Ministry of Interior about their conducts. So far so good

as it came to intent and willingness to achieve, but it is also true that both these gentlemen were leading figures at their turn as chief of Afghan Spy Agency, the National Directorate of Security (NDS) and held different other portfolios in the previous Government headed by Hamid Karzai so they must be aware and should have deep knowledge about weaknesses and strengths of Afghan security and defence institutions.[5]

Despite all possible resources available to the NDS, the agency failed to counter foreign intelligence networks. On 16 August 2018, terrorists attacked the intelligence training centre in Kabul. Several gunmen were firing on a training facility overseen by the National Security Directorate. Corruption and political interference destroyed the agency. Mohammed Gul Sahibbzada diverts the attention of the government towards politicization of the agency and actions:

> There are rumours that ex-National Security Advisor appointed many senior officials in the ranks of Ministry of Defence, Ministry of Interior and NDS' and that 'these appointments were meant to manipulate and serve vested individual political interests when time for such manipulation arrives'. The same is true for all previous political leaders during their tenures at defence and security institutions. This whole phenomenon has taken immense toll on the performance, unity of purpose, disarray in chain of command & control and professionalism at defence and security institutions, which in turn has resulted in the absence of a national security agenda and comprehensive war strategy in the face of ongoing insurgency and war against international terrorism– not to mention security and law & order issues posed by criminal gangs operating in cities under government control. In addition, huge losses in battlefields incurred on Afghan security personnel are mostly because of lack of knowledge and experience of field commanders in battlefields to engage in such fights, hence the number of casualties including death and injuries have been consistent at one thousand five hundred to two thousand per month, turning this 'war on terror' a 'war of attrition' waged by insurgents. Reports

of soldiers dying due to lack of information and intelligence gathering, timely reinforcement, ammunition, food and water in battlefields have a checkered record of performance of our defence and security institutions.[6]

The appointment of these two former intelligence chiefs has come with a lot less fanfare than the departure of the old one, Mr. Amrullah Saleh, who resigned after deep disagreements with President Karzai. Shura-e Nazar led the Northern Alliance capture of Kabul. Alliance members controlled, not the NDS offices as well as the Ministry of Foreign Affairs and the Office for Administrative Affairs. The alliance gave nothing to the nation without corruption and ethnicization of state institutions. The spectrum of intelligence-gathering-capabilities deployed by the Afghan government and its international partners created chaos and misled policy makers in Kabul and Washington on wrong direction. The intelligence that cannot be gotten directly can be secured from allies with that knowledge, though it is not at all clear that the capabilities of Afghanistan's fledgling intelligence services or its willingness to share what actionable intelligence it does have can be decisive. Founder of the Stimson Center, and researcher, Michael Krepon (Herald, 19 April 2018) in his review article on Steve Coll's book identified important flaws in the US-Afghan strategy. He also noted inconsistent political and military approach of former Presidents (George Bush and Barak Obama):

Afghanistan remains a quagmire for the US troops that cannot succeed without good Afghan governance, capable Afghan national forces and a strong partnership with Pakistan. All these factors have been consistently lacking. Washington keeps looking for an exit strategy but this pursuit only increases the resolve of its opponents. Badly conceived and poorly executed wars – and no country's record since Vietnam is worse on this score than the United States'–do not usually end well. Washington never recovered from its confusion over war aims, lingering over plans to defeat al Qaeda as the Afghan Taliban revived them. The Bush and Obama administrations were particularly ill-suited to succeed for separate and overlapping reasons. Quickly after sending the

US expeditionary forces to Afghanistan, the Bigfoot in Bush's national security team turned their attention to Iraq, with disastrous effects on both campaigns. When dollar-releasing spigots were subsequently opened in Afghanistan and Pakistan, the money disappeared into well-greased Afghan construction projects and creative accounting schemes like the Pakistan military are Coalition Support Fund.[7]

The deterioration of law and order continue to force the residents of various provinces of Afghanistan to Pakistan or to an unknown destination. However, on 12 January 2015, CBS News reported potential gains of the Taliban in Helmand and ISIS in Jalalabad, Kunar and Nuristan provinces, the capture of Kunduz, Sangin and parts of Badakhshan provinces, kidnapping for ransom, all raised serious questions over the credibility of NDS, and CIA, war strategies. Moreover, an Afghan army commander abruptly revealed that his office had confirmed information about the existence of 200 foreign militants in Kunduz city, and 3,000 militants in the entire province, where the Taliban had established check posts in villages and towns to target Afghan forces.

In 2015, the Taliban defeated Afghan security forces in Kunduz. The UN report on civilians' deaths seemingly exposed the incompetence of the Afghan armed forces that could not defend the country. This exponentially growing conflict in Kunduz province forced Afghan authorities to enlist local militia fighters to bolster opposition to the Taliban insurgency.[4] In Kunduz, the NDS was unable to spotlight the existence of Taliban either in a hospital or in parts of the city. However, the fall of Kunduz did not come as a surprise, particularly considering the territory already controlled by the Taliban.

On 23 April 2018, Al Jazeera reported the killing of 57 people in a suicide attack on a voter registration centre in the city. The bomber blew himself up in a large crowd queuing to collect their national ID certificates so they could register to vote in long-delayed legislative elections.[8] This attack was the failure of NDS to intercept the bomber. Analyst Anant Mishra (2018) noted the deteriorating relationship between the NDS and the Pentagon over the operational mechanism in the battlefield:

> Additionally, the saga of lost-in-translation and unclear objectives massively affected the relationship between the Pentagon, the NDS, and the North Atlantic Treaty Organization (NATO), which all approached differently the 'war against terror' in Afghanistan. These different visions and perspectives towards the war on terrorism in Afghanistan impacted negatively the Afghan National Army (ANA) and the NDS. This was especially the case after the withdrawal of US troops in late 2014; the challenges faced were beyond the capacity of the NDS. Since then, the Taliban attacks compromised Kabul's control over many territories. ANA endured major casualties during the early days of US withdrawal, forcing it to operate thinly within the territories under their control. The Taliban attacked from across the Durand Line crippling an Afghan effective response. The NDS failure to adequately and systematically collect vital intelligence, especially in rural regions, remains a challenge which hinders its ability to respond to or even identify sudden attacks.[9]

On 14 March 2016, Khan Nashin district of Helmand fell to Taliban, while on 31 December 2016; Taliban continued their attacks against the Afghan National Army. In January 2017, the Marine Corps Times reported Taliban's spring attacks and noted that the US army was going to deploy a task force of 300 personnel (known as Task Force Southwest) for nine months to South-Western part in Afghanistan. However, on 12 February 2017, Daily Huffington Post reported US aircraft conducted around 30 air strikes in Helmand Province, while Military website of the US army reported the death of 60 Taliban fighters, and 8-commanders.[10]

On 23 July 2017, following heavy clashes in Ghor province, Taywara district collapsed to the Taliban.[11] Public order police commander in Ghor said the Taliban stormed the district centre. He also said that a number of security forces and local residents who had been supporting troops were reportedly under siege by the Taliban. However, Local officials from northern Faryab province also confirmed the centre of Kohistan district fell to the Taliban the same day. "Soon we will launch a military operation to re-capture the centre of the district. Currently, security forces are fighting the insurgents in eight districts of the province," said Abdul Karim Youresh.[12]

In March 2017, the Sangin District of Helmand province fell to Taliban[13], and on 29 April 2017, the US army deployed an additional force (5,000) to the Southern Helmand Province, this marked the return of its soldiers to the province since 2014.[14] In the first week of January 2017, Marine Corps Times reported Afghan army sought to rebuild 33 districts spread across 16 Afghan provinces under insurgent control.[15] On 9 February 2017, US Army Commander John W. Nicholson told Congress that NATO and allied forces in Afghanistan were facing a "stalemate" and that he needed a few thousand additional troops to more effectively train and advise Afghan soldiers.[16]

On 18 April 2017, in his New York Times book Review comment, prominent Pakistani journalist Ahmad Rashed warned: "the inconsideration of the Donald Trump administration that barely mentioned Afghanistan, a country where US forces have been engaged in the longest war in American history. Perhaps this is because, after more than fifteen years and $700 billion, the US has little to show for it other than an incredibly weak and corrupt civilian government in Kabul and a never-ending Taliban insurgency".[17] However, on 23 April 2017, CNN reported Taliban's deadly attack on a northern army base that killed or wounded more than 100 people was revenge for the deaths of two of its officials in the region.[18]

On 29 January 2018, ToloNews reported Mohammad Hashim Alokozai's criticism against the Government's failure to identify foreign elements inside the administration.[19] Former Chief of NDS, Mr. Amrullah Saleh said government knew a number of spies within the government institutions. Mr. Saleh claimed that one of the deputies of the National Security Council (NSC) was a Pakistani spy. "One of the deputies of the National

Security Council has links with Pakistan, he is an agent, he is a spy and the government knows it,"[20] said Saleh. Serious criticism was levelled against the government's security strategy following a fresh spate of attacks by the Taliban and Daesh in the country since 2014.[21] Critics argued that government and its security and intelligence agencies failed to identify foreign spies. "These people are collaborating and cooperating with the enemy, we are trying to arrest them, we have arrested dozens of them already from the ranks of the security forces, from inside society and from among the politicians," Minister of Interior Wais Ahmad Barmak warned.[22]

On 11 August 2018, ToloNews reported former head of the National Directorate of Security Mr. Assadullah Khalid's revelations behind the fall of some parts of Ghazni City to militants as the inattention of intelligence agencies. Mr. Khalid said the main reason for the collapse of Ghazni province was negligence and intelligence failure. "We reject government officials' claims. The situation is not what they say. Taliban (militants) are inside the city. The city is burning and the martyrs' bodies are on the streets. From yesterday and before that we contacted officials to address the situation, but no one is listening," Khalid warned. A number of former military commanders also blamed security officials over poor war management. "If the government had the will, it could target the Taliban in security belts outside the city before they launch their attack," Jawed Kohistani, a former military officer said.[23] In August and September 2018, after consecutive terror attacks in Kabul, President Ashraf Ghani ordered the establishment of a security plan into four security zones:

> The measures in this area are not enough and I have directed that Kabul be divided into four security zones, including West of Kabul and that now the Security Coordination Centre is active in western Kabul and will become a core security centre in the future,"[24] Ghani said. Former Chief of National Directorate of Security (NDS), Mr. Amrullah Saleh, believed that dividing the capital into security zones would be a successful plan. Mr. Saleh said the only way to keep the country, especially the capital secure, was to work with the

security forces and for government to gain the people's trust. "People should be put at the centre, as they always have said. Putting people at the centre means that they ask the people who the enemy is and where the gaps are,"[25] said Saleh.

On 25 December 2018, President Ghani assigned the State Minister for Parliamentary Affairs to introduce Amrullah Saleh and Assadullah Khalid to the parliament. President Ashraf Ghani in a decree nominated Amrullah Saleh as Minister of Interior and Assadullah Khalid as Minister of Defence. Saleh and Khalid served as head of the National Directorate of Security (NDS) during former President Hamid Karzai's government.[26] Saleh was appointed as a State Minister for security reforms in 2017, but he resigned from the post after a short time.[27] That decree frustrated Pakistani print and electronic media. On 24 December 2018, Pakistan's English newspaper, the Nation in its comment noted that:

> Mr. Khalid and Amrullah Saleh are known to have visceral hatred toward Taliban (and Pakistan), but are also CIA products. President Ghani may have virtually sabotaged Khalilzad's mission to strike deal with Taliban over his head. This had to happen at some point. Khalid and Saleh are ardent supporters of open-ended war and genuinely believe in military victory over Taliban if only war is fought with grit and tenacity.[28]

In a statement issued by Presidential palace said that according to the decree of 13th section of 64th article of constitution Mr. Assadullah Khaled was assigned as acting Minister for Defence Ministry.[29] Statement said that based on decree of 11th section of 64th article of constitution, Mr. Assadullah Khaled assignation as the nominee of Defence Ministry approved.[30] According to the decree of 13th section of 64th article of constitution, Mr. Amrullah Saleh was assigned as acting Minister for Interior. Statement said that based on decree of 11th section of 64th article of constitution, Mr. Amrullah Saleh assignation as the nominee of Interior Ministry approved.[31]

Daily Outlook reported criticism of Kandahar MP, Muhammad Naeem Lalay Hamid Zai. The MP criticized government for its inability to stabilize the country: "The agenda should be on security. At least twelve terrorist attacks were carried out just in one specific area of Kabul." There are two camps within the Afghan administration. One camp wanted the implementation of strict security measures across the country to prevent terrorists entering cities and towns, while the other wanted security of Kabul only. The failure of Afghan intelligence to tackle security challenges is a matter of great concern.[32]

Officials in Afghanistan said four operatives of the national intelligence agency gunned down their 16 colleagues before fleeing to join the Taliban insurgency in the southern Helmand province. The rare overnight "insider" attack took place at a facility linked to the National Directorate of Security or NDS in the Gerishk district, VOA reported. Mr. Omar Zawak, the provincial government spokesman, confirmed the incident saying the Taliban also assaulted the NDS Centre while the insider attack was under way, sparking fierce clashes with Afghan security guards.[33]

The members of parliament argued that the presence of foreign fighters in the Ghazni city should be documented and reported to the United Nations. Pakistani nationals were reported to have fought along with the Taliban militants in Ghazni province.[34] The lawmaker, Mr. Arfanullah Arfan, said were foreign fighters in Ghazni including Pakistani citizens, calling on the government to do something immediately.[35] "People from Pakistan, Chechnya, Uzbekistan and Tajikistan were involved in the war in Ghazni. We asked the government to report this to the UN Security Council as soon as possible. It should share the evidence with the countries that have fighters in the Ghazni war as well."[36]

On 27 January 2018, an ambulance was used as a vehicle-borne Improvised Explosive Device near the Sidarat Square in Kabul, Afghanistan. At least 103 people were killed and 235 others wounded in the attack. The Taliban claimed responsibility for the attack. On 27 January 2018, attackers blew up an explosives-packed ambulance near an interior ministry building on a busy and heavily-guarded street in Kabul during rush hour.[37] According to the estimates of Watson Institute (August 2016):

> Afghan Civilians 2001-2015, killed 29,818, Wounded- 37,412, From January to June 2016, 1,601 killed and 3,565 injured. Moreover, 30,470 police and military personnel killed and 17,000 injured. The same period shows all but 42,000 Taliban killed and 19,000 injured". However, during the last 15 years, more than 2,371 US soldiers and a Major General killed and 20,179 injured. The same period shows more than 2, 800 US allied forces and contractors killed and 20,000 injured, while unreported wounded contractors are estimated at more than 2,000. All but 111,442 Afghans American, and allied forces and contractors killed during the last 15 years war on terrorism in Afghanistan, and 116,603 wounded. Moreover, on 17 April 2016, New York Times also reported the killing of more than 2,000 civilian and 80,000 displaced in 2016 alone.[38]

The British Home Office Report of 2016 in its paragraph-2.3.4 confirmed that a significant number of people displaced in the armed conflict in Afghanistan. In its paragraph-2.3.5, the report admitted that the displaced women and girls were at risk. Having quoted Long War Journal, in its paragraph 5.1.4, the report further confirms the Taliban control over 40 districts in Afghanistan.[39] The UN report also published its assessment of war causalities. The report noted:

> More than 2900,000 Afghan civilians from all provinces have been displaced during the last 15 years. However, as a result of violence and persecution, Afghan women and children have been under constant threat. In 2015 alone, all but 250,000 Afghans arrived in Europe, while in 2016, 85,000 men, women and children left the country for Europe, Pakistan, US, UK and Iran. International Rescue Committee in its report (2016) admitted the 21 percent of the over one million refugees who have fled to Europe since January 2015 were Afghans.[40]

Internally displaced people were living under open skies without shelter, food and security. On 26 November 2016,

ToloNews reported dozen of displaced Afghan families were living in tents in the Capital of Afghanistan, Kabul. These families were forced to leave their homes in different provinces who sought refuge in the capital amid ongoing insecurity in their provinces.[41] "Four of my relatives were killed. I have nothing here and with my children, I live in a tent and burn plastic to keep warm," said Murad, a displaced resident from Kunduz province. "We do not have warm clothes and fuel for winter. I argue government to help us"[42] said Nasim. Afghan Ministry of Refugees and Repatriation (MoRR) confirmed the displacement of more than 63,000 people from different provinces due to war and insecurity.[43]

On 18 April 2015, Daily Outlook Afghanistan reported a suicide attack in Jalalabad city, in which 33 people were killed, and 100 injured.[44] However, on 24 November 2016, Pajhwok News reported Pentagon's concern at the exponentially growing violence in Afghanistan.[45] Before this attack, on 23 July 2016, Associated Press reported an ISIS attack on Afghan protest in Kabul, in which 80 people were killed and 231 injured.[46] In Ghor province, the ISIS kidnapped 30 civilians-killed 23 and released 7 women and children. Moreover, the Afghan Defence Ministry in its report (2016) noted the killing of 600 civilians in 6 months. The report noted the devastation of 20,000 families by the ISIS terrorist attacks in Jalalabad province.[47]

On 22 November 2016, ToloNews reported the ISIS suicide attack on a Kabul mosque, in which 11 people were killed and 50 injured. The ISIS carried out two more attacks during the Shiite ceremony of Ashura on October 11 in Kabul, and on October 12 in the northern province of Balkh, that altogether killed at least 32 people. The group also claimed responsibility for the attack, took place on July 23, against a demonstration by mainly Hazara Shiites in Kabul, killing at least 85 and injuring 413 people.[48]

On 03 May 2017, Sayed Masood Sadat reported for Asia Foundation about the miseries of Afghan refugees: "After Syrians, Afghans form the largest group of refugees in the European Union (EU), with over 360,000 asylum applications lodged in 2015 and 2016, according to official EU figures. Afghan migrants risk their lives during the months-long journey to reach Europe, which crosses thousands of kilometres in the Middle East and the Balkans. To embark on this perilous journey, the migrants pay human smugglers at least $5,000 per person, which they usually raise by selling their properties or borrowing from friends and families".[49] On 16 June 2017, the Guardian reported Pentagon's intention to send more than 4,000 soldiers to Afghanistan. "The Pentagon wants to send almost 4,000 additional American forces to Afghanistan, according to a Trump administration official, an attempt to break a stalemate in a war that has now passed to a third US commander-in-chief", Guardian reported.[50]

The United States understands the intensity and ferociousness of war in all provinces of Afghanistan, but lurks facts and ground-realities. The Trump administration also understand the shameless failure of the US forces to restore confidence of civil society and respond in a professional means to the Taliban's consecutive attacks across the country. In June 2017, the US Congress in its report on Afghanistan spotlighted the inner pain of the US commander General Nicholson:

General Nicholson, Commander of USFOR-A and RS, assesses that the exploitation of ungoverned sanctuaries outside of Afghanistan by terrorists and Afghan insurgents is the single greatest external factor that could cause failure of the coalition campaign. External sanctuary hampers efforts to bring Afghan Taliban senior leadership to the negotiating table and allows space for terrorist groups like the Haqqani Network to plan coordinated operations against U.S. and coalition forces, the ANDSF, and civilians. External sanctuary allows the Afghan Taliban to rest, refit, and regenerate, thereby perpetuating the cycle of violence. Afghanistan faces a continuing threat from an externally enabled insurgency and as many as 20 total terrorist organizations present or operating in the country, the highest concentration of terrorist groups in the world. These pervasive insurgent, terrorist, and criminal networks constitute a threat to Afghanistan's stability. Revenue from drug trafficking, illicit mining and foreign financial support continues to sustain the insurgency and Afghan criminal networks. Additionally, extortion and kidnappings by low-level criminal networks have increased in some areas of Afghanistan.[51]

The UN Secretary General in its March 2017 report also expressed concern about the deteriorating law and order situation in Afghanistan. Secretary-General openly admitted the failure of US and NATO forces to restore stability in Afghanistan. The UN report described fatalities inflicted by Taliban and other insurgent forces on the people of Afghanistan during the last two years:

> The overall security situation continued to deteriorate throughout 2016 and into 2017. The United Nations recorded 23,712 security incidents, almost 5 per cent increase compared with 2015 and the highest number in a single year ever recorded by UNAMA. While the fighting remained particularly prevalent in the five southern and eastern provinces of Helmand, Nangarhar, Kandahar, Kunar and Ghazni, where 50 per cent of all incidents were recorded, the conflict spread in geographical scope, with increasing Taliban activities in northern and north-eastern Afghanistan, as well as in Farah in the west. The Taliban continued to put pressure on the Government's control of the provincial capitals of Farah, Kunduz, Lashkar Gah, Helmand Province, and Tirin Kot, Uruzgan Province. International and Afghan air support and the deployment of Afghan special forces remained critical to the holding of these cities.[52]

In November 2016, Foreign Ministry of the Netherlands in its research paper reported the killings, and displacement of civilians in Afghanistan. The paper noted some important facts and figures that elucidate the intensity of war. The paper has noted fatalities in several provinces of Afghanistan:

> In the first nine months of 2016, the number of casualties was approximately equal to that in the same period in 2015. Between January and 30 September 2016, UNAMA recorded 8,397 civilian casualties: 2,562 dead and 5,835 wounded. In the same period in 2015, there were 2,681 dead and 5,805 wounded? The number of female casualties fell by 12 percent,

but the number of children who were victims of the conflict (639 dead and 1,822 wounded) was 15 percent higher than in the same period in 2015. Children were particularly affected as a result of ground combat, IEDs and remnants of explosives. UNAMA recorded six parallel legal rulings in which women were accused of moral offences. Ground combat caused the most casualties: 829 dead and 2,425 wounded. In the southern region, the number of victims, therefore, rose by more than 50 percent, mainly as a result of fighting in Helmand and Uruzgan. There were also many casualties in Baghlan and Takhar in the northeast. IEDs accounted for the second highest number of casualties (496 dead and 1,018 wounded). The percentage of casualties resulting from ground combat rose, while that resulting from IEDs fell. Although AGEs were responsible for most of the casualties, the number of casualties at the hands of pro-government forces rose by more than 40 percent. The number of complex suicide and other attacks increased in the first six months of 2016, with 225 dead and 774 wounded. Most attacks took place in cities, the worst-hit being Kabul and Jalalabad (Nangarhar). There were also more civilian deaths as a result of ANDSF air strikes.[53]

When Taliban intensified their military operations across Afghanistan, the US Special Inspector General for Afghanistan Reconstruction (SIGAR) in its report on 30 April 2017 noted the inner frustration of General Nicholson on the deteriorating security situation in Afghanistan. In fact, he was deeply concerned at high-level casualties of the US forces across the country:

Testifying before the Senate Armed Services Committee on February 9, 2017, General John W. Nicholson Jr., commander of U.S. and NATO troops in Afghanistan, characterized the security situation in Afghanistan as a "stalemate," saying that he was particularly concerned about the high level of Afghan National Defence and Security Forces (ANDSF) casualties. General Nicholson underscored the importance of Afghanistan for American national security..... In March 2017, the report also noted the intensity of war in Afghanistan and admitted that from 01 January 2017, through February

24, 2017, more than 807 ANDSF personnel were killed and 1,328 were wounded. Among these, 12 ANDSF service members were reported killed and eight wounded during insider attacks.[54]

The Ghazni attacks showed that Afghan intelligence failed to spotlight the Taliban entrance in the city. The attacks on Ghazni underlined the fact that Taliban's impressive ability to collect and exploit intelligence-helped them surprise their government adversaries. The village and district level intelligence units provide the Taliban with a huge quantity of information regarding American troops' movements and potential Afghan government collaborators. They succeeded in exploiting open source intelligence for sustaining their insurgency campaign.

On 15 May 2018, ToloNews reported Taliban control of a number of check posts in the city and the National Directorate of Security (NDS) and police headquarters. Footage released on social media showed that a number of security forces' vehicles were torched and that the Taliban entered a building used by the security forces. The geographical expansion of the Islamic State in Afghanistan, forced Pakistan to host an unprecedented meeting of heads of intelligence agencies from Russia, China and Iran to discuss counterterrorism cooperation, with particular focus on the build-up of Islamic State. A spokesman for Moscow's Foreign Intelligence Service confirmed that the emergence of IS in Afghanistan prompted the deliberations in Islamabad.[55]

As there is no coherent conflict resolution mechanism in Afghanistan, theory of peacebuilding suggests that attempt must be made to predominate the culture of peace on community level. Conflict resolution experts argue that military wind-down, mediation, talks, and effective peacebuilding measures supported by internal and external stakeholders can help kindle the prospect of peace in Afghanistan. The regional element and facet of war is so well-built that without long-term consensus among Pakistan, Iran, Saudi Arabia, Tajikistan, India, China and Russia, and termination of their financial, military and political support to warring factions, war will not come to an end. Afghanistan neighbours have their own stakes, roles, and actions, and play for the protection of their own interests. India and Pakistan fight their own proxy war by supporting their own factions. Pakistan army and civilian government have different priorities on the issue of peace in Afghanistan.

The army wants to maintain political and military influence, and to prevent India making Afghanistan the training ground of Baloch and Pashtun insurgents' against the country. Iran has its own national interests in Afghanistan, and does not want geographical expansion of Islamic State (ISIS). Iran does not want Saudi Arabia to challenge its interests. India wants to monitor the activities of Pakistani extremist groups in Afghanistan. For this purpose, the country has established four regional consulates. To keep the war ignited several regional players changed their priorities, and established military training centres for warring factions on their soil.

It means they don't want peace in Afghanistan, while a growing body of literature on wars suggests that military intervention never settled violence or long wars. The only way to peace experts suggest is a conventional approach to peace, in which power-sharing is of great importance. On 13 February 2015, in an interview with the Guardian newspaper, General Musharaf vowed that when he was in office, his government sought to eliminate the Karzai's government because he had helped India in establishing its military network in Afghanistan. "India was stabbing Pakistan in the back", he said. Pervez Musharraf also admitted that the Inter Services Intelligence (ISI) cultivated Taliban after 2001. "Obviously we were looking for some groups to counter India," he said. [56]

On 14 January 2019, ToloNews reported regional rivalries in Afghanistan. Unity government warned that attempts of regional states to engage in the rivalry in the peace process in Afghanistan prompted harmful and the issue further complicated the peace process. Meanwhile, US Special Representative for Afghanistan Reconciliation Zalmay Khalilzad arrived in Beijing where he held talks with senior Chinese officials about the peace process in Afghanistan.[57] The India-Pakistan rivalry turned Afghanistan into a battleground, where the two nuclear-armed neighbours tested both their hard and soft power. Indian Prime Minister Narendra Modi government's open-armed policy for Afghanistan irked Pakistan the most.[58]

Prominent Indian analyst M.K Bhadrakumar (19 July 2018) has also documented the involvement of some Arab state in the Afghan conflict: "Curiously, although the newfound Saudi-Emirati pro-activism in Afghanistan is coinciding with the steady expansion of IS-K, the two Gulf states today are preoccupied with weakening the Taliban, whom they had mentored in an earlier era in the 1990s.[59] The Kabul government approved on June 6 the deployment of UAE Special Forces to Afghanistan.[60] On July 11-12, Saudi Arabia hosted an Ulema conference in Jeddah and Mecca, which issued a 'fatwa' against the 'jihad' waged by the Afghan Taliban.[61] Washington encouraged these parallel Saudi-Emirati moves, which implies a concerted attempt to weaken the Taliban whom the US military failed to defeat, with a view to force it to compromise.[62] Russia and China want the withdrawal of US forces from Afghanistan to tackle the ISIS menace with their own swords. The United States, in fact, wants to destabilize the region and prolong its presence in Afghanistan.[63] Mr. Fraidoon Amel in his research paper noted some reservations of Russia and China about the presence of ISIS in Afghanistan:

> More recently, by elevating IS presence in Afghanistan and its level of threat to US enemies such as Russia, China, and Iran, the US is elevating the justification for its own military options intended to go beyond Afghan strategic geography. The US is essentially playing a destabilizing role in the region as it aims at establishing world-tyranny. Its strategy revolves around the so-called Wolfowitz Doctrine which aims at preventing the emergence of a regional or global power that could challenge US's sole hegemonic status. However, US's attempt at establishing its hegemony in Afghanistan and beyond is being challenged by a de facto strategic alliance involving Russia, China, Iran and Pakistan. In other words, the US-NATO coalition is facing a formidable enemy – three of which are nuclear powers – determined to contain US's

hegemonic ambitions in the region. China and Russia are at the forefront of shaping this new geopolitical reality.[64]

What makes the issue of Indian and Pakistanis actions in Afghanistan so thorny is that, to some observers, all three parties have overriding national interests in the situation. Meanwhile, India's interests in Afghanistan typically exist in the context of strategic rivalry between India and Pakistan. India remains wary of the emergence of a fundamentalist Afghanistan that can provide a breeding ground for militants operating in the contested states of Jammu and Kashmir. India's growing presence and influence in Afghanistan undercuts the Pakistani military establishment's long-term obsession with the quest for "strategic depth" against India. However, analyst Mr. Sajjad Ashraf (6 July 2017) noted strategic rivalry between Pakistan and Afghanistan and argued that peace in Afghanistan depends on Pakistan and India relationship:

> Meanwhile, India's interests in Afghanistan typically exist in the context of strategic rivalry between India and Pakistan. India remains wary of the emergence of a fundamentalist Afghanistan that can provide a breeding ground for militants operating in the contested states of Jammu and Kashmir. But India's larger interests in Afghanistan extend beyond Pakistan to its desire for increased trade and energy relations with Central Asia. And when Pakistan disallows the use of land routes through its territory due to its hostility towards India, both India and Afghanistan get parked in the same tent. Peace in Afghanistan is deeply tied to India–Pakistan relations. Islamabad genuinely fears that Afghanistan may well act as India's proxy. Until Pakistan is secure in its relations with India, it will continue to interfere in Afghan affairs to deny India space. As they both jostle for influence, the rift between the two contributes to unsettling Afghanistan.[65]

China, which is currently an economic and military power, is afraid of instability and insecurity in Afghanistan. This fear is due to the possible expansion of insecurities to its Xinjiang province and its economic projects in the region. After the emergence of ISIL in the region, Russia and Iran are the countries that have begun to criticize the US presence in Afghanistan.[66] China wants a peaceful Afghanistan, but the United States wants war to destabilize neighbouring states. The emergence of the ISK (ISIS Khurasan Chapter) has put in danger territorial integrity of neighbouring states. Its networks in Pakistan and Afghanistan forced Russia and China to deploy more troops along the Afghan borders. Geopolitical insight in its Afghan commentary argued that the presence of the ISIS terrorist group in Afghanistan is a threat to peace and stability of the region:

> Continuing competition amongst insurgent groups in this complex geopolitical environment will only serve to obfuscate the peacemaking process. As the current government in Kabul has demonstrated repeatedly, it is incapable of containing, let alone, defeating the jihadist threat it faces, even from local groups. As ISK continues to grow and changes the nature of the insurgency in Afghanistan, it is unlikely that any negotiated settlement or power-sharing agreement, even one including the Taliban, would have the capacity to combat ISK. The width and breadth of the many terrorist groups - entangled in rivalries, loyalties, and defections - in Afghanistan will necessitate a collective regional security strategy - and likely, an international military presence - for many years to come.[67]

On 16 January 2019, ToloNews reported car bomb attack in Kabul that killed five Afghan citizens: "Taliban claimed responsibility for a car bomb attack near a heavily fortified foreign compound in Kabul that killed five people, including an Indian national. The bombing sparked international condemnation as efforts increased to strike a peace deal with the Islamic insurgents to end more than 18 years of war. More than 110 people were wounded in the blast near the Green Village compound, which houses several international companies and charities, in eastern Kabul. Taliban spokesman Zabihullah Mujahid said the militants were responsible for the attack in which he claimed dozens of foreign and Afghan security forces were killed and wounded".[68] On 22 January 2019, Afghanistan Times reported in its editorial page the killing of 100 NDS soldiers in Maidan Wardak province.

The ISIS terrorist group or the Taliban, in its deadly terrorist attack on the Academy of Afghan secret agencies at Maidan Wardak province killed 100 soldiers:

> Almost the victims were youngsters who on completion of education made a mind of serving their motherland which was badly affected in last four decades. Ironic to mention that the deadly terrorist attack occurred amidst peace efforts being brokered by the US through its special envoy Dr. Zalmay Khalilzad....... Though violent acts are in progress in Afghanistan is taking place since 2001 but it was intensified during and after of previous parliamentary polls completed in October 2018. And the Afghan government especially President Ashraf Ghani has exonerated his assignments to "words" whereas in practicality he is yet to take steps for ensuring safety to lives and properties of common men. Now when sensitive installations and institutions like Maidan Wardak are insecure and vulnerable to militants then how it is possible for common men to be safe and sound in his home. Security situation is aggravating day by day in all over Afghanistan and almost people from rural areas now making routes towards urban cities and towns. Since installation of Ashraf Ghani as president in 2014, there is polarization socially, politically and economically.[69]

Russia and China want the withdrawal of US forces from Afghanistan to tackle the ISIS menace with their own swords. The United States, in fact wants to destabilize the region and prolong its presence in Afghanistan. Mr. Fraidoon Amel in his research paper noted some reservations of Russia and China about the presence of ISIS in Afghanistan:

> More recently, by elevating IS presence in Afghanistan and its level of threat to US enemies such as Russia, China, and Iran, the US is elevating the justification for its own military options intended to go beyond Afghan strategic geography. The US is essentially playing a destabilizing role in the region as it aims at establishing world-tyranny. Its strategy revolves around the so-called Wolfowitz Doctrine which aims at

preventing the emergence of a regional or global power that could challenge US's sole hegemonic status. However, US's attempt at establishing its hegemony in Afghanistan and beyond is being challenged by a de facto strategic alliance involving Russia, China, Iran and Pakistan. In other words, the US-NATO coalition is facing a formidable enemy – three of which are nuclear powers – determined to contain US's hegemonist ambitions in the region. China and Russia are at the forefront of shaping this new geopolitical reality.[70]

Chapter - 3

Why the NDS Matters?

The Emergence of the Afghan Intelligence Agency after 9/11

Dr. Diva Patang Wardak

Abstract

Governments in Afghanistan paid little attention to the basic function and importance of intelligence during the last four decades. Immediately after the United States drawdown at the end of 2014, the National Directorate of Security (NDS) faced numerous challenges in tackling certain issues, which will be outlined in detail throughout this article, since the Pakistan Inter-Services Intelligence trained and funded the Taliban on its soil and continues to provide military and financial support to the Taliban and other terrorist groups carrying out attacks against the Afghan Security Forces across the country. The NDS continues to suffer from key intelligence capabilities, especially in gathering intelligence information from remote areas in order to prevent Pakistan's interference in Afghanistan affairs.

The failure of major powers to come to the aid of Afghanistan and strengthen its intelligence agency not only created more extremism, radicalisation, and terrorism but also created insecurity and instability. Consequently, to thoroughly analyse the intelligence operations of the NDS, detailed interviews were conducted with senior political figures. This article argues that the reform of the intelligence agencies is imperative, and the de-politicization of the intelligence process is as much an element of national reconciliation as a consolidation of power. Reforming the intelligence agencies, therefore, requires not only a change in the state, but also a change in the state of mind of the players involved.

Introduction

It is unarguable that the intelligence in Afghanistan consistently fails to obtain and gather information of significant worth which could otherwise prove to be in the best interest of its national security. Poor information gathering is due to undertrained intelligence personnel with limited access to advanced technology. As a result, their ability to gather information is limited and of low quality. Such information gathered from major cities and government departments can lead policymakers and military commanders to wrong conclusions. The basic process to support policymaking is the intelligence cycle, but the National Directorate of Security (NDS) is not well- trained to follow this cycle.[1]

For instance, the Taliban's capture of Kunduz in 2015 was the worst kind of intelligence failure where intelligence cooperation among the NDS, National Security Agency of Afghanistan (NSA), Ministry of Defence (MoD), and Interior Ministry (MoI) was weak. This failure was because the security alerts and intelligence reports regarding the Taliban's plan of capturing the city were not taken seriously, but were simply overlooked by the MoD and MoI.[2] Kunduz' capture should not have come as a surprise given the amount of territory the Taliban was already controlling. However, Kunduz' rapid fall and slow recapture was an intelligence failure: intelligence gathering, processing, and analysis has been a complicated problem ever since the establishment of the NDS with the assistance of the Central Intelligence Agency (CIA).

In addition, another issue that created misunderstanding among the Pentagon, the NDS, and their North Atlantic Treaty Organization (NATO) allies was the conceptualisation of war in Afghanistan where several states viewed the ongoing war against terrorism through different glasses. Because of these different concepts of war, the Afghan National Army (ANA) and NDS faced numerous challenges immediately after the United States (US) drawdown at the end of 2014. Since 2014, the Taliban conducted high-profile attacks, which threatened the control of the Afghan government over its territory. These attacks were planned and launched from safe havens in Pakistan.[3] The NDS continues to suffer from the lack of key intelligence capabilities, especially in gathering intelligence from remote areas to prevent these surprise attacks.

Afghanistan's civil war prompted many national security challenges. The political and military involvement of neighbouring states, warlordism, and the growing power of the Taliban and Islamic State of Iraq and Syria are security challenges that stubbornly prolong the civil war in the country. However, after each terrorist attack, the only statement we hear from responsible security institutions is that attacks are constituted and planned from across the borders. It is very well known that Pakistan is a safe haven for terrorism, but Afghanistan's intelligence institutions never took responsibility either for their intelligence failures or for the incompetency within the NDS and ANA infrastructures which caused misunderstanding between the government and the state institutions in the country. The lack of intelligence and continued intelligence failures in remote areas of Afghanistan stem from the drawdown of the US forces and the shutting of the US and NATO bases since 2012.

Former President General Musharraf admitted that the Inter-Services Intelligence (ISI) supported and trained terrorist groups inside Pakistan and then sent them back to Afghanistan for terrorist attacks.[4] On 13 February 2015, in an interview with The Guardian newspaper, General Musharraf admitted that when he was in power Pakistan sought to create problems for Karzai to undermine his government and that the ISI actively cultivated the Taliban to counter India's action against Pakistan.[5] As stated in a book by Mr. Raje, "Pakistan is a terrorist state, and ISI is its instrument of terror. Both were created virtually simultaneously."[6]

In the 20th century, the ISI exclusively trained over 150,000 mujahedeen fighters, while the CIA funded the ISI to train them, as well as training the Pakistani army and ISI personnel.[7] General

Musharraf confirmed his country's involvement in terrorism, that the Pakistani ISI trained and funded the Taliban on its soil, and that it continues to provide military and financial support to the Taliban and other terrorist groups in carrying out attacks against the Afghan National Security Force (ANSF) across the country.[8]

Additionally, Ex-Pakistan Ambassador to the US Husain Haqqani confirmed that his country is sponsoring and supporting terrorism.[9] On 14 July 2016, the former chief of the NDS Rahmatullah Nabil leaked documents which show that the money provided by the US government to Pakistani military for fighting terrorism is in fact spent by Pakistan's ISI for promoting and supporting terrorism.[10] For instance, the ISI has been accused of playing a role in major terrorist attacks across Afghanistan and the world, including the 9/11, Mumbai train bombings, Indian Parliament attack, Mumbai terror attacks, and Kabul International Airport attack, as well as giving shelter to most of the terrorist leaders such as bin Laden, Mullah Umar, and many more. Because of the involvement of Pakistan and other neighbouring countries in the internal affairs of Afghanistan, the security agencies, including the NDS are fighting on various fronts.

Unfortunately, all Afghans are paying the price for the failure of intelligence and for fighting the war for others. It is clear that Afghanistan became a failed state, and Afghans suffered a humanitarian emergency. Afghanistan became an object of charity and neglect for the US and other major powers. Regional powers, particularly Pakistan, as well as private networks, smugglers, drug dealers, and terrorists, treated it as an open field for manipulation and exploitation. The failure of major powers to come to the aid of Afghanistan and strengthen its intelligence agency not only created more extremism, radicalisation, and terrorism but also created insecurity. The Russians were intensely involved in Afghan internal politics until 1978, seeking to overthrow the local ruling leaders in order to further their regional interests.[11] Both the Russians (Soviet Union) and Americans had very similar objectives; however, it is difficult to compare the CIA with the KGB (Russian Committee for State Security) as they used completely different intelligence methodology and approach.

In contemporary international politics, intelligence plays the most important role in the protection of state security. Experts view intelligence as more than classified and organised information; it can include technical issues such as the transcription of intercepted conversation and verification of the reliability of information. In modern studies, experts view intelligence as a real struggle with human opponents to gain some advantages.[12] Another thing that prompted confusion among security experts is the basic task of an intelligence agency during war and peace.[13]

In the Western world, governments view intelligence not only as an advance warning about looming threats but also as an umbrella—a range of activities from planning and information to analysis, all conducted in secret.[14] However, it is important to emphasise that the achievement of a reformed security sector of Afghanistan is very much a function of the extent to which the national unity government can broadly be perceived as legitimate.

To deeply analyse the intelligence operations of the NDS, the author conducted detailed discussions with former Afghan President Hamid Karzai in London, former Army Chief General Sher Muhammad Karimi in Kabul, government officials, and Afghan intelligence experts and researchers and consulted classified documents. Because of very limited academic literature and secrecy, very little is written about the NDS. In its normative dimensions, this article tries to answer questions related not to the technicalities of intelligence and cover operations, but to the political ways which they could be made accountable and why the NDS matters after the 9/11 attacks. Afghan intelligence agencies relied on human intelligence because of the lack of intelligence equipment and funds.

The information they are collecting about the insurgent threat in remote districts through farmers, teachers, shopkeepers, and village elders is of low quality and unauthentic. Similarly, the literature on the Afghanistan intelligence agencies is scarce and is often of poor quality; therefore, writing on Afghan intelligence is not an easy task as there is very limited information available to writers and researchers in libraries. There is not much scholarly research on Afghanistan intelligence and not much is spoken about it. Hopefully, this article will greatly benefit the academy of intelligence and future research.

Afghanistan Security Services during the communist regime (1978–1992)

Afghanistan is a mountainous, landlocked state of about 652,230 km2 bordered by China, Iran, Pakistan, Tajikistan, Turkmenistan, and Uzbekistan. In 2015, the population of Afghanistan was about 32.5 million. The largest ethnic group among the population is the Pashtuns, followed by Tajiks, Hazaras, Uzbeks and others. The main languages spoken are Pashto and Dari.[15] Afghanistan has a lot of natural resources such as gas, petroleum, coal, copper, chromate, talc, barites, sulphur, lead, zinc, iron ore, salt, precious and semiprecious stones and arable land.[16] As Afghanistan is a landlocked state with lots of national resources, the NDS is continuously facing challenges from the neighbouring countries. The biggest factors affecting the NDS were the almost complete absence of international forces on the battlefield and the Pakistan-sponsored terrorism. Furthermore, Daesh, another new actor in the war, also presented a dangerous and new, though geographically limited, threat to the population. The mass migration from Pakistan, the intelligence source of information shrieked, the working methods changed from civilian intelligence to the militarised way of operation.

The governments in Afghanistan paid little attention to the basic function and importance of intelligence during the last four decades. Various intelligence agencies were established with the technical support of the KGB and GRU (Russian Military Intelligence Directorate) to make effective the war against the mujahedeen. However, Wazarat-e-Amniat-e-Daulati (WAD) and Khadamar-e Aetela'at-e Dawlati (KhAD) had established friendly relation with the KGB and GRU, because they had deep influence on Afghan intelligence operations. From 1980 to 1992, these secret agencies played a vital role in countering insurgency in Afghanistan, but after the fall of Dr Najibullah's government in 1992 and the collapse of the whole infrastructure of the state, Afghanistan lost its state intelligence agencies.[17]

The 1980s saw much upheaval and fictionalisation in Afghan politics and bureaucracy. The successful governments in Afghanistan established four intelligence agencies (Da Kargarano Amniyati Mu'asasa [KAM; Workers Intelligence Service], Da Afghanistan da Gato de Satalo Adara [AGSA; Safeguarding Agency of Afghan Interests], WAD, and KhAD) to ensure the stability of the country.[18] President Noor Muhammad Tarakai was in power for a limited time, while Hafizullah Amin's politics forced a division between the communist party and intelligence agencies into two factions (Khalq and Parcham). However, the AGSA, which was established by Mr. Tarakai, was dissolved because of his differences with Hafizullah Amin.

In 1979, President Amin established another secret agency named "Da Kargarano Amniyati Mu'asasa".[19] Hafizullah Amin used KAM against its opponents and the change of name did not mean that the terror exercised by the AGSA was stopped. The agency continued to torture and killed thousands of Afghan civilians. The AGSA and KAM received direct assistance from East Germany and the Union of Soviet Socialist Republics (USSR) but never established the degree of sophistication shown by KhAD.[20]

The Council of European Relations (2001) reviewed Afghan intelligence KhAD from a historical perspective, in its well-researched report, which gives us some fresh information about the function of secret services. On 11 January 1980, the government announced that KhAD would replace KAM. KhAD was removed from the Khalqi-dominated MoI and made a department of the Office of the Prime Minister and later transformed into the Ministry of State Security, WAD, in 1986.[21] Its director general, Dr Najibullah, reported directly to the KGB. Additionally, according to one estimate, by 1987 WAD employed 15,000 to 30,000 professionals and about 100,000 paid informers and each KhAD official had one or more KGB advisers.[22] On the other hand, the ISI trained about 83,000 mujahedeen between 1983 and 1993 with the support of the CIA and sent them to Afghanistan to fight against the Soviet Union.[23]

KhAD was responsible for the security of the state and most importantly to ensure the continued existence of the communist regime and was working on uniting all tribes and ethnic minorities in collaboration with the Ministry of Nationalities and Tribal Affairs. However, KhAD was also known as KGB secret police, imposing pervasive terror on urban areas as the government tried to impose a totalitarian system in those areas under its control.[24] The agency also funded religious leaders and established a separate directorate named the Directorate of Religious Affairs. The political role of KhAD was of great importance, as Afghan President Dr Najibullah as the head of the political directorate sought to convince all political factions that the Soviet war in Afghanistan was a just war. For all its efforts, the Soviets and the Afghan government made remarkably little progress towards re-establishing state control or even state presence in most of the countryside.

During the KhAD years (1980s), torture was introduced under the instruction of East German and Soviet KGB officers, who reportedly provided modern electrical torture devices.[25] Mass secret executions without trial began and thousands started to disappear. The treatment of prisoners changed since the establishment of the KGB-controlled KhAD and it became part of a scientific system of intelligence rather than just a form of sadistic punishment. Lots of training centres were established for orphaned children under the control and direction of the secret police, KhAD (WAD), since the children did not have any relatives to object.[26]

According to Rosanne Klass, more than 60,000 Afghans were sent to the Soviet Union between 1980 and 1984. By the end of 1985, more than 10,000 members of KhAD had received special training by the KGB.[27] As the NDS was lacking experienced intelligence officers since the CIA was not producing the huge number of qualified intelligence officers that the KGB did, the NDS had no option but to use the KGB-trained officers or inexperienced officers. This is an issue that needs to be addressed and reform is needed. The reform of the intelligence agencies is imperative and the de-politicisation of the intelligence process is as much an element of national reconciliation as consolidation of power.

Furthermore, KhAD formed widespread networks of spies and informers, and established militia and tribal units close to the border to observe activities, to interdict resistance lines of supply and movement, and to guard regime personnel. Tactically, the KGB developed tribes to penetrate resistance groups, sabotage resistance operations, spread rumours and disinformation, and create suspicions and enmity both within and among the various resistance groups and between the residence and local tribes and communities.[28] These agents set one tribe against another, encouraging and bribing powerful tribal chiefs, leaders, and dissidents of all sorts to exploit their personal oppositions, and they also persuaded or bribed them to restrain their respective tribes and communities from anti-communist activities. The Soviets' intention was to deprive the Afghans of their cultural heritage and identity and to transform the country into a passive future instrument of Soviet policy.

Where did America go wrong?

In the 19th century, America viewed Afghanistan as strategically unimportant, but in 1922, Cornelius Van H. Engert, the first American diplomat to visit Afghanistan, wrote a detailed report in which he strongly recommended recognition of the country's importance.[29] However, his report was filed away and ignored. The US refused to recognise Afghanistan as an important country until 1934 as a diplomat, Wallace Murray, assured the American Congress that the US could not extend recognition to Afghanistan because it was probably the most fanatic hostile country in the world.[30] This attitude prevented the US government from opening a diplomatic mission in Kabul until 1942. When in 1953 Daud Khan, the Prime Minister, asked Washington's aid to modernise Afghanistan's army, the Eisenhower Administration refused his request.[31] This is where America went wrong again. If it had agreed to offer military assistance, Afghanistan would not have turned to Moscow.

However, the US Agency for International Development, and its predecessor the Technical Cooperation Agency, in 1960 provided assistance to fund the Helmand and Arghandab Valley Authority following up on the work done by an American company on Helmand River on contract to the Afghanistan government.[32] Helmand River meanders through southern Afghanistan, representing 40% of the country's water resources. The US assistance of approximately $80 million continued and they were officially involved in this project from 1949 until the Soviet invasion in 1979.[33] The main reason for the development was to settle new farmers on land reclaimed through irrigation. This was a good opportunity for the US to make its relationship strong with Afghanistan.

The successful Soviet penetration of Afghanistan started when America failed to respond to the real economic and security needs of a friendly and pro-western Afghanistan and to understand the internal Afghan politics of the Pashtunistan problem. The US for the next two decades watched with remarkable calmness as the Soviets gradually increased their armed forces in Afghanistan, dictating to KhAD, training their own army, getting a foothold in the educational system, building a strategic highway system, gaining control of resource development and ultimately achieving an economic hammerlock on the country.

Between 1953 and 1963 the Soviet economic, military, and cultural programmes were set up as to satisfy the needs of Afghans themselves, but were in fact mainly set up to serve the Soviet political, economic and strategic interests.[34] By 1978 the Soviets had completed 71 separate projects, were working on 52, and had agreed on 60 more. The Soviet Union had invested more than three billion dollars in Afghanistan.[35] They had also trained 5000 students in Soviet academic institutions and 1600 in technical schools, plus 3725 Afghan military personnel.[36] Daud Khan's regime made all this possible, and the inadequate American diplomatic response failed to prevent it time and again.

The CIA gave birth to the NDS

After two decades of consecutive wars, in 2002, the NDS was established by the CIA and Pentagon to help them in countering the Taliban insurgence and collect intelligence in cities and remote districts.[37] This new agency was the successor to KhAD.[38] During USSR presence in Afghanistan, KhAD was the strongest intelligence organisation, resourceful, trained and operated as a professional intelligence in the battlefield; however, KhAD subjected many to prolonged incommunicado detention without charge or trial for interrogation and torture,[39] whereas the present NDS is a strong, capable organisation but lacks professional and skilled staff, as well as has limited funds.

Since the establishment of the NDS, no reforms were introduced to make it a professional intelligence agency or to adopt the CIA structures. The country is in need of a well organised intelligence agency to provide important information on the activities of insurgents. The NDS is not a new intelligence agency but an agency with a different name and funder. In May 2016, in an interview during his visit to London, the former President Hamid Karzai stated: "NDS' job is to gather, analyse and share intelligence, and to give advice in support to foreign policy. Intelligence must not be a repressive tool in the country but a national security tool."[40] In Afghanistan, the main source for intelligence collection is interaction with tribal elders and villagers through local commanders. Sometimes, because of its demonstration of ineffective intelligence, the NDS faces criticism from parliamentarians and media.

The NDS does not fall under the MoD or MoI command, but liaises closely with the ANSF at every level [41] and is overseen by the NSA but reports directly to the President. The NDS as an organisation is accused of not sharing all its information with the police department and defence ministry and of not providing reliable information to policymakers. There were also instances of policymakers not taking intelligence seriously, acting late or not trusting the intelligence. The other major weakness of the agency is the lack of modern ways of intelligence analysis.[42] Historical records suggest that the areas where the intelligence cycle most frequently fails are in the assessment process and the policy interface rather than in collection. For the conceptual framework of intelligence studies to advance further, it is essential to make a clearer distinction than is usually made at present between the roles of intelligence communities in authoritarian and democratic regimes. Afghanistan intelligence is in need of modern intelligence systems to change the nature of authoritarianism within the organisation.

On the function of the NDS in war zones, in an interview, the former Chief of Army Staff of Afghanistan General Sher Mohammad Karimi stated: "NDS is presently fighting against terrorists and provides information to the army and police, and working closely with intelligence department of the army and police. The agency is using Special Forces against terrorist networks directly, depending on the situation. The strength of NDS is based on limited funds provided by the US and NATO member states. The nature of the enemy in the region demands covert and unconventional special operations in response. Today countries are using intelligence extensively and it needs special operations to deny their access to the homeland."[43]

Because of the flawed intelligence operations, distrust between the government and the NDS is exacerbated when agency officials refuse to hear the Commander in Chief (President). The controversial nature of the NDS emerged in debates in national and international forums, when chiefs of the agency started acting like politicians criticising the President, neighbouring states, and the parliament. This kind of behaviour raised many questions as to whether the NDS is an intelligence agency or a political party.

Amidst these controversies, former President Hamid Karzai changed three NDS chiefs, but no change occurred in the mindset of the agency officers. In fact, according to Mr Musa Khan Jalalzai, the NDS was divided between the Presidential office and the Northern Alliance.[44] Therefore; it can be argued that the NDS operations in 2015 lost the confidence of the Afghan government and international community when the Taliban captured most of Kunduz province, a big intelligence failure by the NDS. To prevent intelligence failure, intercourse between the three levels of intelligence—strategic, operational, and tactical—is necessary. Intelligence failure can be broadly defined as misunderstanding the prevailing situation or the developing law and order scenario. To fix the machine, the government needs to introduce a reforms package.

On the oversight and legal aspect of intelligence operations, General Karimi stated: "NDS must obtain permission from the court for any of the actions they need to take. It is important to note, anyone in the intelligence field must understand power, responsibility and commitment (Moka-lafiyat, Masuliyat and Selahiyat)."[45] When intelligence planning and operations fail, it means something is not working in the machine properly. Normally, intelligence failure occurs due to preventable conditions, such as lack of understanding, capabilities, coordination, cooperation, and poor distribution of intelligence among the intelligence agencies.

Additionally, General Karimi stated: "Every country small or big, strong or weak has security forces (army, air force, navy, police, intelligence and many other related auxiliary organisations). One of the elements of security is the intelligence organisation. Intelligence organisation is usually called Department of Security or National Security or State Security. It functions in accordance with national policies. It is both offensive and defensive. Our state security agency, the NDS, is mainly defensive. When the Taliban were defeated in 2001, the reform of the security sector was one of the key issues. The US was directly responsible for the reorganisation of the army and NDS and later for the police as well."[46] The Afghan government and the ANSF will need an integrated approach to both internal security and human intelligence (HUMINT), as Afghan intelligence plays a critical role in supplementing International Security Assistance Force (ISAF) and US collection and analysis capabilities, mainly at the local level where HUMIN is critical.

Also, the NDS mainly deals with national security cases and kidnapping and the NDS detainees do not follow the requirements of the Interim Criminal Procedure Code.[47] As the primary intelligence organisation of Afghanistan, the NDS shares information with ministries of Afghanistan and with provincial authorities. Like most ANA officers, the NDS personnel are mainly either ex-Soviet trained or ex-mujahedeen. Testifying before the US Senate Armed Services Committee in February 2016, General Campbell said the Afghan National Defence and Security Forces (ANDSF) still suffers from capability gaps in aviation, combined-arms operations, and military intelligence, and added, "those capability gaps notwithstanding, I still assess that at least 70% of the problems facing the Afghan security forces result from poor leadership."[48]

General Campbell further noted that dozens of poor performing officers have been replaced. But even the best of leaders cannot do their jobs without a clear understanding each day of how many personnel, and with what skills, are present for duty.[49] Afghan author and journalist Musa Khan Jalalzai in his article in 2014 has pointed to the failure and incompetency of the NDS to deliver: "Intelligence failure in several districts of the country occurs when an attack happens without warning. A majority of the Afghan intelligence agencies have never been in schools, colleges and universities, while their appointments have been made on a political and ethnic basis. They happened to be more like politicians and less like secret agents."[50]

Notably, the NDS is one of the most capable branches of the ANSF; however, it is clear that the NDS activities do need to be fully integrated with those of the ANSF and ISAF, and that there have been coordination problems in the past. The role of the NDS in intelligence operations nowadays is very important as its agents belong to various tribes, sects, ethnicities, and regions. The NDS has managed sources in every district, tribe, and region. The NDS fights in the front line and against subversions as it protects military and civilian in salvations.

Even 15 years after the US and its allies routed most al-Qaeda militants and other terrorist groups; the country is again becoming a haven for extremist groups. As stated by the former President

Karzai in an interview with Russian television (RT): "there is no security, no end to extremism and radicalism rather we see more insecurity, extremism and radicalism."[51] Likewise, General Campbell informed the Senate Armed Services Committee (SASC) in February 2016 that Afghanistan had not achieved an enduring level of security and stability that would allow for a reduction in US support. Also that month National Intelligence Director James R. Clapper told the SASC that the intelligence community believes "fighting in 2016 will be more intense than 2015, continuing a decade-long trend of deteriorating security."[52]

Since the majority of the US troops left Afghanistan, the drones and surveillance balloons to monitor remote areas of the vast and rugged country are all gone. According to The Wall Street Journal report, as of September 2015, all but about 20 of the installations that anchored the extensive intelligence-gathering network have been closed, bull-dozed or handed off to the Afghan government.[53] Furthermore, Mr Karzai stated: "The fight against terrorism will not succeed unless we fight it in their sanctuaries, their training grounds, their motivation and their financial resources."[54]

Besides, the US Department of State's publication Country Reports on Terrorism 2015 stated: "the Afghan government does not have a comprehensive formal national countering violent extremism (CVE) strategy, but has begun the process to develop one. The Office of the National Security Council has designated a team to take the lead in coordinating the government's CVE engagement. Various ministries and offices have CVE issues incorporated in their portfolios. The government continues to support activities designed to prevent radicalization."[55] Radicalised terrorists from various groups use different terrorist tactics to pursue their goals. Methods used included suicide bombers, vehicle-born improvised explosive devices, ambushes, kidnappings, beheadings, and targeted assassinations.[56]

Although the Congressional Research Service noted that the US spent about $1.6 trillion in Iraq and Afghanistan to win the war against terrorism,[57] the result has not been very positive. According to the Special Inspector General for Afghanistan

Reconstruction (SIGAR) quarterly report published in April 2016, as of 31 March 2016 the US Congress had appropriated more than $68.4 billion to support the ANDSF. This accounts for 60% of all US reconstruction funding for Afghanistan since fiscal year 2002.[58] The total Afghanistan Security Forces Fund request for fiscal year 2017 is $3.45 billion, which is less than the previous year's appropriation of $3.65 billion.[59]

Although so much money is spent to improve security and bring peace, the challenges of the security forces are multiplying. There are many factors as to why so many NATO countries and the CIA failed to accomplish a change of intelligence culture and professionalise the NDS in the last 15 years. The resources invested by the CIA to bring a change were not used in the right approach as well as CIA specialist and Special Forces Units alike were being reassigned to the Iraq theatre. Not many of the CIA personnel knew the Afghan Intelligence culture and the US analysts increasingly believed that support for religious militancy within Pakistan's military and ISI was one of the key obstacles to formulating a sound approach towards Afghanistan. As President Obama remarked in his December 2009 West Point address, "success in Afghanistan is inextricably linked to our partnership with Pakistan."[60]

The US and NATO response has always been behind the curve and ignoring it to wage war in Iraq. It was a fatal error to allow the insurgency to grow so strong that defeating it would be brought into question and cost so many lives. There are other terrorist groups expanding such as al-Qaeda in the Indian subcontinent and ISIL/ Daesh. As Afghanistan is largely unmonitored and the NDS is failing to monitor all the doors to the country, it is highly likely that extremists from Islamic states, al-Qaeda, Daesh, and other militant groups can find safe haven inside the country's borders. As long as the Afghan government faces obstacles such as complex organisational structures, weak inter-ministerial coordination, corruption, lack of territorial control, and safe havens for terrorist groups operating on its soil, the ongoing challenges will continue to remain. Terrorist attacks are always unexpected and dramatic.

Both Afghanistan and the US have long acknowledged the importance of developing air power. However, despite the fact that this was pointed out as a critical capability gap, the Afghan Air Force is still far from fully capable, let alone self-sustaining. According to the SIGAR quarterly report published on 30 April 2016, the impact of the lack of a well-equipped and capable Afghan Air Force became all too clear in the aftermath of the fall of Kunduz on 28 September 2015 to the Taliban. Despite the end of the US combat operations and a transition to a mission focused on training, advising, and assisting, the US forces were once again called upon to provide air support to the Afghan forces.[61] The Afghan forces were able to clear the city of Kunduz from insurgents, but required the US air power and other intelligence support in the operation. This was a capability gap, which needs to be addressed to prevent similar attacks in the future.

Conclusion

Historical records suggest that the areas where the intelligence cycle most frequently fails are in the assessment process and the policy interface rather than in collection. It is essential that the NDS, and the CIA that is funding it, more clearly differentiates between the role of intelligence communities in authoritarian and democratic regimes. It is, of course, impossible to change the history of the AGSA, KAM, KhAD, and WAD; the Afghanistan regimes at the time were heavily dependent on those intelligence services. The successful Soviet penetration of Afghanistan started when America failed to respond to the real economic and security needs of a friendly and pro-western Afghanistan and failed to understand the internal Afghan political requirements.

With the establishment of the unity government in Afghanistan, relations between the government and intelligence agencies remained under strain. Pakistani intelligence discussing with the NDS authorities about intelligence sharing and cooperation was the cause of many controversies. Furthermore, the fight between the Indian intelligence (Research and Analysis Wing) and the ISI is a bigger challenge for the NDS and CIA who want to stabilise the country. Abuse of intelligence is another challenge in Afghanistan with intelligence agencies behind the political opponents of the government.

With the NDS lacking experienced intelligence officers and the CIA unable to produce the numbers required, the NDS had no option but to use the KGB-trained officers or inexperienced officers who may also have criminal background. This is an issue that needs to be addressed and reform is needed. Moreover, Afghanistan is still at the very beginning of a process whose success is still uncertain. Change is never easy, and redirecting intelligence agencies to uphold a democratic process is a real challenge. While change is possible, it will be slow, frustrating, and painful. The reform of the intelligence agencies is therefore imperative, and the de-politicisation of the intelligence process is as much an element of national reconciliation as consolidation of power.

Reforming the intelligence agencies requires not only a change in the state, but also a change in the state of mind of the actors involved, and it must be understood in the larger context of civil-military relations. In the case of Afghanistan, this requires building trust – particularly difficult not only because of past relationships between civilians and intelligence agencies but also because of the structural contradictions it presents. The lack of trust is precisely why the agencies need to be controlled. The Taliban and al-Qaeda are not the only militant groups that appear to be exploiting the intelligence gap.

Thousands of central and south Asian Islamic militants have crossed into Afghanistan undetected this year after their havens in Pakistan were attacked. Significant reductions in counterterrorism capabilities aided the expansion of extremist groups. The lack of intelligence about militant activities in remote areas of Afghanistan stems from the drawdown of the US forces and the shutting of the US and NATO bases that began in 2012. Afghanistan became an object of charity and neglect for the US and other major powers. Regional powers, particularly Pakistan, as well as private networks, smugglers, drug dealers, and terrorists, treated it as an open field for manipulation and exploitation.

Pakistan's interests might not have changed much as it had hoped that the Taliban would provide it with strategic depth, a secure neighbourhood, and, potentially, oil resources from the north of the country, so as to be able to conclude the Kashmir question with India. In addition, Pakistan, as a principle supplier of weapons and fuel to the Taliban, is not in an awkward position.

The failure of major powers to come to the aid of Afghanistan and strengthen its intelligence agency not only created more extremism, radicalisation, and terrorism but also created insecurity beyond the Middle East. The Kunduz attack laid bare capability gaps within the ANSF. The government forces were able to clear the city of insurgents but despite the end of US combat operations and a transition, the US forces were once again called upon to provide air support to the Afghan forces.[62]

In spite of all these failures in Afghan intelligence, the government never tried to introduce intelligence reforms or fix the broken window. While there are more heart breaking stories about the intelligence failure that cannot be accommodated in this article due to limited space, it does provide evidence of the need to professionalise the NDS and its agencies.

(Journal of Intelligence and Terrorism Studies, University of Buckingham, Centre for Security and Intelligence Studies (BUCSIS), Buckingham, United Kingdom, 19 January 2017-Copyright-2016, Patang Wardak. Dr. Diva Patang Wardak has received her Master in Intelligence and Security Studies. She is a PhD Scholar at the University of Buckinghamshire, UK.

Chapter - 4

National Directorate of Intelligence (NDS) GRU, CIA, Taliban, and the ISIS Terror Group

Future of Afghanistan is in danger by different fundamental threats. The emergence of Russian Taliban, the ISIS terrorist group in Jalalabad, Fatimid sectarian group, Zainabia Brigade, ethnic and sectarian conflict, Pakistan based terrorist groups, and the confrontations between China and the United States are new threats that have embroiled the country in a cogent conglomeration. Russia recently made regional visits and discussions over Afghanistan-the-tragic-Kunduz incident that intimidated the Central Asian states and, above all, Russia. The Intensification of war in Afghanistan could keep Russia busy on developing new weapons technologies. Russian national interests are also permanently, and even existentially, threatened by the ISIS terrorist group in Afghanistan and Central Asia. The current war in Afghanistan reminds one of a chess game in which several stakeholders are moving with an illusion of an absent opponent. Analyst Elkhan Nuriyev (Russia in Global Affairs, 2018) highlighted confrontations among Russia, the West and China in his recent paper:

> Against a markedly different geopolitical backdrop compared to the Cold War era, the sharp deterioration of Russian-Western relations has a negative impact on the security environment in today's vastly turbulent Eurasia. Not for the first time in its long history, big geopolitics is emerging as a powerful tool in shaping the Eurasian security system. As

always, Eurasia, which sits at the heart of a knot of strategic issues that surround international politics, is dominating the global chessboard. Several major players – the United States, Russia, the EU, China, and the Islamic world – have arisen today in the Eurasian chess game. Realizing that the emerging global order is being shaped by various twists and turns in the Eurasian geopolitics, they all vie for regional pre-eminence. Each of them pursues its own strategic goals in this resource-rich continental landmass. Each actor plays on its own and against each other, without siding openly with anyone for the moment.[1]

The situation in Afghanistan is rapidly deteriorating. The Unity government in Kabul has lost control of its territory-handing it into the hands of the ISIS and Taliban militants. In his Valdai Discussion paper, Alexei Fenenko (2017) argued that domestic stakeholdarism, Taliban and the ISIS are causing irksome in Afghanistan:

> The country's problems are aggravated by contradictions inside the ruling regime. During a recent visit to Kabul, US Secretary of Defence James Mattis accused Russia of supporting the Taliban and even of supplying it with weapons. Moscow categorically rejects these accusations.......There are several reasons for this, the expert believes. First, the Afghan Government proved to be more solid than it was thought. Second, there is no agreement among its Islamist opponents, as there are constant conflicts between Al-Qaeda, Taliban, ISIS and other groups. Moreover, the so-called Tribal Zone has always been only under the nominal control government of the Afghan state. Finally, there is the problem of the Durand Line, which at one time determined the division of the border between Afghanistan and Pakistan, has become more acute.[2]

Moreover, Afghan Foreign Ministry on 02 October 2018 warned that the United States and Russia's tension on Ukraine can move to Afghanistan, which will have "negative repercussions" for the country if they begin here. In his remarks, Mr. Hekmat Khalil Karzai, the Deputy Foreign Minister said:

> The tensions are slowly moving from Ukraine toward Afghanistan. It will be a bad situation for Afghanistan when the tensions officially begin in Afghanistan," said Karzai. "Our goal should be to once again strengthen the consensus that Afghanistan's stability should be important for Russia even now," he said. "We should not expect China to put pressure on Pakistan 'automatically', because such an expectation is improper. We should recognize China's benefits (for us). China has invested $48 billion in CPEC (China–Pakistan Economic Corridor) only. How much it has invested in Afghanistan? What is the difference between China's benefit in Afghanistan and Pakistan? We should recognize this[3], said Karzai.

With the geographical expansion of the Islamic state, and the emergence of Khurasan group in Jalalabad, Russia and China comprehended that these developments were a direct threat to their national security and territorial integrity. Russia established its own Taliban, and adorned the group with sophisticated weapons to counter the Islamic State and exponentially growing US influence in Afghanistan and Central Asia. China supported the Russian plan. Russia also reinvented its old intelligence and political contacts in Afghanistan, while China deployed its army alongside Afghan-China border. Russian military intelligence (GRU) organized its old cadre in Afghanistan and created an environment, in which neither the US and NATO military commanders, nor Afghanistan's army commanders have been capable to cruise between small and big cities in open air.[4]

However, confinement of their forces, officers and commanders in forts is evident from the fact that when the US Foreign Minister splashed-down in Bagram Airbase in 2018, he was taken to NATO headquarter by helicopter. When he desired to meet Afghan President to discuss the prospect of US policy in South Asia, he again demanded a helicopter to the Presidential Place. Concurrently, he snubbed US commanders for their failure to bring stability in Afghanistan. The US and NATO allies were unable to patrol town and cities. They were inescapable in their forts and underground nests, while Russian and Chinese intelligence agencies were visiting people of all walks in cities and towns through their proxies.

Russia has already promoted friendly relations with Pakistan, China, Iran, and India, and stretched out its political and military influence across Central and South Asian regions. On the intra Afghan scene, Russian intelligence approach had already shifted throughout the 2000s from supporting Northern Alliance to prioritizing the national level and diversifying contacts to extent to all key Afghan communities. More recently, following the geographical expansion of Islamic State, Moscow even established communication with insurgent groups in Afghanistan.[5]

Afghan officials in 2018 warned that Russian intelligence was supporting the Taliban. After weeks of intense battles in the western Farah province in 2017, Afghan army's 207th Corps commander uncovered Russian intentions in Afghanistan. "Many large countries are involved in the Afghan war. We can name Russia, who is actively meddling in Farah, and we have seized Russian-made weapons, including night vision sniper scopes," Commander Mohammad Naser Hedayat, warned. Russia's recent push for influence in Afghanistan follows a pattern across the region, where Moscow has challenged American influence in Libya, Turkey, Syria and the Gulf.

US officials have often accused Moscow of supporting the Taliban. In December 2016, Gen Nicholson criticised Russia and Iran for establishing links with the Taliban to "legitimize" the group. Since then a number of high-ranking US officials made similar claims, some suggested Russia was also arming the Taliban. In a recent interview, Gen. John Nicholson, the senior U.S. and NATO commander in Afghanistan, said that he witnessed "destabilizing activity by the Russians" includes providing financial support and military weapons to the Taliban. Secretary of Defence James Mattis argued that funnelling weapons into the country was a violation of international law "unless they were coming to the government of Afghanistan."[6]

An active role of Russian intelligence in Afghanistan is bound to further complicate the geopolitics of the region. Although Russian diplomats emphasized that their contacts with the Taliban were limited to peace negotiations, Western officials claimed the Russian-Taliban ties prospered beyond that. From Afghanistan to Libya, the US Pentagon officials were increasingly concerned by mounting Russian military and diplomatic activity they believed was aimed at undermining the US and NATO. On 06 July 2018, ToloNews reported members of Helmand Peace Convoy protest outside the Russian embassy in Kabul. A spokesman for the convoy, Bismillah Watandost, told ToloNews that Afghans still realize the pains they suffered during the Soviet invasion in 1980s. "People of Russia should ask their government that why they interfere in Afghanistan's war? Why the (Russian) government provides equipment to the warring groups? Why their advisers have met with a number of groups?" asked Watandost.

The US and NATO mission in Afghanistan ultimately failed due to their kill and dump policy, which alienated Afghan citizens from their puppet governments. Eighteen years on, US commanders, Ministers, and guests have been unable to travel by car, or visit markets and shops openly. On 05 September 2018, US Secretary of State snubbed NATO commanders on the ground that they failed to bring peace and stability to Afghanistan. Mr. Zabihullah Noori (2017) in his article critically noted the failure of the Afghan government in tackling Taliban insurgency:

> Afghan forces are losing ground to insurgents. Taliban fighters have reached the doorsteps of Kabul. The Afghan government is dysfunctional with all its three branches of power acting illegally and against the Afghan Constitution. The international community's financial and military efforts in Afghanistan will be in vain if it does not engage fully and impartially in resolving the current political dispute among different parties. The dissatisfaction of major players within the government can lead to a civil war and the collapse of the

political system, which will only pave the way for the Taliban and Daesh to gain more territory.........A major turn back to democracy in the formation of National Unity Government (NUG), was the demolition of true political opposition. Since both front-runners running the government, there's no real opposition to hold them accountable to the people. Instead of taking measures to improve security, the government continued to cover up the shortcomings of the security officials, partly for ethnic and partisan biases. The government's culture of impunity to officials made the security officials even more irresponsible and indifferent to the situation. While this foul approach encouraged the Taliban and ISIS to become even more proactive.[7]

Author and journalist, Steve Coll in his New York Times analysis (2018) uncovered frustration of US authorities and failure of their forces to stabilize Afghanistan and defeat the Taliban. Mr. Coll critically analyzed failed strategies of political and military establishments about the peace process in Afghanistan:

The Trump administration undertook the latest rethinking of the war in August. President Trump's advisers again reviewed its causes: opium, corruption, ethnic factionalism and, above all, the support and sanctuary provided to the Taliban by Pakistan, through the covert action arm of its powerful spy agency, the Directorate for Inter-Services Intelligence. Why is this problem so hard? Why, since the Sept. 11 attacks, has the United States been unable to prevent Pakistan, a notional ally that has received billions of dollars in aid, from succouring the Taliban at such a high cost in American lives and Afghan misery? One major reason is American war aims in Afghanistan have been, and remain, riddled with contradictions and illusions that Inter-Services Intelligence can exploit. President Bush, President Barack Obama and President Trump have all offered convoluted, incomplete or unconvincing answers to essential questions: Why are we in Afghanistan? What interests justify our sacrifices? How will the war end? Mr. Trump is departing from his predecessors by getting tougher on Pakistan. His administration is withholding as much as $1.3 billion worth of annual aid to Pakistan until it does more to pressure the Taliban.[8]

Mr. Coll's study of Pakistani politics, military establishment and war in Afghanistan encouraged him to write a book on Pakistan's intelligence (ISI) role in the Afghan conflict. Pakistan has remained a key actor, especially its intelligence service, during the last 18 years war on terrorism in Afghanistan. Mr. Steve Coll highlighted the gloomy political culture that governs the relations between the US intelligence, Afghanistan and Pakistan. His book, "Directorate S" refers to a branch within the Inter-Services Intelligence (ISI) that deals with Afghanistan. In his analysis of the Afghan war, he noted important aspects of the US policies and strategies in Afghanistan:

> The leaders of Inter-Services Intelligence understood that they could wait Washington out. Mr. Obama made this obvious when he announced in 2009 that American troops would start withdrawing and handing off the war to Afghan forces in 2011. Pakistan's generals, led then by the Army chief Gen. Ashfaq Parvez Kayani, a former director of the spy agency, privately told American and NATO military leaders that they would fail. "Given the number of troops you have and the time constraints, you won't be able to do it," General Kayani said, according to a participant in the meeting. He meant that the American-led effort against the Taliban would not be decisive and that Afghan forces would never cohere enough to win. General Kayani wanted a less ambitious plan aimed at clearing radicals out of the Afghan-Pakistan border. Considering Inter-Services intelligence's role in the conflict, however, his prediction of American failure could be heard as much as a threat as a forecast. Pakistan's objective has been to prevent Afghanistan's violence from spilling over its border and to prevent India from gaining influence in a neighbouring country.[9]

In May 2018, Taliban attacked Afghanistan's Ministry of Interior in Kabul. The attack reportedly began when two vehicles were driven at the Interior Ministry's gate. The Afghan government also suffered casualties. This was the biggest failure of Afghan and US intelligence agencies to intercept terrorists reaching Interior Ministry. Both the Taliban and the Islamic State claimed responsibility for multiple operations inside the Afghan capital in 2018. On 30 April, 2018, two suicide bombers attacked Afghan intelligence headquarters, where nine journalists were killed, and six others wounded.[10] In 2014, establishment of Islamic State of Khorasan (ISK) in the Afghanistan-Pakistan region encouraged various extremist groups to join its ranks. Amira Jadoon, Nakissa Jahanbani, and Charmaine Willis in their analysis joint analysis have argued that this group can make alliances with regional and local group to expand its geographical influence:

> Expanding into new operational theatres can be a rewarding yet risky venture for transnational terrorist groups. Establishing a meaningful presence in a new region often depends on a new entrant's ability to build alliances, especially in militant-saturated areas like Afghanistan and Pakistan. Excessive rivalries, however, can get in the way. Islamic State Khorasan's (ISK) arrival in the Afghanistan-Pakistan region in 2014-2015 triggered a number of defections from regional militant organizations and individuals eager to exploit the ISK brand. A notable tide of pledges of allegiance followed, which included six Tehrik-i-Taliban Pakistan (TTP) leaders who publicly expressed their commitment to Abu Bakr al-Baghdadi in October 2014. Other groups' reactions ranged from pledging bay's to offering general support or remaining neutral. However, ISK's attempts to set up shop in the Afghanistan-Pakistan region by poaching discontented militants and establishing links with opportunistic leaders of local groups have also met resistance, often resulting in bloody clashes. Most notably, ISK militants have continually clashed with Taliban fighters in Afghanistan and the Federally Administered Tribal Areas of Pakistan (FATA).[11]

If the NATO member states had trained the NDS in a professional streak, the agency could have countered terrorism and espionage war in the continent. But unfortunately, Afghan intelligence (NDS) has been in turmoil and its security sector reforms proposals remained in procrastination-old intelligence infrastructure of cold war era resisting it. The NDS lack process, collection and analysis skills due to its limited access to remote areas in Afghanistan. However, Ghulam Farooq Mujaddidi (2017) spotlighted weaknesses and failure of NDS and its lack of resources to counter Taliban insurgents:

> Right after toppling the Taliban regime in late 2001 for refusing to handover Osama bin Laden–the perpetrator of the 9/11 attacks – the U.S.-led international community embarked on a state-building mission in Afghanistan. Part of their mission was – and still is – to build the ANDSF. Although their intention was noble and realistic, their approach has been misguided and wrong. Rather than prioritizing the ANDSF brain, the NDS, they have concentrated their efforts on building the ANDSF's body parts, namely the Afghan National Army (ANA) and the Afghan National Police (ANP). Due to this historical mistake, NDS – the main organ of the ANDSF – remains highly under-resourced and ill-equipped to tackle the challenges emanating from terrorist groups, as well as to counter unfriendly neighbouring countries' malicious intelligence interventions and activities inside the country. The number of high-profile attacks carried out since last year against hard ANDSF targets in the Afghan capital alone says it all about the status and competence of the NDS.[12]

On 11 March 2017, Mr. Amrullah Saleh was appointed by Presidential Decree to introduce significant reforms in the security sector. The appointment was made in terms of article 64 of the constitution. Mr. Saleh's duties included advice to the president on the appointment of new security officers, monitoring and implementation of a professional growth plan for high officers and giving advice on bringing about reforms in security departments.[13] Mr. Saleh failed due to his limited experience in intelligence studies. Afghan intelligence (NDS) also failed to counter Taliban with poor training and technology. The NDS became corrupt by the U.S. money and old technology, faces crucial gaps in intelligence collection and analysis, as well as a strong leadership. Analyst Javid

Ahmad (12 February 2018) describes incompetent operational mechanism of Afghan intelligence agencies:

> The agency's human-intelligence presence across Afghanistan is insufficient and weak, its surveillance and reconnaissance capabilities are deficient, and its sabotage activities are negligible. In fact, the Taliban's network of informants in many provinces is arguably stronger and more credible than that of the NDS, all while the insurgency miraculously manages to maintain its operational security. At the same time, Afghan intelligence and security operations are often not in sync, and tactical operations typically lack intelligence-gathering components that produce information for future operations. Afghan forces have been trained as operators, not intelligence collectors, so they rely on NDS for information. Crucial pieces of information are often missing, however, mainly because the NDS places little attention to its analytical functions to efficiently process and analyze intelligence collection. At times, the security directorate's sources and ownership of information and its reliability have been dubious. The directorate's primary sources of information in the field tend to be local commanders, militia leaders, strongmen, and tribal elders who often provide erroneous or biased information to advance their own agendas, including settling personal vendettas. In other cases, NDS officers collect unreliable, low-quality intelligence from local villagers, shopkeepers and farmers that is often difficult to validate. Corruption is also a problem. The spy service has been accused of nepotism and ethnic favouritism and has increasingly become politicized and factional. A large number of the agency's personnel are recruited through political connections, rather than professional channels. Many NDS personnel maintain loyalty to their ethnic leaders rather than the agency and tend to act more like political leaders than spies. Few are trained in the arts of intelligence to effectively manage sources, recruit assets, analyze large volumes of information, and write time-urgent assessment reports.[14]

Growing concerns among NDS leaders about increased infiltration of insurgents and Iranian and Pakistani double agents within their ranks resulted in the arrests of more than a dozen NDS agents in Pakistan. Indian analyst, Manish Rai, also raised the same question of ethnic composition and incompetency of the Afghan intelligence (NDS) in his article (2018), and argued that this type of composition poses challenges to the ability of the agency:

> The Afghan government has weak intelligence. Afghan forces require a robust intelligence collection and targeting capability if they want to turn back the tide of a reinvigorated Taliban insurgency. Afghanistan intelligence agency i.e. National Directorate of Security (NDS) not only suffers from an inability to share and disseminate actionable intelligence, but also is plagued by accusations of favouritism and nepotism. While its ethnic composition is dominated by Panjshiris Tajiks from Panjshir; a group affiliated with the former Northern Alliance. The NDS ethnic composition poses challenges to the intelligence agency's ability to infiltrate the Pashtun groups most likely affiliated with the continued insurgency in Afghanistan. There is also urgent need to increase more advanced voice intercept capabilities and cross communication between the National Directorate of Security (NDS) and security forces in the field.[15]

The failure of Afghan intelligence and CIA has also been highlighted by Karen McVeigh (2017). The Pentagon report noted failure of US forces to adorn Afghan intelligence with modern technology for intelligence collection: "The report, by the Special Inspector General for Afghanistan Reconstruction (SIGAR) said there was "no indication of improvement in overall intelligence operations" as a result of five contracts for training and mentoring, worth hundreds of millions of dollars, run by Legacy Afghanistan R&D and Afghanistan Source Operations Management (ASOM)".[16] However, an Afghan PhD scholar, and Journalist Ihsanullah Omar Khail (May 2018), has also noted some aspects of the NDS intelligence approach and argued that the ANP, ANA and NDS lack proper training. He also noted some flaws in the system of institutions:

> After US commanders mingled their ethnic militias into the Afghan National Army (ANA), Afghan National Police (ANP) and National Directorate of Security (NDS), these militias lacked proper military training, as they were all the products of civil war and a large number of them were deeply involved in maintaining ties with the political party Jamiat-e Islami. Meanwhile, most generals in the Afghan army are inclined to their personal interests and political views rather than to the national interest of the country. Many Afghan army generals are of Tajik ethnicity and at the same time have strong bonds to Jamiat-e Islami. The ANA, ANP and NDS are increasingly politicized by factions in Kabul and ethnic-based polarization. Most army men including generals even lack high-school diplomas and rose to the highest position within a speedy timeframe.[17]

The system with the largest contribution to Afghan intelligence success was the National Information Management System to share real-time intelligence and provides decision makers with the ability to make informed and time-sensitive decisions, but CIA and Pentagon did not develop this system for the NDS, and kept the agency dependent on US intelligence. Analyst Ghulam Farooq Mujaddidi (23 June 2017) views NDS as an incompetent agency and notes that it cannot thwart deadly Taliban attacks:

> While high profile attacks against hard targets take months of planning, surveillance, and coordination, NDS is unable to detect and thwart these deadly attacks during any of the preparatory stages. But this is not the only problem; NDS seems to gravely suffer in the intelligence-gathering field as well, and thus misses important developments in the country – not to mention its failures to prevent new and/ or root out existing Taliban infiltrators in ANDSF, who turn their guns on coalition troops. This has caused massive mistrust between foreign troops and Afghan security forces. Last year, an impostor was able to use ANA helicopters and

armoured vehicles, travelling from province to province with ANA transportation and protection after tricking an ANA corps commander along with several other high-ranking ANDSF officials with fake certificates of appreciation from the Presidential Palace. This wasn't his first time though; he had been engaging in such activities for more than a decade before his arrest. Nor was he the first person to do so. Before him, a "shopkeeper" disguised as a prominent Taliban leader and negotiator made it to the Presidential Palace and met with the former Afghan president, and another man posing as a "peace messenger" severely injured the former head of the NDS itself, to name some high profile cases.[18]

There were different concocted stories cruising around the NDS quarters. Researcher and analyst Anant Mishra noted in his paper the inability of the Afghan intelligence (NDS) to counter Taliban insurgents, or collect high-value information beneficial for the Afghan army. He also notes the NDS inexperienced operators and intelligence officers to guide military operations of the country's army:

Intelligence agencies in Afghanistan are outstandingly failing to collect information of high value beneficial for Afghan's domestic security. Deploying under-trained and inexperienced intelligence officers with limited knowledge of technical tools or key operational skills results in the collection of inadequate information [as well as inefficient] flow and management. With amateurish operational skills, these agents are unable to collect vital information for state security; some, even in the best of their experience, collect poor quality intelligence. Information collected from major known terror outfits and key government institutions could force policymakers and military leadership to make wrong decisions. The main objective of intelligence gathering is to maintain a swift flow of information, but the NDS officers are not well versed in this task. For example, the successful capture of Kunduz (a province in northern Afghanistan) by the Taliban did not occur because of their weapons superiority or technical expertise in battlefield; it happened because of massive failure of intelligence cooperation and coordination between the NDS, the National Security Agency of Afghanistan (NSA), the Ministry of Defence (MoD), and the Interior Ministry (MoI).[19]

The Afghan government and its intelligence agencies have long-standing worries that Pakistani intelligence (ISI) has been carrying out an operation inside Afghanistan through Afghan Taliban since 2004. This was further confirmed by many reports and books recently published in the United Kingdom. Writer Sandy Gall (2012) in his book elucidated the ISI involvement in Afghanistan, and noted the allegations of Afghanistan that ISI has been recruiting fighters and suicide bombers for the Afghan Taliban among the 1.7 million registered and 1-2 million unregistered Afghan refugees living in refugee camps and settlements along the Afghan-Pakistan border in Pakistan many of whom have lived there since the Soviet war in Afghanistan.[20]

An Afghan refugee living in Pakistan revealed that ISI once asked him to either receive training to join Afghan Taliban or for him and his family to leave the country. He explains: "It is a step by step process. First they come, they talk to you. They ask you for the information.... Then gradually they ask you for people they can train and send [to Afghanistan].... They say, 'Either you do what we say, or you leave the country. Another Afghan refugee, Mr. Janat Gul told the UN Office for the Coordination of Humanitarian Affairs, that Afghan refugees which had been successfully recruited by the ISI were taken to Pakistani training camps which had previously been used during the times of the Soviet war in Afghanistan.[21]

On 24 June 2015, Dawn reported Afghanistan's intelligence allegations against ISI officers who helped the Taliban carrying out an attack on parliament. Afghan intelligence services spokesman Hassib Sediqqi said that an officer of Inter-Services Intelligence helped the Haqqani network carrying out the attack outside parliament in Kabul, which killed two people and wounded more than 30. Mr. Sediqqi said the suicide car bomb which was used in this attack was manufactured in Peshawar, adding that Afghan authorities were made aware of the attack on 10 June and had deployed extra security.[22]

On 25 June 2015, Express Tribune reported Pakistan Foreign Office repudiation against Afghan intelligence claims that an officer of Pakistan's spy agency, the Inter-Services Intelligence, and the Haqqani Network were involved in the attack on the Afghan parliament. Afghanistan's intelligence agency, the National Directorate of Security (NDS), alleged that the brazen attack on the parliament building in Kabul was planned in Peshawar. "We reject these allegations. These allegations have been levelled against ISI and its officers in the past as well," Foreign Ministry spokesperson Qazi Khalilullah said.[23]

However, on 13 February 2015, Dawn reported Mr. Musharaf's interview with the Guardian in which he admitted that during his tenure as the head of state, Pakistan had tried to undermine the government of former Afghan President Hamid Karzai because Karzai had helped "India stab Pakistan in the back". Mr. Musharaf revealed that: "Obviously we were looking for some groups to counter this Indian action against Pakistan, Definitely they were in contact, and they should be. In President Karzai's times, yes, indeed, he was damaging Pakistan and therefore we were working against his interest. Obviously, we had to protect our own interest," Musharraf said.[24] The CIA's handouts about the cash President Karzai received from CIA and MI6 was reported by the New York Times. Failure of the US and Britain's intelligence raised questions important question.[25]

Chapter - 5

Pakistani Deep State, Democratic Forces, Tug-of-War, and Terrorism Afghanistan

Pakistan is jiggling on the brink. The Scimitar of the jihadist ideology of miltablishment is not either effective to destabilize south or Central Asia. The country's domestic policy is in dire straits. Disgruntlement and inner-pain of fighting soldiers and officers in Waziristan and Baluchistan is exacerbating by the day, which made them schizophrenic. Patience of Baloch and Pashtun leaders has now dematerialized to tolerate the search and stop policy of armed forces and the abduction of their children, women and tribal elders by intelligence agencies. They are dying of starvation and diseases in hospitals and desets[1].

Broken-down ethnically, the garrison state is now tottering under heavy burden of debt and poverty[2]. National debt of the country has soared past US$100b. Prime Minister Imran Khan with his porringer at hands has been cruising across Asian continent-beseeching for financial help to pay for the debt interest since 2018.[3] To that end; the Prime Minister supplicated the IMF for bailout package to treat the wounds of his teetering-tottering state. Pakistan needs to pay back $100b to China by 2024 of total investment of $18.5b.[4] Alike Baluchistan, Sindh, and FATA, Waziristan is in turmoil. The ISIS, Taliban and Jihadists returned to the region and continue to target civilians and military installations. The Nexus of Mullah and miltablishment is making things worse. The deep state is expanding its sphere of influence to all state institution to gradually undermine democracy, and prosper its private criminal enterprise[5].

In his Asia Times column, Mr. Imad Zafar noted nexus of jihadists, wealthy individuals and the army in Pakistan: "The nexus of mullah, property tycoons and businesses men and serving and retired bureaucrats and opportunist politicians have all lent their support to the invisible forces in order for the deep state to maintain a successful business enterprise"[6]. They must know that the invisible forces are in trouble while they lost the confidence of civil society. Pakistani intelligence agencies are undergoing deep crisis of national security management, and professional credibility. Contest of strength between ISI and the IB, and misplaced sense of patriotism[7]; poor politicized and sectarianized organizational management, and their inefficient approach to national security threatened the territorial integrity of the staggering state[8]. The uninterrupted militarization of public mind and thought, and the enfeebled operational mechanism of civilian intelligence in the country-to that end, every movement, action and way of thinking of Pakistan's political leadership have become militarized, and seek a military solution to every bigger and minor issue[9].

Expanding the theatre of their illegal business of forced-disappearance to cover major foreign and domestic policy areas, the agencies have assumed more controversial proportions than ever before. Normally, the prime task of intelligence agencies is to lead policy makers on the right direction, but the case here in Pakistan is different[10]. The agencies are misleading political leadership and policy makers on the wrong direction, and making alliances of radicalized elements in support of miltablishment.[11] In all previous democratic governments of the country, even Cabinet Minister never stumped out to question secret agencies about their illegal prisons, and kidnapping for ransom. Those who dared to ask generals and spy masters about the wrecking they inflicted on the country were retired, killed, or transferred to remote regions[12]. Civilian and military intelligence agencies in Pakistan face numerous challenges, including widespread lack of civilian support, faith in oneself, sectarian and political affiliations, and the war in Waziristan, and Baluchistan where their circumference of intelligence information collection has shrunken[13].

In most parts of the country, intelligence information collection faces numerous difficulties since the Taliban and other militant groups returned to FATA region. Having failed to defeat insurgent forces in Baluchistan and Waziristan, the agencies started translating their anger into the kidnapping of innocent civilians with impunity. Amnesty International called upon the Pakistani authorities to immediately carry out independent and effective investigations with a view to determining the fate and whereabouts of all missing people, where they are in the custody of the state to either release them or charge them with a recognizable criminal offence. Anyone reasonably suspected of criminal responsibility for enforced disappearances must be held to account through fair trials.

Enforced disappearance is frequently used as a strategy to spread terror within society. The feeling of insecurity and fear it generates is not limited to the close relatives of the disappeared, but also affects communities and society as a whole. Democratic governments in Pakistan established several commissions in yesteryears to force intelligence agencies for releasing illegally detained citizens. Human Rights Commission of Pakistan has already called on intelligence agencies to help the commission in recovering kidnapped activists. Mr. Abubakar Siddique (01 June 2018) has documented number of kidnapped citizens by intelligence agencies of Pakistan:

> In its recent report issued on May 31, the Commission of Inquiry on Enforced Disappearances said it has received 5,177 cases of alleged enforced disappearances since its inception in 2011. This number highlights the magnitude of enforced disappearances in Pakistan. During the past 15 years, families of separatists, members of ethno-nationalist political parties, peace activists, members of Islamist factions, and critics of the military have frequently accused authorities of either orchestrating enforced disappearances or failing to help in finding their loved ones. The north-western Khyber Pakhtunkhwa Province together with the merged areas of the former Federally Administered Tribal Areas has the highest number of cases. The commission's data says that out of 2,157

reported cases in the region, the commission has resolved 967 cases and is still working on 983.[14]

Baloch, Pashtuns and Sindhis are oppressed communities of Pakistan. Enforced disappearance, extrajudicial killings, and confinement of political prisoners are very common in Pakistan. According to the Voice for the Baloch Missing Persons (VBMP): "people have continued to go missing under Mr. Khan Government. "Around 1,200 people have gone missing only in 2018 but 450 of them were picked up since Imran Khan became PM". Pakistan's Supreme Court in multiple judgments, acknowledged the role of security and intelligence agencies in enforced disappearances and secret detentions-holding that the practice constitutes a violation of the "fundamental rights" recognized by the Constitution of Pakistan as well as international human rights law.

Faisal Siddiqi in his analysis (06 February 2017) argued that the issue of enforced disappearances is a difficult moral and political one, and Pakistanis should have the courage to recognize that there are no choices between good and bad solutions in such difficult issues. "We must make these tough choices". Pakistan's security agencies have been repeatedly blamed for supervising enforced disappearances to suppress criticism. In recent years, a number of abductions, allegedly by the agencies, have taken place notoriously in major cities of Pakistan. On 18 July 2018, Mr. Justice Shaukat Aziz Siddiqui of Islamabad High Court publicly called on the military's top brass that ISI has been involved in corrupt practices including providing aid in the commission of offences and receiving their share from crime money. "I am constrained to observe that local police is in league with the mighty agencies who have disrupted the civic fibber of the country," Siddiqui said in a written order concerning a petition about the missing people".[15]

Radio Free Europe reported the removal of Justice Shauka Siddiqi due to his criticism against ISI, and its illegal influence on courts proceedings: "Justice Shaukat Siddiqi was removed as judge of a high court in the capital, Islamabad, through an order issued overnight by the president of Pakistan, the Law Ministry announced on 12 October 2018. The Supreme Judicial Council, a body that oversees complaints against judges, had recommended Siddiqi's removal after a secret trial for "defaming a state institution," the ministry said. Siddiqi had accused the Pakistani Army's spy agency, Inter-Services Intelligence (ISI), of manipulating the elections that brought Prime Minister Imran Khan to power in July -- an accusation that was also made by Khan's opponents.

Sectarian policies of General Zai-ul Haq created more trouble for the military and civilian agencies. During the Zia military regime, the process of radicalization began in military barracks, and intelligence infrastructure, and a major change occurred when Zia-ul-Haq instructed military and its intelligence units to take on combatant mullahs with them to the frontline. Soldiers and officers were also required to attend Tablighi Jamaat classes. The purpose was to indoctrinate young officers. All military, civilian and policing agencies were regularly participating in Tablighi congregation to purify their soul for the Afghan and Kashmir jihad. With the Afghan war came to an end, and jihadists returned to Pakistan, a new wave of terrorism and radicalization challenged the authority of the state, and weaken the resolve of secret agencies.

The Inter-Services Intelligence (ISI) never tried to intercept their violent actions against civilian and military installations. The ISI's intransigence and remorselessness to cooperate with civilian intelligence agencies on national security issues often prompted internal tug-of-war. The ISI never extended hand of cooperation to civilian intelligence agencies, or even considering Intelligence Bureau (IB) as an older civilian brother during the last two decades. This unending tug-of-war forced former Prime Minister Nawaz Sharif to restructure the IB and make it more effective to counter ISI's influence in democratic institutions. The greatest challenge Prime Minister Nawaz Sharif faced was on the national security front. The miltablishment was not happy with his national security approach and his silence over the arrest of Indian spy Kulbhushan Yadav[16].

The Intelligence Bureau is the country's main civilian agency that functions under the direct control of the Prime Minister-tackling terrorism, insurgency and extremism. The way military intelligence has operated in the past was not a traditional way. The IB has been the victim for its democratic stance. Inter-Services Intelligence, Military Intelligence and other units mostly concentrated on countering democratic forces, instead of tackling national security challenges[17]. When intelligence war among military and civilian agencies intensified, the blame-game became the main nucleation of literary debates in newspapers and electronic media that this war of interests making thing worse.

On April 3, 2014, Pakistani newspapers published news stories about the resolve of the Prime Minister to restructure the country's intelligence agencies, generating a hope that he wants to reinvent the real concept and culture of civilian intelligence in his country. The Intelligence Bureau, which never received attention from either civilian or military governments during the last 65 years, was now trying to stand on its feet and challenge the militarization of the intelligence mechanism in Pakistan. The Prime Minister, newspapers reported, allocated huge funds to the Intelligence Bureau to recruit and employ more agents to meet internal and external challenges the country faces.[18]

The list of problems faced by the Pakistani intelligence machine is long. The Intelligence Bureau also played a political role in the past. In 2008, a case was filed in Pakistan's Supreme Court against the alleged involvement of the agency in destabilizing the Shahbaz Sharif government in Punjab.[19] The Intelligence Bureau also spied on journalists and politicians in a non-traditional manner, which badly affected its professional reputation. The Prime Minister now realized that a legislative and structural umbrella was a must under which intelligence agencies must function without military and political interference, while remaining committed to their central mission.[20]

On February 25, 2014, former Prime Minister Nawaz Sharif approved and published the National Internal Security Policy (2014-2018) and introduced a new mechanism to counter internal and external threats. The involvement of the army and air force in tackling insurgency in the tribal areas and Waziristan caused misunderstanding, while Prime Minister was also forced to drink in a poisonous bowl. Mr. Sharif was in a state of muzzy-fuzzy on the killings in Waziristan, but unable to explain his inner pain. Pakistani military was relying on US drone attacks against Taliban and innocent civilians, but never gave any importance to the intelligence reports of the country's agencies.[21]

The use of force in one's own country against one's own people always sends uncomfortable signals. In the intelligence relationship between policing intelligence, the Intelligence Bureau, Inter-Services Intelligence and Military Intelligence, lack of trust has been a longstanding concern in civilian circles. Majority of the members of intelligence agencies of the country belong to different sectarian groups. This illegal affiliation also directed intelligence operations on sectarian bases. Poor data collection with regard to the activities of militant sectarian organizations and their networks across the country is a challenging problem. Many criminals who joined terrorist groups are not tracked and profiled effectively. Many terrorists currently arrested have not been recognized properly, and these groups continue to propagate their agendas through their weekly, daily and monthly publications.[22] In his well-written report, Monish Gulati has outlined the basic role of intelligence in the modern world:

> Intelligence agencies must be clear about the challenges to the security of the state. Their ambit will perforce need to extend the entire gamut of collecting intelligence on internal security, external security, military intelligence—both tactical and strategic, economic and commercial intelligence as well as new data in science and technology related issues. Intelligence is essential but its purpose must be to inform action. It has a broader range of applications in the context of modern day threats."[23] In view of the aforementioned established mechanism of intelligence, Pakistani intelligence agencies now need to change their way of operations in countering extremism and militancy across the country. The Prime Minister's decision to restructure the intelligence infrastructure received worldwide appreciation. Mr. Sharif was in a position to take stern steps and wanted to improve the operational capabilities of his country's intelligence agencies.

The creation of an effective intelligence infrastructure to meet internal and external challenges must necessarily be taken as a long-term policy.[24]

The civilian watch-dog under instruction from a ruling Pakistan Muslim League-N, whose grip on power looked ever more shaky-had been carrying out round-the-clock surveillance of judiciary, opposition parties, and military intelligence for sometimes. It is known the officials from the military's Inter Services Intelligence (ISI) agency had their phone calls listened to at the height of civil-military tension in 2014, following an attempt on the life on the Geo-TV anchor Hamid Mir, who said he suspected ISI involvement.[25] The bubbling rivalry between the IB and ISI boiled over in June 2017 when a joint investigation team (IJIT) probing alleged money-laundering by the Sharif family made a written complaint to the Supreme Court that the IB was Wiretapping JIT members, including ISI and military intelligence personnel.[26] The JIT further reported that the IB was hampering its inquiries, adding that military-led intelligence agencies were not in "good terms" with the IB. It said that IB had collected intelligence on members of the JIT from the National Database and Registration authority (NADRA) and presented it to Nawaz to use it against them[27].

All civilian and military agencies followed a specific mindset. Their sectarian affiliation and dearth of electronically trained manpower, lack of professional surveillance approach, and lack of proper intelligence sharing culture, raised serious questions about their credibility, and weak national security approach[28]. These and other things also caused failure of National Counter Terrorism Authority (NACTA), to effectively counter the exponentially growing radicalization and extremism in Pakistan[29].

Military and civilian intelligence agencies did not cooperate with NACTA in its war against radicalized forces. As a matter of fact, NACTA established a Joint Intelligence Directorate and appointed 413 competent officers from ISI, MI, IB, and policing agencies to help democratic government in dealing with extremism and Talibanization in four provinces, but neither government paid long-term attention to support it financially, nor military establishment helped it to trains its operational managers.[30]

Under the NACTA Act, the agency was entrusted to the board of governors (BOG). The Prime Minister is its chairman, while Defence, Finance, and Foreign Ministers, Law Minister, Members of Senate and National Assembly, Chief Ministers of four provinces, Prime Minister of Kashmir, Interior Secretary, Director General Federal Investigation Agency (FIA), all Chiefs of intelligence agencies, and chiefs of Police Department from all provinces were given membership of National Counter Terrorism Authority (NACTA). On 25 September 2018, Prime Minister Imran Khan chaired first meeting of the board of governor of NACTA. Mr. Khan expressed dissatisfaction over the performance of NACTA, and ordered the establishment of a special committee to oversee its performance and make it competent.[31] Journalist and expert Imad Zafar painted a hard-featured and ominous image of the army deep state in his all-inclusive article. He mainly focuses on the army political and bureaucratic role in state institutions:

> As per the constitution of Pakistan, every democratic government is answerable to the people of Pakistan. But in reality, they are actually answerable to the GHQ............ Every single Prime Minister in Pakistan can only do their job smoothly if they completely surrender in the matter of defence, interior strategic decisions and foreign policy. It means the rule for civilian governments are already decided and they have been told to go by the book, not to cross the red-lines defined by the defence establishment. This makes it a "state within a state" that instead of ruling the country from the front prefers to politicians and civilian governments to implement its decision and exercise power[32].

In 2017, Prime Minister Nawaz Sharif tried to take control of foreign and internal policy of the country, but was disqualified by the Supreme Court. He desired to lead Pakistan's India and Afghan policy on right direction; but he was intercepted, humiliated, and his movements were salami-sliced[33]. Retrospectively, former President Asif Ali Zardari tried to bring ISI under democratic control; he met eyeball-to-eyeball and faced the same fate. He was pushed around that his crippled and torturous body would be shifted to hospital by an army ambulance. The consecutive militarization and Talibanization of society, and instability led to the catastrophe of disintegration and failure of the state, while most part of these challenges was further inflamed by the US war on terrorism, and international military involvement in Afghanistan.[34] Pakistan's weak and unprofessional diplomatic approach towards Afghanistan prompted deep crisis, including the closure of trade routes and diplomatic impasse[35.]

To punish Afghanistan's National Army, Pakistan's intelligence agencies have been providing with sophisticated weapons to Taliban and other extremist organizations to make the war in Afghanistan disastrous and unfavourable since 2001. Military establishment of the country continues to train, arm, and transport terrorist groups inside Afghanistan to target civilian and military installations, and make lives of women and children vulnerable. The ISI has often been accused by Afghan army of playing a role in major terrorist attacks. Pakistan (Vanda Felbab Brown, 5, 01 2018) has long been a strenuous and troublesome state to Afghanistan struggling to limit political influence of India there, and organize radical to create war like situation in Kashmir[36].

The war brought instability, hater, disparities and destruction due to regional rivalries. Peace is a far away dream in Afghanistan. Robert Kaplan (2012) warned in his book that if Taliban control Afghanistan, radicalization will get strong and Pakistan's sphere of influence will expand from India's border to Central Asia: "An Afghanistan that falls to Taliban sway threatens to create a succession of radicalized Islamic societies from the Indian-Pakistani border to Central Asia. This would be, in effect, a greater Pakistan, giving Pakistan's Inter Services Intelligence the ability to create a clandestine empire composed of the likes of Haqqani and the Lashkar-e-Taiba".[37.]

Moreover, Afghans understand that Pakistan army pursued its own agenda in Afghanistan in ways the country purveys funds and sanctuaries to Taliban on its soil. Its support to Haqqani

THE INTELLIGENCE WAR IN AFGHANISTAN

networks, and the ISIS, prolonged the Afghan war that caused catastrophe[38]. These and other misgivings and premonition caused great diplomatic and foreign policy challenges. Today, the country's leadership feels isolated, and no one likes to dance to its tango. These and other afflictions and suffering forced civilian leadership to recalibrate foreign policy of the country. On 28 February 2018, Dawn reported the country's National Security Committee (NSC) decision of recalibrating foreign policy to make it more effective and regionally focused[39]. Pakistan's nuclear marketing across the globe also caused embarrassment, mortification, and shame[40]. Pakistani scholar and Professor Pervez Hoodbhoy in his research paper uncovered the clandestine support of armed forces to sectarian religious groups against democratic governments:

> For three decades Pakistan's military establishment has stoutly denied supporting violent religious groups irrespective of whether a group's target lay across national borders or, instead, its goal was to achieve specific political objectives within Pakistan. But today the military's attitude is more ambivalent. Both serving and retired senior army officers are now openly expressing support for some groups. These include the newly emerged religious parties opposed to the PML-N government, notably Hafiz Saeed's Milli Muslim League (MML) and Khadim Hussain Rizvi's Tehreek Labbaik Ya Rasool Allah (TLYRA). Religious groups have already made their debut on the national scene and their initial successes—as in the NA-120 by-elections—are considerable. In a video that went viral, the serving DG of the Punjab Rangers, Maj-Gen Azhar Naveed, can be seen handing out coupons of Rs1000 to TLYRA demonstrators while assuring them support—"kya hum bhi aap kay saath nahin hain?"[41] On 25 December 2017, Afghan Minister of Interior, Wais Ahmad Barmak warned that Daesh in Afghanistan receive support from Pakistan and majority of the fighters belong to Afridi and Orakzai tribes based in Pakistan[42].

The Miltablishment and its secret agencies have been using jihadists in Kashmir and Afghanistan to achieve strategic goal since 2001. In Afghanistan, Pakistan backed Taliban are fighting to control natural resources sites in different province of the country in order to support their war machine. Pakistan army has already constructed a road from Chitral to Badakhshan province spick and span to make access easy to natural resources extracting sites. Expert Mr. Sanjeeb Kumar Mohanty and Jinendra Nath Mahanty in their research paper picked an argument on the military-Mullah Alliance, and their business of jihad in South Asia:

> The military-madrassa-mullah nexus has deliberately manipulated and encouraged jihadism by preferring a tactical deployment of jihadi groups in Kashmir and Afghanistan for expansion of regional influence......The internal situation in Pakistan has also deteriorated throughout these decades because of its focus on building up the militancy and grooming Islamic extremist groups as weapons in its eternal obsessive struggle against India. The military-militant cabal is the main problem of Pakistan today. The Abbottabad raid and the Mehran Naval Base attack in May this year were strong enough pointers in this direction. The two incidents were symptomatic of a large malaise that has been eroding the army's professionalism for quite some time. The signs of this malaise could be seen in the army leadership's obstinate hatred towards India, which has been driven primarily by paranoia and self interests.[43]

Pakistan's support to Taliban is for two reasons; to establish its political and military influence in Afghanistan, and push India back to the borderline of South Asia.[44] Pakistan is freethinking that its good Taliban are those who fight against Afghanistan and India, while it's bad Taliban are those who fight against its own army. This criterion for the identification of good and bad Taliban by miltablishment and the ISI is viewed by military experts as a left-handed game[45]. On 27 November 2013, former Prime Minister Nawaz Sharif appointed war criminal General Raheel Sharif as a Chief of Pakistan Army, who later on resisted his government pressure to introduce security and intelligence sector reforms.[46] This change of face didn't make effective war against Taliban. Warlord General Raheel's mission of killing innocent Pashtuns in Waziristan failed to eradicate militancy.[47]

Moreover, a large number of his army officers and soldiers refused to fight against civilian population. Warlord Raheel Sharif refused to negotiate with tribal leaders, and refused to respect parliament and democratic norms. He himself designed the policy of kill and shot for Waziristan; killed women and children with impunity, and kidnapped tribal elders[48]. The army failed to develop a true ethnic representation process or motivate Baloch and Sindhis to join the ranks of armed forces, but gained a good experience in the killing of innocent civilians. In Baluchistan, thousands Baloch men and women disappeared in a so-called military operations in yesteryears, while bodies of thousands of missing persons began turning up on roadsides. Since the killing of Akbar Bugti in 2006, more than 35,000 Balochs men were kidnapped or forcefully disappeared by Pakistani intelligence agencies and the police, in which 1500 were students and teachers.[49] Mr. Dhruv C. Katoch explains the operational mechanism of Pakistan's backed jihadists and their involvement in neighbouring states:

> The integration of "terror" into the military concept of war and strategy and involvement of civilians in a total holy war naturally led to the evaluation of the idea of non-state players who could be acting in connection with the military as part of their pre-action preparation, including striking "terror" in the heart of the enemy. The launching of various civilian militant groups during Zia-ul Haq's time could be traced to the evolution of this military doctrine. Sipah-e-Sahaba Pakistan (SSP) and its militant wing the Lashkar-e-Jhangvi were floated to quell Shiite and Christian opposition to pro-Sunni Islamization measures and the promulgation of Blasphemy Law, respectively. Pretty soon this doctrine of "terror" was married to 1976 Whitepaper on Kashmir brought out by Z.A Bhutto regime and Kashmir specific terror groups were launched, beginning with JKLF and then JI floated Hizb-ul Mujahideen and others[50].

The miltablishment and the ISI view Afghan Taliban as a good Taliban, and perceive their fight against Afghanistan as a welcome development. The army also perceives the Quetta Shura as a strategic asset, according to a recent interview of former army Chief General Musharaf (13 February 2015): "Hafiz Saeed, Haqqani, Osama Bin Laden, and Al-Jawahiri are our heroes".[51] In his most explosive interview with India Today Magazine (11 Feb 2016), former Pakistan President Pervez Musharraf pointed straight at the Inter-Services Intelligence for training Lashkar-e-Tayyeba and Jaish terrorists. "Inter-Services Intelligence (ISI) trains Jaish-e-Mohammad (JeM) and Lashkar-e-Tayyeba (LeT) terrorists," said Musharraf.[52] The issue of good and bad Taliban and their fight against Afghanistan and has been investigated and elucidated by Mr. Dhruv C Katoch in his research paper:

> The Pakistan army views Afghan groups such as the Quetta Shura located in Quetta, Baluchistan and the Haqqani network located in North Waziristan, as "strategic assets". The Afghan Taliban is supported by the ISI to maintain influence over Afghanistan post an American drawdown of forces from the area as many Pakistan's military establishments continue to think of the Afghanistan landmass as the backyard of Pakistan and an area which will provide them strategic depth in the event of hostilities with India. Pakistan has also encouraged and promoted terrorist organisations such as the LeT, JuM, and HuM which it views as strategic assets to be used against India. These terrorist groups have been waging a proxy war against India over the past two decades in Kashmir at very little cost to Pakistan-a policy of bleeding India with a thousand cuts-but keeping the conflict below perceived Indian threshold levels. While the army is concerned and active in addressing the Pakistan Taliban, it actively aids and abets the Afghan Taliban and the terrorist groups created by it to be used against India[53].

However, War criminal General Raheel ordered armed forces into North Waziristan, while shifted Afghan Taliban commanders to safe houses. The so called challenge to Pakistan's sovereignty in Swat and Buner was addressed with brute force only after the Taliban appeared to be on a triumphant march to Islamabad.[54] The insurgency in South Waziristan was tackled on a war footing after years of procrastination, but the writ of the Tehrik-e-Taliban Pakistan still runs in North Waziristan. The issue of ethnic representation within the armed forces also raised serious concerns. Some experts say this is not a national army and view it as the club of Punjabi generals[55].

Lashkar-e-Taiba is a salafi jihadist organization that fights Indian army in Kashmir to further Pakistan's foreign policy objectives. Its broader objectives include librating Kashmir, and engaging Indian army in a long and an unending war. The Lashkar-e-Taiba was established in 1989 in Kunar province of Afghanistan as the military wing of the Pakistan-based Islamist fundamentalist movement Markaz al-Dawa wal Irshad. The LeT maintained several charities such as Falah-e-Insaniyat Foundation; Idara Khidmat-e-Khalq; Jamaat al-Dawa; Jamaat-i-Dawat; Jamaat Daawa, Paasban-e-Ahle-Hadis, and Milli Muslim League.[56] South Asia expert Ashley J. Tellis (2012) has viewed LeT with different perspective:

> Thought the international community first began taking notice of the terrorist group Lashkar-e-Taiba (LeT) after its spectacular coordinated bombing and shooting attacks in Mumbai, India, in November 2008. The group was established in 1987 at a time when Pakistan was in the throes of Islamic ferment. Then, LeT had access to a steady supply of volunteers, funding and-most important of all—concerted state support. Long bolstered by Pakistan's Inter Services Directorate, this Wahhabi group promotes the vision of a universal Islamic caliphate through tableegh and jihad—preaching and armed struggle.[57]

Lashkar-e-Toiba follows salafi faith. The only trained extremist organizations that fight against India in Kashmir receive military training from Pakistan army. Terrorist organisations like al Qaeda, LeT, Taliban, and Arab extremists and Takfiri jihadists in Pakistan and Afghanistan are posing security threat to the country. They train suicide bombers across Asia and the Middle East. Religious and political vendettas are being settled by using suicide bombers against rival groups or families in Pakistan.[58] This generation of fear and panic is controlled by extremist elements and non-state actors in Waziristan, Kabul and Quetta. Pakistan is also an epicentre of terrorism. Terrorists are being trained by Pakistan to further its foreign policy agendas in India and Afghanistan. But sometimes, these groups turn their weapons on the armed forces of Pakistan. This controversial, but faith based connection between Pakistan army has now weakened after the kill and dump policy of the rogue army in FATA and Waziristan regions. Mr. Alok Bansal, (28 June 2001) has highlighted some aspects of this regular business of Pakistan army with jihadist militias:

> Despite the denial of the Pakistani state, there have been clear pointers to the presence of sympathisers and collaborators of Islamic radical organizations within all three armed forces of Pakistan. Every single attack on a military installation bore clear marks of collusion by elements from within. Many Pakistan Air Force (PAF) and army personnel including six officers were convicted for attempts on General Pervez Musharraf in December 2003, when he was the President. An army soldier, Abdul Islam Siddiqui, was hanged on August 20, 2005, after an in camera Court Martial for triggering an explosion to target Musharraf in Rawalpindi. On another occasion, an anti-aircraft gun was discovered on the flight path of General Musharraf's plane, when he was taking off from Rawalpindi Air base on a pitch dark night......... In 2010, two former army officers along with two serving officers including a colonel were convicted by a court martial for planning an attack on the Shamsi airbase, which is used by the Americans to fly their drones. Even before Brigadier Khan, two serving army officers were court-martialled for links with Hizb-ut-Tahrir.[59]

In the past, terrorists attacked Pakistan's nuclear installations. In 2007, they attacked two air force facilities in Sargodha, associated with nuclear installations. On 21 August, 2008, terrorists attacked the Ordnance factories in Wah. In July 2009, a suicide bomber struck a bus that may have been carrying A Q Khan Research Laboratory scientists, injuring 30 people. Moreover, two attacks by Baloch militants on suspected Atomic Energy Commission facilities in Dera Ghazi Khan have also drawn international attention to the security of the country's nuclear installations.

On 10 October, 2009, nine terrorists, dressed in army uniform, attacked the GHQ. In June 2014, two suicide bombers killed high ranking military officers linked to Pakistan's nuclear programme in Fateh Jang.[60]

Pakistan has all the signs and symptoms of ailing state that may not be able to sustain itself at the current rate of deterioration. It feels wretched from the crisis of self-reliance at home. People, an important constituent of the elements that defines a State, are fast losing faith in their institutions. The democratically elected governments has been shamelessly accusing of inability and inefficiency in handling the tottering state since the last four decades. Professor Yunis Khushi in her paper highlighted some aspects of internal and external squeezing on Pakistan:

Pakistan is at war with itself. This partial civil war is caused due to misadventures of many internal and external forces. All these forces are working on their agendas without worrying about the future of Pakistani people and implications of these deadly agendas on South Asia region and rest of the world. Among the internal forces, religious parties are promoting extremism, jihad, and intolerance and preparing Muslim youth from Ghalba-e-Islam (promulgation of Islam in the whole world). This job is being done in 2.1 million religious seminaries spread all over Pakistan. Initially, the religious parties were providing jihad training to youth in collaboration with those who were heading jihad and providing training to Mujahedeen and these Mujahedeen were being exported to Afghanistan and Kashmir to fight freedom war. But, all this was being done with dollars from CIA via ISI. Net result is that Mujahedeen, which were created by CIA and ISI, are now fighting against Americans in Afghanistan, and against Pakistan army in Swat, Waziristan and other tribal areas of Pakistan.[61]

Poverty-stricken and economically failing Pakistani state has become the headache of its neighbour. Pakistani commentator, Jan Muhammad Achakzai in his recent article (25 December-2018) warned that Pakistan needs to specify its direction of either join the path of Singapore and Malaysia, or join the club of failed states:

Pakistan is facing worse challenges never seen before", is more relevant today than ever before; economically failing state, dysfunction political system, corrupt political elite, unemployed youth bugle, extremism both religious and now ethnic mix intend to denuclearize Pakistan, the only Muslim country to have nukes, and the list goes on. The most worrying aspect of all is the lack of capacity of the current system to cope with these challenges. Even worse is the agony of realizing that the current system is beyond repair. It is so rotten that any fix will take decades which we do not have to wait for. Whereas the country is going to be on the edge not after a decade from now, not five years from today but the likely year is going to be 2019, as it will determine our direction to join the path of the countries like Singapore and Malaysia, or enter the club of failed states; Syria, Iraq, and Libya[62].

Chapter - 6

Pakistan Army ISI, IB, Forced Disappearance and Terrorism in Afghanistan

On 19 January 2019, Diva Radio reported a demeaning incident of Pashtun families in North Waziristan. "Soldiers do not feel foolishly; say it is okay", Hayat Khan said. In a video released in social media, Hayat Khan, a lonely child, said that: "Pakistani soldiers left behind the main screen and entered his house without permission. The soldiers said its okay."

Political and economic instability immersed Pakistani establishment after Prime Minister Nawaz Sharif was illegally deposed. In March 2018, Pakistan's parliament passed constitutional amendment-reinstating, secret-military-courts to try terrorism suspects for another two years. Intelligence agencies have been embroiled in enforced disappearances and extrajudicial killings[1]. On 20 August 2018, International Crisis Group documented brutalities, abuses, and extrajudicial killing in FATA region during the so-called military operation against militant groups: "Military operations had displaced hundreds of thousands in the tribal belt. Most have returned, but to destroyed homes and livelihoods. Rights abuses, including extrajudicial killings, enforced disappearances and custodial deaths continue, as collective punishment. For example, after a December 2017 killing of two soldiers, the military imposed a curfew in North Waziristan's Hamzoni town, preventing access to hospitals and forcing women and children out of their homes during search operations".

The army set to fire houses, offices, markets, and looted everything-soldiers and officers desired in North Waziristan.[2] The human rights crisis in Baluchistan is deeply underwhelming while business of forced disappearances and extrajudicial killings of Baloch men and women has stretched out to all parts of the province. The most significant human rights issues included extrajudicial and targeted killings, disappearances, lack of rule of law, including lack of due process; poor implementation and enforcement of laws.[3] The insurgency in South Waziristan was tackled on a war footing[4] after years of procrastination, but the writ of the Tehrik-e-Taliban Pakistan still runs in North Waziristan.[5]

In a startling revelation, Mr. Umar Daud Khattak, a separatist Pashtun leader accused the rogue army for using Pashtun women as sex slaves. He claimed that Pakistan Army, in the garb of conducting a military operation in the Swat and Waziristan region, committing grave human right abuses, and is targeting young Pashtun women. "The Pakistan Army abducted hundreds of Pashtun women and put them in a Lahore prostitution centre as sex slaves, during military operations in Swat and Waziristan," Khattak warned. He further said that Pakistan raises money by pushing Pashtun women into the flesh trade, adding that there are proof and evidences to support his claim.[6]

On 24 September 2014, Dawn reported humiliation of Waziristan women by Pakistan rogue army. "I saw a woman crying for help for her injured husband who got his ribcage broken while collecting ration. But the so-called social and cultural taboos did not allow her to move her husband to a nearby hospital," said Maryam Bibi, a social worker while sharing her experience of working at an internally displaced persons camp. Maryam Bibi said during her visits to the IDP camps she noticed that the second wife was not allowed to get herself registered for aid because she did not have documents to show her the member of a particular family. Amnesty International in its report of 2016 and 2017 noted serious violation of human rights in all provinces of Pakistan:

security forces including the Rangers, a paramilitary force under the command of the Pakistan Army, perpetrated human rights violations such as arbitrary arrests, torture and other ill-treatment, and extrajudicial executions. Security laws and practices, and the absence of any independent mechanisms to investigate the security forces and hold them accountable, allowed government forces to commit such violations with near-total impunity.[7]

According to the UNHCR, about five hundred thousand people from the area fled to Afghanistan to escape atrocities of the Pakistani army," Khattak said, adding that the Pakistani army wants "to use the area for terror camps" and is, therefore, trying to "evict" the Pashtuns.[8] The North and South Waziristan areas of FATA were the site of large military operations in 2009, and 2014 after the Pakistan Taliban took control of swathes of territory in the region. The Pashtuns are being targeted by the Army as many of them have been abducted and extra-judicially killed. The Guardian reported Pakistan army war crimes in Baluchistan:

> In Baluchistan, mutilated corpses bearing the signs of torture keep turning up, among them lawyers, students and farm workers. Why no one investigating is and what have they got to do with the bloody battle for Pakistan's largest province? The bodies surface quietly, like corks bobbing up in the dark. They come in twos and threes, a few times a week, dumped on desolate mountains or empty city roads, bearing the scars of great cruelty. Arms and legs are snapped; faces are bruised and swollen. Flesh is sliced with knives or punctured with drills; genitals are singed with electric prods. In some cases the bodies are unrecognisable, sprinkled with lime or chewed by wild animals. All have a gunshot wound in the head. While foreign attention is focused on the Taliban, a deadly secondary conflict is bubbling in Baluchistan, a sprawling, mineral-rich province along the western borders with Afghanistan and Iran.[9]

Wall Street Journal has also reported war crimes of Pakistan army in Waziristan. The journal documented miseries of innocent people in Waziristan: "An army unit ordered more than 20 truck drivers out of a restaurant in North Waziristan and then killed them execution style. No trial, no jury.[10] On 12 December 2012 Amnesty International reported abuses by armed forces in FATA region: "Abuses by Armed Forces and Taliban in Pakistan's Tribal Areas" relates that the army arbitrarily detains people in the tribal areas for long periods without charge and without due process of law.[11]

Prominent separatist leader from Pakistan and President of World Baloch Women's Forum, Naela in an exclusive interview to Ashok kumar of OneWorld South Asia revealed that Pakistan was treating Baloch women in the same ways as ISIS (Islamic State in Iraq and Syria) to contain the freedom movement led mostly by women. Women and children, if they survive, are the worst sufferers when Pakistani Army bombs residential areas in Baluchistan, Naela said. "Women are taken to the rape cells where they face the most brutal handling by the Pakistani soldiers. Like in Bangladesh and Afghanistan, people have seen how Pakistani army behaves with women or how insensitive it is towards them. They use rape as tool of oppression and as a tool of occupation. They are throwing acids on Baloch girls to stop them from coming out because Baloch girls are leading the liberation moment as most of the men are up in the mountains as part of the Baloch Army". Naela said.[12]

Since the killing of Akbar Bugti in 2006, more than 25,000 Baloch men were kidnapped or forcefully disappeared by Pakistani intelligence agencies[13] and the police, in which 1500 were students and teachers. On 29 November 2013, nineteen personnel of Paramilitary force[14], who had allegedly taken away 35 detainees[15], were directed by the Supreme Court to appear before the CID office in Quetta[16].

There are numerous stories of Pakistan army war crimes in North Waziristan and Baluchistan province circulating in print and electronic media showcase the real hidden agenda of Miltablishment. In Baluchistan, thousands innocent Balochs were killed, kidnapped, and their houses were destroyed. Pakistani intelligence agencies and the police created bigger problems of ethnicity and sectarianism by kidnapping, torturing and forcefully disappearing Baloch and Pashtun leaders in Khyber Pakhtunkhwa and Baluchistan provinces. On 25 September 2017, Dawn reported the Senate Functional Committee on Human Rights Chairperson, Nasreen Jalil, accusations against law enforcement agencies of abducting people and "asked" them to investigate the missing person's case. "They [disappeared individuals] are not even presented in court and [only] their tortured corpses are found later," she alleged. The PPP leader, Senator Mr. Farhatullah Babar also warned that parliament, Supreme Court and other institutions have failed to resolve the issue. "The people involved in abductions are not punished despite the evidence against them," he said.[17] In his article, prominent Pakistani analyst I.A Rehman spotlighted some weaknesses of the government and law enforcement agencies in resolving the issue of missing persons:

> The horrible phenomenon of enforced disappearances in Pakistan has been in public debate for more than 25 years and there is hardly any aspect of the matter that has not been discussed threadbare and from different points of view. If the demand for an end to enforced disappearances, criminalization of the practice punishment of the perpetrators and payment of compensation to victim families has been made from various national and international forums, there have also been suggestions, though from a tiny minority, for giving the security forces powers to detain indefinitely dangerous criminals who in many cases are victims of enforced disappearance (ED).[18]

Court proceedings after 9/11, and the information provided by different authorities confirm that ISI and the army had adopted the policy of enforced disappearances as a long term measure for 'national security'/counter-terrorism strategy.[19] Enforced disappearances have been adopted as a strategic tool as opposed to a mere short term tactic.[20] This is supported by the fact that in several legislative measures introduced at the behest of the national security institutions, the focus has been to provide 'legal' cover rather than prohibit and criminalize the practice as required under the constitutional framework and international law.[21] In his recent article in the News International, Mr. Sher Ali Khalti noted important facts of missing persons in Baluchistan and Khyber Pakhtunkhwa provinces:

> According to data available with TNS, the Commission received 4113 cases of missing persons up till June 30, 2017. About 2857 out of 4113 cases were disposed of till July 30, 2017. Around 377 hearings were held in the country and despite that 1256 persons are still missing in the country. In Khyber Pakhtunkhwa, 1582 cases of missing persons were received. Around 666 missing persons were traced and 831 cases were disposed of till July 30, 2017, yet 751 missing persons are to be produced. In Punjab, 862 cases of missing persons were received, 450 missing persons traced and 617 missing persons' cases were disposed of while 245 persons are still missing. Sindh Province ranks second on the list of missing persons. 1055 cases of missing persons were received, 766 traced and 1005 cases of missing persons were disposed of and 50 persons are still missing. In Baluchistan 291 cases of missing persons were received, 108 missing persons traced and 193 cases of missing persons were disposed of and 98 persons are still missing. 45 people in Islamabad, 48 in Fata, 5 in Gilgit Baltistan and 14 persons in Azad Jammu Kashmir are still missing.[22]

Pakistan is notorious for widespread enforced disappearances, with state agents finding it an easy way to keep persons in their custody indefinitely, torture and kill them without any evidence. Since 2001, the higher courts failed to recover missing persons; the military and other institutions, accused of enforcing disappearances, have arrogantly refused to obey court orders.[23] The case of Zeenat Shahzadi, who was pursuing Ansari's case, is no less serious than Qandeel Baloch's, the model who was killed because she wanted to live by her own lights.[24] On 07 January 2017, social activist Samar Abbas reportedly went missing. He was one of the founders of the Civil Progressive Alliance, a campaign created to counter the dominant public narrative after the Peshawar Army Public School attack in 2014, when six gunmen affiliated with the Tehrik-i-Taliban killed 141 people, including 132 school children.[25] On 30 August 2017, World Sindh Congress and Asian Human Rights Commission (AHRC), Voice of Baloch Missing Persons (VBMP) and Right snow in their joint statement on the International Day of the Victims of Enforced Disappearances reported thousands of cases of forced disappearance in Pakistan:

> From 31st December 2010 to 31st March 2017, the highest number of enforced disappearance cases was reported from Khyber Pakhtunkhwa province (1486 cases), followed by Sindh (1031), Punjab (819), Baluchistan (282), Islamabad Capital Territory (138), Federally Administered Tribal Areas (113), Azad Jammu & Kashmir (40) and Gilgit-Baltistan. The Edhi Foundation has reportedly buried a total of 58,261 unidentified and unclaimed bodies between 2005 and 2012 in the country, including 12,561 bodies in 2005, 4,819 bodies in 2006, 6,611 in 2007, 6,692 in 2008, 6,491 in 2009, 6,493 in 2010, 7,854 in 2011 and 6,738 in 2012. The Edhi Foundation claimed that they used to bury more than 100 unclaimed bodies a month in Karachi during this period.[26]

On 25 January 2019, in Friday Times column, politician Farhatullah Babar criticized policy of forced disappearances and proceedings of Military Courts in Pakistan. Mr. Babar also raised the question of military courts twice allowed two-year terms, and argued that Military Courts have been disastrous for fundamental rights in the past. Proceedings during the past four years were secret and opaque in a massive violation of the right to a fair trial:

> Military courts are disastrous for fundamental rights. Proceedings during the past four years have been secret and opaque in a massive violation of the right to a fair trial. The Peshawar High Court recently overturned scores of convictions awarded by military courts. The International Commission of Jurists (ICJ) in a recent report Military Injustice in Pakistan called yet another extension in the tenure of military courts a "glaring surrender of human rights and fundamental freedoms." The ICJ has also documented some serious fair trial violations in military courts. These

include denial of the right to counsel of choice; failure to give convicts copies of judgment recording evidence and reasons. There are no rapporteurs to publicly record the proceedings, let alone public hearings in military courts. Even charges against the accused have not been disclosed. According to the report more than 97 per cent of convictions are based on "confessions" by the accused. In the absence of anti-torture legislation and given the opaque internment centres, it is not hard to imagine how confessions have been extracted. More seriously, there is a disturbing nexus between military courts and enforced disappearances. This has been highlighted both in the ICJ report and in recent proceedings before the Peshawar High Court.[27]

On 30 July 2017, MQM held a large demonstration in front of White House against paramilitary operation to suppress Mohajirs, enforced disappearances and extra judicial killings of MQM workers in Karachi. The demonstration was attended by MQM Convener Nadeem Nusrat, members of Coordination Committee; office bearers along with large numbers of workers, supporters and members of Pakistani Diaspora from all walks of life, including ladies, elders and youth.[28] The demonstrators demanded that Pakistani establishment should stop these cruel tactics of "unlawful kidnapping" of Mr. Hussain's relatives in order to cause him to bow his head down, a wish of their which will never fulfill. They held banners and placards demanding US government to take notice of worst form of human rights violations, enforced disappearances, extra judicial killings, inhumane torture, ban on political and social activities of MQM, Media blackout of MQM's founder and leader Altaf Hussain.[29] MQM's founder Altaf Hussain joined the participants via tele-conferencing and addressed the participants in a brief speech. In this address, he went on to condemn the role of Pakistan Army and ISI in Karachi, particularly against the Muhajir community.[30]

A fact-finding mission of the Human Rights Commission of Pakistan to Swat documented accounts of extrajudicial killings by the rogue Pakistani army in 2009. However, the discovery of mass graves in Swat points to the unabated suffering of the civilian population. The report of the three-day mission documented a number of Swat residents evidences of having seen mass graves in the area, including at least one at Kookarai village in Babozai tehsil and another in an area between Dewlai and Shah Dheri in Kabal tehsil. The witnesses to mass burials said at least in some cases the bodies appeared to be those of Taliban militants.[31] The mission expressed grave concern over the "worrying development and also over credible reports of numerous extrajudicial killings and reprisals carried out by the security forces. Bodies were dumped throughout the valley–bloated corpses were found floating down the rivers while others dangle from electricity poles with notes warning of dire consequences for the Taliban and its supporters. Some villagers claimed that state security forces even warned them against giving a Muslim burial to fallen Taliban fighters – in Islam the dead must be buried immediately".[32]

Since the discovery of the mass graves, government remained unhelpful in getting to the truth behind the mass graves. The government sometimes deviated from the actual issue by disputing the actual number of the bodies found in the mass graves while, on other occasion, it blamed India for being involved in this gruesome episode.[33] A mass grave was discovered in Tootak, Khuzdar by a shepherd after which the locals converged there to recover bodies.[34] The number of the bodies found, which the middle class government representatives are at pains to limit to 13, while reports filtering out put the number at around 150 and more. The Baloch are systematically being marginalized to make their suppression easier and the illegal exploitation of their resources justifiable.[35]

The killing of thousands of tribal leaders in FATA destroyed leadership among the ethnic Pashtuns. For more than a decade, Pakistan army in Federally Administered Tribal Areas (FATA) relied on the targeted assassination of powerful tribal chiefs as a cornerstone of its strategy to establish control and protect the sanctuaries of terrorists[36] On 15 November 2017; Dawn reported fifteen bullet-riddled bodies were discovered by the Levies force in Baluchistan's Kech district. A senior administration officer who spoke to Dawn News on condition of anonymity said that the

Levies found the bodies in the Gorak area of tehsil Buleda. "All the victims received multiple bullets from a close range," he said.[37]

On 11 February 2015, after learning that 4,557 bodies were found in the country over the past four years, the Supreme Court asked the federal government to effectively address in a coordinated manner the handling of unclaimed bodies as well as the issue of missing persons.[38] A bench comprised of two-judges of Supreme Court, headed by Justice Jawad S. Khawaja, took up an application of Nasrullah Baloch, chairman of the Voice for Baloch Missing Persons, who invited attention of the court towards lack of a proper system for handling of mutilated or unclaimed bodies found at different places in Baluchistan.[39]

The detainee men, women and young children were abused, raped, humiliated and then killed in secret prisons established by Pakistani intelligence agencies and the army in Waziristan, FATA, and Baluchistan. Soldiers and officers of Pakistan army kidnapped girls and women from Swat, Momand and FATA as well. Minor children were killed in front of their parents. The FATA Senator Maulana Gul Naseeb accused rogue army of kidnapping girls and women from Swat and Momad agencies. Moreover, Supreme Court of Pakistan ordered law enforcement agencies to arrest those criminal army officers responsible for the enforced disappearance, but they didn't arrest them because of their affiliation with ISI and military intelligence.[40] The army has been facing many difficulties in conducting effective counter-insurgency operations, even though, it has deployed more than 150,000 soldiers in the Khyber-Pakhtunkhwa and FATA, and has suffered over 15,700 casualties, including over 5,000 dead since 2008. Total casualties including civilians numbered 80,000 since 2001.[41]

After the 16 December 2014 attack on Peshawar school, the army started the ball rolling to legalize enforced disappearances and kidnapping by exerting pressure on Prime Minister Nawaz Sharif to announce National Action Plan (NAP), the license of kill and dump.[42] On 06 January 2015, Pakistan National Assembly and the Senate passed the 21st Amendment to constitution, which formally established Military Courts.[43] The NAP was established on 25 December, 2014, in reaction to 133 children being murdered by terrorists. The first point in the NAP is the controversial lifting of the moratorium on the death penalty. After the establishment of NAP, the army began punishing innocent Pashtuns in Waziristan, Baluchistan and FATA, and political activists in Sindh and Punjab.[44]

Thousand were forced to leave their houses, and thousands were killed and kidnapped in daylight-bombed their houses, and kidnapped their relatives. Torture cells were established and law enforcement agencies were empowered to kidnap citizens with impunity. Pakistani American analyst, Shuja Nawaz in his research paper raised important points about the disengagement of parliament and civil society in the war against militancy and terrorism:

> But there were few opportunities for the public to understand the details of what was being done and the relationship between the actions of the military inside FATA and the actions being taken by the civilian authorities in the rest of the country. Periodic meetings between the civil and military leaders were reported briefly, largely through the shorthand tweets from the military PR outfit. Parliament did not appear to seek, nor was it granted, regular briefings or reports on the ongoing operations. Against this backdrop, it was not surprising that the general public was not fully engaged in the effort against militancy and terrorism.[45]

In December 2017, after announcing a 23-party "Grand Alliance" called the Pakistan Awami Itehad (PAI), Asia Times reported former military dictator General Pervez Musharraf admitted that he had been the greatest supporter of Lashkar-e-Toiba (LeT) in the past. The rise of Hafeez Saeed's MML, and the Tehrik Labbaik Ya Rasool Allah (TLY) against PML-N can be attributed to the military establishment's bid to contain the civilian leadership.[46] Miltablishment shamelessly supported Faizabad set in and in the tail-end, gave money to every participant. Security experts view these counter-measures as flawed and brutal for the reason that this unprofessional security approach cannot restore the confidence of minorities, ethnicities and political parties.

Notwithstanding the enforced disappearances of thousands innocent people in Punjab, Khyber Pakhtunkhwa, Baluchistan and Sindh provinces, lawlessness, terrorism, target killings, insurgency and alienation of citizens from the tattering state still exist in different forms, and the side-effects of their proposed panacea further aggravated and conflagrated.[47]

Writers, bloggers, commentators, and columnists who have been lambasting and disparaging the role of Pakistan army, and law enforcement agencies in enforced disappearance, torture, and extra-judicial killings in four provinces receive death threats, or kidnapped by agencies since the past two decades.[48] The exponentially growing trends of kidnapping for ransom by police and intelligence agencies is a new development in Pakistan, which further exacerbated the pain of political activists, members of human rights groups and civil society.[49] This campaign of consternation now reached at a crucial stage where political workers and parliamentarians have raised this issue on various forms, and besmirched the criminal inattention of the country's armed forces, judiciary and political parties.[50] On March 2017, journalist Kiran Nazish in her investigative report on forced disappearance in Pakistan astonished civil society about the male practiced of police and intelligence agencies:

On December 2, 2017, 40 years old Raza Khan, a Pakistani political activist, disappeared from his home. When Raza wouldn't answer his phone, Khan's brother went to his residence in Lahore. He found the lights on, the curtains drawn and the doors locked-but no sign of Raza. The intelligence agencies hold so much power that even the police can't touch them, an officer at Peshawar police headquarters told me the police see several abduction cases a week but can't write up official police report. "We have orders not to meddle in such cases that might be part of anti-terror campaign" he told me.[51]

The issue of secret prisons managed and established by police, army, and intelligence agencies still remains untouched, while the conscience of Pakistani politician, religious clerics, mullahs and so-called jihadists have died, and they have criminally kept close-mouthed.[52] There are numerous secret prisons managed by intelligence agencies in houses, field-intelligence-units, secret basements, military farms, and forests.[53] This wave of harassment and consternation has ruined the lives of millions Pakistanis, who never liked the way intelligence agencies and the armed forces maintain security and law and order management in the country. Civilian and military intelligence agencies are deeply involved in kidnapping of writers, journalists, and critics of military establishment and since the promulgation of National Action Plan (NAP).[54]

In history of law enforcement, and counterinsurgency operations across the globe, no match of Pakistani methodology, modus-operandi and flawed security approach can be found.[55] Thousands young girls, boys, students, adults, political workers are missing, while bodies of thousands innocent men and women have been found in hospitals, farms houses, roadside, deserts, forests and plains in Baluchistan and Khyber Pakhtunkhwa provinces.[56] In March 2014, after repeated court orders, Minister of Defence registered First Information Report (FIR) against the army officers allegedly responsible for the disappearances of innocent citizens.[57]

On 29 August 2013, the News International reported a gang of Pakistan's naval intelligence involvement in kidnapping for ransom in Karachi: "Some officers and an activist of the naval intelligence had formed a gang which was kidnapping traders and industrialists and receiving a huge ransom. The kidnapped persons used to be kept in the headquarters of naval intelligence, adjacent to the Chief Minister's House, the newspaper reported".[58] The News International also reported fisheries trader, Mr. Javed's kidnapping for ransom. His life was spared after immediate payment of Rs.2 million and some negotiations in which it was also agreed that he would be freed after a payment of another Rs.3 million. Subsequently, the members of Javed's family boarded a taxi and arrived at the Nehr Khayyam in Clifton in pitch darkness where they found a motorcyclist who had covered his face and who had come to receive the ransom payment. The News noted.[59] However, on 29 August 2013, the News International also documented the involvement of a gang of Pakistan naval intelligence in kidnapping for ransom:

> In the meantime, the SSP South, Nasir Aftab, who had been present in plainclothes along with the family of the kidnapped man, opened fire on the man who was going back after receiving the ransom money. A bullet hit him on his leg and he fell. Nasir Aftab and some cops, who had been hiding in a bush, then grabbed the accused. He was taken to the Clifton police station in an injured condition, and during initial investigations made a shocking disclosure that he belonged to the naval intelligence and that two assistant directors of the naval intelligence, Ashfaq and another unknown, had been present at the venue where the accused had gone to receive ransom money, but they escaped from the venue when they heard the gunshot, the SSP and a CPLC team contacted the high officials of naval intelligence and recovered the kidnapped person from the headquarters of the naval intelligence. The SSP Nasir Aftab and CPLC chief Ahmed Chinoy confirmed the arrest of the accused and the involvement of assistant directors in the gang, but they refused to divulge more information". The Newspaper reported.[60] After this report, leader of the Awami National Party (ANP), Senator Zahid Khan called for the court-martial of intelligence officials if they are found to be involved in extortion. JUI-F leader, Senator Haji Ghulam Ali questioned how intelligence agencies could stop India if they could not even stop kidnappers entering their headquarters. The Newspaper reported.[61]

On 01 April 2018, Dawn reported mysterious death of Rezwan Attique, a Group Captain of Pakistan Air Force. His wife had submitted a petition to the Islamabad High Court along with attached copy of Punjab Forensic Science Laboratory, which spotlighted injury marks on her husband body. The petition cited Secretary of Defence, Chief of Air Staff, and Deputy Chief of Air Staff, and Air Intelligence Director General as respondents. The officer wife requested Islamabad High Court to form a joint investigation team. In response to a petition filed by Attique's widow, Tanzeela Khan, PAF's Director legal service Sohail Ahmed stated that the woman's husband had committed suicide as he feared the consequences of an inquiry into his alleged corruption, Dawn reported"[62].

Pakistani human rights groups remained hushed and wordless. They were under threat and under pressure from the army and intelligence agencies-taking the issue of forced disappearance and kidnapping to the court. Similarly, courts were tight-lipped, close-mouthed, and tongue-tied to investigate cases of extra-judicial killings of innocent Pashtun and Baloch activists. They are frightened and panic-stricken to raise the issue of mass graves, torture and humiliation by police and law enforcement agencies. Prominent human right activist and senior journalist, I.A Rehman also noted the attitude of law enforcement authorities to recover missing persons:

> The lack of satisfactory progress on affording relief to the victims of enforced disappearance makes it necessary to revisit their case. The more one looks at the monthly reports on the cases pending before the Commission of Inquiry on Enforced Disappearances, the more alarmed at the unmitigated suffering of the people affected one becomes. Let us look at these reports for the last three months — December 2016, January and February 2017. The commission inherited 138 cases from the earlier body. It has received 3,718 complaints since March 01, 2011, when it started working; raising the total number of cases to 3,856.[63] Mr. I.A Rehman also uncovered more details about forced disappearances in Khyber Pakhtunkhwa, Baluchistan and Waziristan, where rights groups and journalist were not allowed to report war crimes:

> The commission claims to have traced 1,953 people in all. Three hundred and fifty-four cases have been deleted from the list on the ground that information about the disappeared persons was incomplete and another 309 cases were dropped for other reasons. The largest group of persons traced so far belonged to Sindh (714 out of 1,025 people reported to have

disappeared), followed by KP (626 out of 1,461), Punjab (398 out of 799), Baluchistan (102 out of 281), Fata (51 out of 113), Islamabad (49 out of 131), and Azad Kashmir (13 out of 40). As for Gilgit-Baltistan, none of the six disappeared have been traced.[64] The UN General Assembly has repeatedly described enforced disappearance as "an offence to human dignity" and a grave violation of international human rights law. In its report, the International Commission of Jurists also elucidated kidnapping and abduction within the matrix of Pakistan's Panel Code:

Pakistan's Penal Code Sections 359 to 368 relate to the crimes of "kidnapping" and "abduction". The crime of kidnapping is of two kinds: kidnapping from Pakistan and kidnapping from lawful guardianship, and is punishable with a maximum of seven years imprisonment and a fine. The crime of "abduction" is regulated by section 362 of the Penal Code and is defined as "whoever by force compels, or by any deceitful means induces, any person to go from any place." Section 364 prescribes a punishment of ten years imprisonment for the crime of "kidnapping or abducting in order to murder". Section 365 relates to kidnapping or abducting "any person with intent to cause that person to be secretly and wrongfully confined" and prescribes a punishment of a maximum of seven years imprisonment.[65]

However, Amnesty International in its report warned that enforced disappearances caused serious violation of human right, and called on Pakistani authorities to immediately carry out independent and effective investigations with a view to determining the fate and whereabouts of all missing people.[66] On 07 December 2017, Dawn reported the Senate Standing Committee on Human Rights decision to summon recovered missing persons for an in-camera session to ask them directly who they had been picked up by. The committee also decided that once the victims have recorded their statements, representatives of the apex Intelligence Agencies; Inter-Services Intelligence, Military Intelligence and the Intelligence Bureau must be summoned before the committee and asked to explain their actions.[66]

Asian Human Rights Commission that celebrated the International Day of Victims of Enforced Disappearance on 30 August 2016 spotlighted Pakistan as a notorious country for enforced disappearances of individuals: We have also found the mass grave of disappeared persons particularly from Baluchistan.[67] We found grave of over 100 persons that were recorded, there was an inquiry ordered but the report has not been made public. Interior Minister of Pakistan said that there were around 1,000 bodies that have been found in a mass grave", senior researcher at Asia Human Rights Naved said.[68]

On 09 February 2018, Dawn reported attention of US Congress to the forced disappearances of political activists in Pakistan. That special hearing of the House Subcommittee on Asia and the Pacific, lawmakers also accused Pakistan of continuing to allow Afghan extremists to destabilize the government in Kabul, a charge raised at a Senate hearing as well.[69] Dawn noted lawmakers also backed President Donald Trump's 04 Jan 2018 decision to suspend security assistance to Pakistan.[70] In recent years, the newspaper reported intelligence agencies responsible for these disappearances broadened their crackdown to include social media and other political activists, rights defenders, and reporters.[71] On 19 February 2018, Daily Times reported the illegal detention and forced disappearance of several political activists by intelligence agencies in Gilgit Baltistan.[72]

In January 2018, law enforcement authorities killed Prof Dr Hasan Zafar Arif and Mr. Naqeebullah, a young man from Waziristan in a fake encounter in Karachi. Sindh Home Minister Sohail Anwar Siyal took notice of the death of Mr. Naqeebullah, and ordered Deputy Inspector General South to personally conduct a "clear and unbiased" inquiry into the matter and submit a detailed report to the Ministry. Mr. Naqeebullah was killed by SSP Rao Anwar, in a fake encounter. The police claim that the deceased was a militant affiliated with the banned Tehreek-i-Taliban Pakistan (TTP) but it is totally baseless, while relative of Mr. Naqeebullah disputed SSP Anwar's claim.[73]

Cold War between Inter Services Intelligence (ISI) and Intelligence Bureau (IB)

On 26 September 2017, Pakistani newspaper-Dawn reported a serving Assistant Sub-Inspector of Intelligence Bureau (IB), Mr. Malik Mukhtar Ahmed Shahzad's petition against the Intelligence Bureau, in which he points the finger at senior officers of not taking action against terrorism suspects. However, he filed a petition before the Islamabad High Court (IHC) requesting the matter to be referred to Inter Services Intelligence (ISI) for a thorough investigation.[74] The Assistant Sub-Inspector (ASI) told the court that he had often reported the link of IB officers and terrorist groups from various countries but no action was taken against these officers. "However, to the petitioner's utter dismay, no action was ever been taken by IB in this respect despite concrete evidence provided to it in the form of the intelligence reports", the petition said.[75]

Upon thorough intelligence gathering process, it transpired that certain high officials of the IB themselves were directly involved with the terrorist organizations, having linkages with hostile enemy intelligence agencies" the petition warned.[76] He also said that the matter was even reported to the IB director general, who also did not take any steps[77] It the petition, he warned that some IB officials travelled to Israel and had direct links with Afghan intelligence which, it was found later, had links with another terrorist group from Kazakhstan.

"These terrorists used to disguise themselves as citrus dealers in Kot-Momin and Bhalwal, Sargodha. The business was a mere camouflage," the petition warned.[78] According to his petition, the son of Joint Director Intelligence Bureau (Punjab) was dealing with the said terrorist groups. The petition named certain IB's officials who were on the payroll of foreign intelligence agencies which included a Joint Director General, Directors and Deputy Directors. The petitioner said that senior IB officials also facilitated Afghan nationals in getting Pakistani nationality.[79]

On October 01 2017, Intelligence Bureau (IB) told Islamabad High Court (IHC) that answering the queries posed by one of its officials would affect Pakistan's relations with several countries and compromise the secrecy of the agency's internal structures.[80] The bureau submitted its reply in response to the petition of Malik Mukhtar Ahmed Shahzad that accusing senior IB officials of having links with different terrorist organizations from neighbouring and Central Asian countries, as well as protecting terrorists. In its reply, IB claimed that the official seeking an Inter-Services Intelligence (ISI) probe against senior bureau officials was a habitual litigant and had tried to tarnish the repute of the intelligence agency in the past as well.[81] The issue was also highlighted by some parliamentarians like Senator Farahatullah Babar who moved a calling attention notice urging the Interior Minister to take notice of the IB official's allegations. The calling attention notice pointed out that the head of the banned Jaish-i-Muhammad Maulana Masood Azhar and Afghan Taliban Chief Mullah Mansour Akhtar were facilitated by certain quarters. Mr. Babar also claimed that during NA-120 by-election in Lahore, a candidate backed by banned militant outfits was allowed to contest, in violation of the law.[82]

"The petition should be dismissed on the grounds of being frivolous, as it demands the disclosure of details pertaining to secret operations and task objectives,"[83] The News quoted the IB as stating in its reply."If disclosed, these details will compromise national security as they will expose the administrative units of the department," the reply further said. The News International also mentioned that IB's response that the employee in question has "frequently caused trouble" for the department, having submitted 14 petitions against the agency in the past.[84] On 28 September 2017, Dawn reported Islamabad High Court warning about the intelligence war in the country. Mr. Justice Shaukat Aziz Siddiqui sought a reply from the Interior Secretary to the petition filed by an IB assistant sub-inspector.[85]

The agency, Dawn noted came under fire from Pakistan Tehreek-i-Insaf (PTI) leader Imran Khan after its head allegedly met ousted Prime Minister Nawaz Sharif in London. A list of politicians allegedly having links with terrorists was also attributed to the IB.[86] The Nation reported petitioner's allegations that he received threatening calls after having filed the petition and requested the court to provide him and his family members with security. Justice Siddiqui then ordered police to deploy reasonable security for the protection of the petitioner and his family.[87]

On 27 September 2017, a news item in Dawn further conflagrated war between military and civilian intelligence agencies. Members of the Federal Cabinet took serious notice of the airing of a "false report" on a private television channel claiming that former Prime Minister Nawaz Sharif had directed the Intelligence Bureau (IB) to keep vigilance over some 37 legislators, mostly belonging to the ruling PML-N, allegedly for having links with banned terrorist and sectarian outfits, Dawn reported.[88]

The Prime Minister later directed Law Minister Hamid to probe the issue and ensure action against the channel through the Pakistan Electronic Media Regulatory Authority (Pemra) for the "malafide reporting". Dawn reported.[89] On 06 October 2017, Prime Minister Shahid Khaqan Abbasi met the Director General of the Intelligence Bureau (IB), the law Minister along with several members of parliament allegedly investigated by the Intelligence Bureau (IB) for links to terror outfits.[90] DG IB Aftab Sultan briefed members of parliament on the issue, clarifying once again that the bureau is not responsible for the list, which purportedly named lawmakers with links to terrorists and was alleged to have been sent to IB by Prime Minister House when Nawaz Sharif was in office.[91] The civilian-military distrust can also be seen in Dawn's report as the IB often accuses ISI of interfering in its affairs. A former top intelligence chief told media that according to the Telegraph Law, "only Intelligence Bureau (IB) is allowed to tap someone's phone, and that too, only based on real fears, only after the prime minister's permission."[92]

Experts view these challenges of Pakistan's intelligence agencies as a bigger bang that shocked the whole region. These developments gave India more courage to tell the international community that Pakistan had been the exporter of terrorism since 1980s. However, on 23 September 2017, Indian Minister of

External Affairs Sushma Swaraj in her address to the 72nd Session of the United Nations General assembly warned that Islamabad had given the world "terrorists" while India was producing top-notch doctors and engineers.[93] "Why is it today India is a recognized IT superpower in the world, and Pakistan is recognized only as the pre-eminent export factory for terror?" Sushma Swaraj told the General Assembly. "We produced scholars, doctors, engineers. What have you produced? You have produced terrorists," she said. Indian Prime Minister Narendra Modi stepped up a drive to isolate Pakistan diplomatically after the Uri army base attack in Sept 2016 in which 19 Indian soldiers were killed.[94]

Chapter - 7

Tongue-Lashing on Intelligence Sharing between the Afghan NDS and Pakistani Intelligence-ISI

Pakistan's intelligence agencies have no second-thought in supporting Taliban and other extremist organizations to make the war in Afghanistan disastrous and unfavourable since 1990s. Military establishment of the country continues to train, arm, and transport terrorist groups inside Afghanistan to target civilian and military installations, and make lives of women and children vulnerable. The ISI has often been accused of playing a role in major terrorist attacks. Pakistan (Vanda Felbab Brown, 5, 01 2018) has long been a difficult and disruptive neighbour to Afghanistan, hoping to limit India's influence there, and cultivating radical groups within Afghanistan as proxies.[1] New attempt of President Trump to bring peace to Afghanistan through dialogue was glorified by Afghani and Pakistani politicians, but some neighbouring states dressed-down this attempt. The US diplomat Mr. Khalilzad was given the task of bringing peace to the region, but most of the Afghan politicians are critical of his mission.[2]

These developments slowly changed the mental outlook of Pakistan's military establishment, when Foreign Minister Shah Mehmood (December 2018) acknowledged India's stake in Afghanistan.[3] This change in Pakistan's behaviourism was good handwriting on the wall. Throughout Pakistan's history, military establishment never accepted India's role in Afghanistan. Moreover, on 24 December 2018, Chief of Army Staff (COAS)

General Qamar Javed Bajwa said that Pakistan supports Afghan-led peace plan to help bring lasting peace in the neighbouring state.[4] In his Diplomat Magazine article (22, 12, 2018), Mr. Samuel Ramani noted some aspects of his Shah Mehmood's statement:

> On December 11, Pakistan's Foreign Minister Shah Mehmood Qureshi surprised international observers by acknowledging India's stake in Afghanistan and asking New Delhi to help end the war in Afghanistan. To justify his calls for India-Pakistan cooperation in Afghanistan, Qureshi emphasized the "shared responsibility" of all regional powers to end the conflict and urged India to follow the "solution through dialogue" approach advocated by the United States, Pakistan, and the Taliban. Despite Pakistan's change in rhetoric toward Indian involvement in Afghanistan, India's reaction to Qureshi's statement was predictably sceptical. Mumbai-based newspaper The Economic Times acknowledged the symbolic significance of Qureshi's statement but also claimed that Islamabad would react negatively to expanded Indian involvement in Afghanistan, due to its long-standing fear of strategic encirclement. Indian Foreign Minister Sushma Swaraj refrained from commenting on Qureshi's statement, while her description of Qureshi's "googly remarks" on Sikh rights continued to circulate widely across Indian social media outlets.[5]

Mainly, the country considers Afghanistan as India's proxy against its army. Pakistan played a very unfair role in Afghanistan by dealing with terror groups such as the Taliban and Lashkar-e-Toiba. In December 2018, Foreign Minister Shah Mehmood Qureshi said that Prime Minister Imran Khan welcomed US President Donald Trump's letter seeking Pakistan's cooperation for reconciliation process in Afghanistan. Let's see the feature of its cooperation, and wait how Pakistan can help the United States in bringing Taliban to dialogue.[6] On 05 January 2016, Abdul Manan Bhat also criticized nexus of Pakistan and Saudi Arabi and their role in promoting Salafist-Wahabi ideology:

The nexus of Saudi Arabia and Pakistan strategically orchestrated the birth of one of the most repressive regimes in the modern world - The Taliban. Through its unrequited financial endorsements for madrases, Saudi Arabia viewed Afghanistan strategically significant in two ways, as the brooding ground for the Wahhabi school of Islam, previously alien to Afghan society, and, as a deportation alternative where the local Saudi extremists could be expelled to. Saudi Arabia, therefore, donated the worst of its possessions to Afghanistan, an archaically, unsuitable radical ideology and the most extreme elements, even by Saudi Arabian standards, to implement it.[6]

The war brought instability, hater, disparities and destruction due to regional rivalries. Peace is a far away dream in Afghanistan. Robert Kaplan (2012) warned in his book that if Taliban control Afghanistan, radicalization will get strong and Pakistan's sphere of influence will expand from Indian border to Central Asia: "An Afghanistan that falls to Taliban sway threatens to create a succession of radicalized Islamic societies from the Indian-Pakistani border to Central Asia. This would be, in effect, a greater Pakistan, giving Pakistan's Inter-Services Intelligence the ability to create a clandestine empire composed of the likes of Haqqanis and the Lashkar-e-Taiba".[7]

Afghanistan is not the only place where Pakistani leaders have flirted with terrorist clients; Pakistan has also helped Kashmiri extremists to constitute attacks against Indian forces. Retired US Army colonel, Robert Cassidy (31 January 2018) in his Modern Institute analysis expostulated that Afghanistan is not graveyard of empire, but Pakistan is the graveyard for strategy in Afghanistan due to the country's support to Taliban and other extremist organizations:

Afghanistan is not the graveyard of empires, although it is true that the country has been more readily invaded than stabilized or pacified. But it is not possible to defeat an insurgency and bring peace to Afghanistan when the Taliban's sources of strength—the group's senior leadership, resources, and recruits—remain protected in Pakistan's sanctuary. Pakistan remains a graveyard for strategy in Afghanistan because its protection and support of the Taliban prevent a winning US strategy in Afghanistan. Until the US-led coalition strategy induces Pakistan to stop mobilizing the Taliban in Pakistan for export and use in Afghanistan, operational forces will continue to face a continuous flow of Taliban into Afghanistan from the sanctuaries of Pakistan. No change in Pakistan's affinity for Islamists means that strategy is dead. This portends a prolonged stalemate without end.[8]

The abrupt announcement of the Trump administration on 20 December 2018, about the withdrawal of US troops from Afghanistan prompted an institutional fight between the State Department and Department of Defence. Secretary of Defence General James Mattis resigned.[9] Mr. Trump requested Pakistan to bring Taliban to the table, but some states such as Qatar, Saudi Arabia, Russia, and China don't like Taliban and their terrorist activities. On 26 December 2018, Dawn published some parts of the report of US Defence Department that highlights the importance of the engagement of regional states:

China's military, economic, and political engagements in Afghanistan are driven by domestic security concerns that terrorism will spread across the Afghan border into China, and also by China's increasing desire to protect its regional economic investments. Iran seeks a stable Afghan government that is responsive to Iranian goals, the elimination of ISIS-K, the removal of the US/Nato presence, and the protection of Iranian concerns, such as water rights and border security, and "Russia is engaging a wide range of actors in Afghanistan, including the Taliban, to secure its interests in Central Asia and to expand its influence in the region," the report warned.[10]

Criticising the role of the US and its envoy Zalmay Khalilzad, former Afghan intelligence chief Amrullah Saled told India Today Magazine (18 October 2018): "All the five Taliban representatives who the US envoy met in Doha had flown in from Pakistan which means that they are backed by the Pakistani state."[11] India

Today was told that US officials met with Taliban members Mullah Shahabuddin Dilawar, Qari Din Mohammad Hanif, Sher Mohammad Abbas Stanikzai, Dr Mohammad Naeem Wardak and Abdul Salam Hanafi in Doha.[12] Writer Mr. Sahar Khan analysis further elucidated Pakistan's role in Afghanistan:

> Why does Pakistan continue to sponsor militant groups in the face of considerable U.S. pressure to stop? This question has plagued U.S.-Pakistan relations for decades. President Trump has rebuked Pakistan, inflaming an already tense relationship when he tweeted about decades of U.S. aid to Pakistan with "nothing but lies & deceit" in return. The Trump administration subsequently reduced security and military aid to Pakistan, campaigned to add Pakistan to an intergovernmental watch list for terrorism financing, and imposed sanctions on seven Pakistani firms involved in prohibited nuclear activities.[13]

Mr. Sahar Khan also explained Pakistan's rational interests behind the support of extremist organizations inside Afghanistan. Pakistan wants a friendly government in Afghanistan to expel India from the country. Pakistani law enforcement agencies and some politicians are of the opinion that India trains Baluch and Pashtun insurgents inside Afghanistan:

> Unfortunately, these policies are unlikely to be effective in changing Pakistan's behaviour. Pakistan's military establishment and intelligence agencies consider militant sponsorship an important mechanism for maintaining Pakistan's sovereignty and national identity. Pakistan's civilian institutions, too, have evolved to facilitate militant sponsorship by routinely legitimizing expansive executive powers, limiting judicial oversight, and violating civil liberties in the name of the national interest. Pakistan's civilian and military institutions, therefore, are much more closely aligned on matters of state sponsorship of militant groups than most U.S. policymakers and academics think and therefore less susceptible to outside pressure.[14]

In August 2018, Pakistani militants and Taliban attacked Ghazni city, inflicted huge financial destruction, and killed countless innocent civilians. The VOA (16 10, 2018) reported simplification of Afghan commanders about the involvement of Pakistani militants: "Dozens of Pakistani nationals were among more than 400 militants killed in fierce battles in south-eastern Ghazni province in the past several days. During the Taliban attack in Ghazni, over 400 terrorists were killed, including 70 Pakistani nationals whose bodies are ready to be transferred to Pakistan in Jahangir Bazar, a local market located between Muqur and Gelan districts of Ghazni province, Mr. Wahidullah Kalimzai, Governor of Ghazni province told VOA News".[15] Prominent journalist Ankit Panda (14, 10, 2018) has argued that the United States strategy to stabilize Afghanistan failed due to the absence of radical changes in the country's approach to the Afghan conflict:

After 17 years of war, the weekend's events show that the Taliban—through seventeen years of war and two leadership transitions since 2015—remains a threat to the Afghan government's ability to successfully administer territory across the country. Ghazni in 2018, Helmand in 2016, and Kunduz in 2015 tell parts of this story. More significantly, the United States' existing strategy in Afghanistan—articulated almost exactly a year ago in a major speech by U.S. President Donald J. Trump—falls short of providing a negotiated solution to the crisis facing Afghanistan today. Absent a radical change in the United States' approach—such as a willingness to unilaterally sit down and talk to the Taliban—there will be more horrifying Taliban sieges, each of which will extract a terrible humanitarian toll and chip away at the Afghan government's control. There are some hints that the Trump administration is exploring talks, with a recent trip to Doha by a senior U.S. State Department official, but broader signs of a change in strategy aren't apparent.[16]

Pakistan's support to terrorist organization, its war against Afghanistan, and its resentment towards neighbours, economically failing state, poverty, extremism and radicalization, all these catastrophes have been elucidated in the article (25, 12, 2018) of analyst and commentator Jan Muhammad Achakzai who put in two cents that the country needs to determine it direction:

> Pakistan is facing worse challenges never seen before", is more relevant today than ever before; economically failing state, dysfunction political system, corrupt political elite, unemployed youth bulge, extremism both religious and now ethnic mix with provincialism, hot but unstable western and eastern borders and a foreign hostile intend to denuclearize Pakistan, the only Muslim country to have nukes, and the list goes on. The most worrying aspect of all is the lack of capacity of the current system to cope with these challenges. Even worse is the agony of realizing that the current system is beyond repair. It is so rotten that any fix will take decades which we do not have to wait for. Whereas the country is going to be on the edge not after a decade from now, not five years from today but the likely year is going to be 2019, as it will determine our direction to join the path of the countries like Singapore and Malaysia or enter the club of failed states: Syria, Iraq, and Libya".[17]

The melodrama of intelligence sharing between Pakistan and Afghanistan remained an embellishment of print and electronic media when Afghan civil society, parliamentarian, government officials and media initiated campaign of hee-haw across the country that Pakistani intelligence agencies (ISI, IB, MI) within realm of possibility wanted to hijack the war on terror for their own interests. The National Directorate of Intelligence (NDS) and the ISI played a critical role in the war on terror in the region, and were still struggling to defeat the Taliban. The Afghan National Directorate of Security (NDS) and the Pakistani Inter-Services Intelligence (ISI) were looking at each other with suspicion and derision due to their changing approaches to the current war in Afghanistan.[18]

In 2015, former Prime Minister Nawaz Sharif visited Kabul and signed a deal of intelligence sharing between the two states. The memorandum signed in Kabul was a successful story, while under that agreement; the two intelligence agencies were directed to cooperate in counter-terrorism operations. An essential element of the accord was a provision for a joint probe of the terrorism suspects. The ISI had to equip the NDS and train its personnel. "MoU signed by ISI and NDS included intelligence sharing, complementary and coordinated intelligence operations on respective sides," Pakistan military spokesman Major General Asim Bajwa tweeted. Afghan President Ashraf Ghani during his trip to Pakistan visited the army headquarters in Rawalpindi as a mark of increasing trust between the two sides, but India reacted differently.[19]

Speaking at a news conference, India's National Security Advisor, Ajit Doval, criticized the intelligence sharing agreement between Pakistan and Afghanistan and said that the agreement between the Afghan National Directorate of Security (NDS) and Pakistan's Inter-Services Intelligence (ISI) was based on faulty assumptions. "What Pakistan wanted was to get an assurance and put pressure on Afghanistan, so that they will not allow their territory to be used for any security related work by India," Doval said. "That is the crux of it. This is based on a faulty assumption that India probably uses Afghan soil or Afghan nationals for its security purposes." Doval warned. India's reservations about the agreement were shared by many Afghans, who continued to distrust the ISI, which had long provided covert support for the Taliban.[20]

On 08 February 2016, Pakistan and Afghanistan decided to discuss the revival of an agreement between their top spy agencies to reset their relationship bedevilled by trust deficit and sporadic blame games. Diplomatic sources in Islamabad admitted that the issue was highlighted in talks between Lieutenant Gen Rizwan Akhtar, the Director General of the Inter-Services Intelligence (ISI), and Masud Andrabi, the Director General of Afghanistan's National Directorate of Security (NDS). Mr. Andrabi visited Islamabad to explore the possibility of intelligence and security cooperation with the ISI. Both sides, however, refused to acknowledge the meeting of their intelligence chiefs.[21]

On 15 January 2018, the NDS arrested a government employee in the western province of Herat for alleged spying for Iran. Mr. Jilani Farhad, the spokesman for Herat's governor, told RFE/RL that the man, identified as Assadullah Rezai was detained and sent to Kabul for further investigation. Mr. Rezai worked for nearly two years as a provincial expert on municipal affairs in Herat Province, which borders Iran.[22] A senior provincial government official said Rezai had been under surveillance for several months. Mr. Rezai transferred classified government documents to Iranian intelligence services.

On 17 January 2017, Al Arabia News reported Iranian support to Taliban, which became more apparent in May 2016, when the group's top leader, Mullah Akhtar Mohammad Mansour was killed by US drone in Pakistan while returning from Iran. The Jahan News, an Iranian outlet close to the Revolutionary Guards, confirmed that he had stayed in Iran for two months prior to his death and had meetings with Iranian officials. In May 2015, an Iranian news website tied to the Revolutionary Guards reported that a Taliban delegation visited Iran and several editorials have been published in the governmental press to justify Iran's support to Taliban.[23]

On 31 January 2018, Geo-News-TV reported visit of Afghan Interior Minister and Intelligence Chief to Islamabad for further cooperation between the two states. "Afghan government had requested that a high-level delegation comprising Interior Minister and NDS chief would like to visit Pakistan with a message from Afghan President and for discussions about cooperation between the two countries. Delegation is here and will have talks today," Foreign Office spokesperson Dr Mohammad Faisal tweeted.[24]

On 30 April 2018, the Guardian reported the killing of ten journalists in a coordinated double suicide bombing in Kabul and a shooting in Khost province. Nine journalists died in the Afghan capital when they gathered at the scene of the first of two blasts. Ahmad Shah, a BBC reporter, was shot dead in a separate incident in Khost province, near the border with Pakistan. In Kabul, a suicide attacker riding a motorbike blew himself up in the Shash

Darak neighbourhood, near the NATO headquarters and the US embassy. A second bomber, holding a camera and posing as a journalist, struck 20 minutes later, killing rescue workers and journalists, including an Agence France-Presse photographer. Afghan intelligence blamed ISI for its support to terrorist groups inside Afghanistan.[25]

On 11 June 2018, Afghan and Pakistani military officials met in Islamabad to boost bilateral cooperation on security level amid ongoing efforts to establish the joint working groups as part of the Afghanistan Pakistan Action Plan for Peace and Solidarity (APAPPS). Director General of Pakistan and Afghanistan military operations met amid growing interaction between the military officials to finalise deployment of liaison officers (LOs), establishment of Ground Coordination Centres (GCCs) for intelligence sharing and to monitor cross-border movement of militants.[26] Before this meeting, in 31 May 2017, Afghan intelligence blamed that Taliban-affiliated militants with the help of Pakistani security services for a truck bombing in Kabul that killed 90 people. Up to 400 others were injured when the suicide attacker drove into the capital's diplomatic quarter during the morning rush-hour before setting off explosives.[27]

This incident created a misunderstanding between the two states. Pakistani ISI was aware of the unwelcomed developments in Afghanistan. The threat of Islamic State in Afghanistan created consternation in South and Central Asia. Regional states expedited intelligence sharing on the movement and activities of Daesh. In July 2018, in light of increasing strength of the Islamic State in Afghanistan, four high profile spy chiefs met in Pakistan to discuss how to counter the extremist group's influence. Sergei Ivano, spokesperson for the Russian Foreign Intelligence revealed that the meeting was held under the auspices of Pakistan's Inter-Services Intelligence (ISI), though the huddle was not reported on mainstream media. The meeting was attended by Russian Foreign Intelligence Director Sergei Naryshkin and comes months after Russia's growing allegations against the USA for supporting the ISIS in Afghanistan. This gathering was indicative of the fact that intelligence war in Afghanistan had intensified. Pakistan army through ISI have been accused of recruiting fighters and suicide bombers for the Afghan Taliban.[28]

Regional states and their intelligence agencies are operating in Afghanistan for their national interests. Professor Marvin G. Weinbaum in his paper (June 2006) blamed regional powers for intelligence war and political instability in Afghanistan:

> As is often stated, Afghanistan stands in a dangerous neighbourhood. Responsibility for much of the political instability and misery of its people can be traced to external powers seeking to realize their own strategic, ideological, and economic interests in the country. The close and more distant neighbours of Afghanistan have regularly intervened in its politics and economy. Foreigners have sometimes acted on behalf of domestic clients and have organized and armed them to dominate large portions of the country. Although renowned for resisting foreign intruders, Afghans cannot thus be absolved of responsibility for much of the fratricide and destruction that has occurred in recent decades. Still, the aggravating role of outside states, near and far, has also made civil conflicts more sustained and lethal.[29]

On 18 August 2018, Pajhwok Afghan News reported the NDS officials blamed ISI for its involvement in Ghazni City.[30] President Ghani warned Pakistan Army Chief General Qamar Javed Bajwa: "You have signed a significant document with us. You have assured me in several phone calls that everything will become normal after elections Pakistan. I want answers how Pakistani fighters penetrated Ghazni". With regard to the killing of Pakistanis fighting alongside the Taliban in Ghazni City, he warned Prime Minister Imran Khan in strong words: "You have received coffins. You being a Pakhtun should probe the matter and give me a reply".[31]

On the other hand, the National Directorate of Security (NDS) accused Pakistani ISI of plotting the Ghazni attack. The NDS claimed it retrieved documents of ISI involvement in the Ghazni fighting. The ISI had tasked Lashkar-e-Toiba to execute the attack.[32] This swing and oscillation in relations between the two states caused misunderstanding. Prime Minister Imran Khan and General Bajwa did not respond to the allegations of NDS and Afghan President. Intelligence sharing agreement between Pakistan and Afghanistan was fundamental to the establishment and preservation of security and stability in the region, but Afghan parliamentarians rejected this idea and said ISI does not want peace in Afghanistan.

Retrospectively, the MoU signed between the two states in May 2015 was considered of vital importance because both states were fighting terrorism and insurgencies. Since Pakistan Army chief war criminal General Raheel Sharif declared in Kabul that the enemy of Afghanistan is the enemy of Pakistan, the two states entered a new era of long-term friendship. The threat of the Taliban and Islamic State (ISIS) significantly changed the direction of intelligence sharing between the neighbours. Although the threat of the Taliban and ISIS was by no means new, the scope and global reach of their networks, both leading up to and following the terrorist attacks in New York, made intelligence sharing a top priority for the war on terrorism in Afghanistan.

Secret agencies of Pakistan and Afghanistan strived to negotiate MoUs, setting out the modalities of intelligence exchange. Since General Musharraf's revelation in February 2015 about the involvement of the Inter-Services Intelligence agency (ISI) in a suicide bombing in Afghanistan, a new perception developed that the ISI is behind all the misadventures and grievances in Afghanistan. If we look at the statements of certain Pakistani generals and religious clerics, the fear and reservations of the Afghan leadership seem justified.[33]

Former Afghan President Hamid Karzai expressed deep concern over the signing of the MoU. The office of the former President issued a statement calling on the government to cancel the memorandum. Senate Chairman Fazal Hadi Muslimyar criticised ISI and termed Pakistan an enemy of Afghanistan. In a bid for peace with the Taliban, President Ghani ordered director of the National Directorate of Security (NDS) to end the propaganda campaign against the ISI. The NDS chief and advisor for national security exchanged harsh words in an official meeting.[34]

Dr Abdullah also demanded an amendment in the MoU's text; he was informed about the contents of the Memorandum by former President Hamid Karzai. The signing of an intelligence sharing MoU between the ISI and NDS caused growing concern at all levels in the country. Warlord Abdul Rasool Sayyaf also criticised the MoU and said that the deal will only benefit Islamabad. Former chiefs of the NDS, Mr. Amrullah Saleh and Asadullah Khalid asked the government to revoke the memorandum. The National Solidarity Party (NSP) also criticised Islamabad for its interfering in Afghanistan through an intelligence agreement.[35]

The MoU was also criticised by Indian National Security Advisor Mr. Ajit Doval. On May 23, 2015, Doval said that the memorandum was based on a faulty assumption: "What Pakistan wanted was to get an assurance and put pressure on Afghanistan so that it will not allow its territory to be used for any security related work by India."[36] Ethnic and political divisions within the NDS and political confrontations were causing the deterioration of the security situation in Afghanistan. In all parts of the country, fighting ISIS was a big challenge for the Sovietised intelligence of the country. Afghanistan wanted to settle all issues with Pakistan to tackle the threat of the Taliban and ISIS effectively but, unfortunately, Pakistan abruptly changes its position and continued to send hundreds of proxies into Afghanistan.

On May 24, 2015, Khaama Press reported President Ashraf Ghani position and adopted an un-compromisable attitude towards Pakistan. The President warned that Pakistan supported an undeclared war with Afghanistan. He made these remarks at the nomination ceremony of Muhammad Masoom Stanekzai as the new Defence Minister of Afghanistan: "The war has been imposed on us and Afghans are determined not to ever bow to the imposed war. "We will respond to the imposed war with war." This is the first time that the Afghan president has clearly given this message to Pakistan. In these circumstances, the trust deficit between the two states could be further exacerbated because Afghanistan does not want to eliminate India's political influence.[37]

"Pakistan is a well-wisher of the Afghan government and its people. We are committed to the recent agreement on intelligence sharing to root out the menace of terrorism," Pakistan responded. "We would keep ignoring such allegations just to help the new Afghan government regain its strength against terrorists," a Pakistani official said.[38] Several Afghan MPs opposed the MoU during debate session in the Wolesi Jirga (lower house of parliament). They warned that it would not benefit Afghanistan.

After lawmakers sought a clarification from the National Security Council (NSC), the first deputy speaker of the Wolesi Jirga, Mr. Zahir Qadir, asked parliamentary panels to summon NSC officials to explain.[39] According to ToloNews, MP Rahman Rahmani told the House: "During (Pakistan Prime Minister) Nawaz Sharif's trip to Kabul, three Pakistani intelligence officers also arrived and you sign a shameful intelligence sharing agreement. By signing this agreement you have made yourself blind and dumb." The deputy head of parliament's internal security commission, Mohammad Faisal Sami, said: "The government should have endorsed its defeat to Pakistan before signing this agreement and announce it publicly."[40]

Members of parliament sought copies of the text, which had not been made public, and warned that they would invalidate the agreement if their conditions were not met. The NDS chief Rahmatullah Nabeel, who reportedly opposed the deal, appeared before a closed-door session of parliament, while national security advisor Hanif Atmar did not attend. The Kandahar Inspector General the late Abdul Raziq criticized the agreement in remarks saying that: "the actions of the national unity government will have negative impacts on the morale of security forces".

Another lawmaker Shukria Barakzai strongly criticised the MoU and demanded revoking of the agreement immediately. She said signing such an agreement meant Afghanistan recognized the Durand Line as legal border between the two countries. Speaker Abdul Rauf Ibrihim said Afghanistan suffered the most due to Pakistan's hidden policies and meddling in Afghan affairs. He said Pakistan was solely responsible for the killing of innocent Afghans in the bombing and other incidents of violence. "The agreement is not in the interest of Afghanistan. It will not end the ongoing wave of violence in Afghanistan," the speaker noted.

The NSC in its statement said the signing of a memorandum of understanding between the National Directorate of Security (NDS) and Pakistan's Inter-Services Intelligence or ISI on intelligence cooperation is important for Afghanistan. Without going into details, the statement said that some dubious sources had been providing misleading information to the NSC and the media. The NSC said it was concerned that the country's high interests were being used for personal gains and character assassination and that the NSC considered it mandatory to explain few words about the agreement in order to remove common fears.[41] The memorandum included a number of traditional points: intelligence data sharing, joint development and coordination of anti-terrorist operations on both sides of the Pakistani-Afghan border. The ISI said that Pakistan army will train Afghan specialists, etc. At the same time, Pakistan consistently emphasized the fact those they "... strictly adhere to the policy of non-interference in the affairs of Afghanistan."[42]

Despite mutual accusations, the ISI-NDS signed the Agreement in May 2015. Pakistan was as much as Afghanistan interested in eliminating armed outbreaks in the Af-Pak region. The army launched large-scale military operations in June 2014 to destroy foreign and local militants. Most of the extremists crossed the Hindu Kush to enter the Afghan territory, which significantly strengthened anti-Kabul armed opposition. It continues to create a major threat to the social and economic reforms planned in the Pakistani province Khyber Pakhtunkhwa. This could put the end as the long-term appeal of the military community to the Afghan authorities on exchanging the intelligence data has been implemented.

The success of the Afghan peace process hung on the Pakistani military and the ISI being brought on board. Pakistan and Afghanistan were said to be cooperating in "ways not known before." Soon after the December 16 massacre in a Peshawar school, troops from both sides conducted coordinated operations along the border. The decision on the ISI-NDS pact was taken by Mr. Ghani, not the Afghan government. Reconciliation was a top priority for the Afghan President. Realizing that the peace process could be a non-starter without the Taliban on board and recognizing that he will need the ISI to get the Taliban leaders to the negotiation table, he took the gamble of shaking hands with Pakistan. Indeed, it was with these considerations in mind that he roped in China, a close ally of Pakistan's, to broker the peace process, no doubt hoping that China will push Pakistan to cooperate with the peace process.

On February 2016, Intelligence agencies of Pakistan and Afghanistan held talks in Kabul and tried to reduce the trust deficit between the two neighbours. Director General of ISI Lt Gen Rizwan Akhtar said he would travel to Afghanistan for a meeting with the acting chief of the National Directorate of Security (NDS), Masoud Andarabi. The meeting took place as Pakistan had called on Afghanistan to act against the terrorist group involved in January 20-Bacha Khan University attack. Islamabad alleges that terrorists planned and directed the terrorist activity using Afghan soil and telecom infrastructure.[43]

Latif Mehsud, a Pakistani terrorist was arrested by NDS, who later on made shocking revelation against the Indian and Afghan intelligence involvement in Pakistan. He categorically told investigators that RAW and NDS were behind the killings in the country. Mr. Latifullah was the deputy of TTP high command in Waziristan. On 08 August 2015, a truck bomb killed 400 civilians in Kabul due to the NDS failure to intercept a monition laden truck on the border. The NDS accused ISI for the attack, while Pakistan arrested 90 NDS agents from Peshawar, Gilgit and Baltistan, Karachi and parts of Baluchistan province.[44] On 01 February 2016, Afghan military commander claimed that Pakistani forces were fighting in Baghlan province. General Murad Ali said they kill innocent civilian and loot their belongings.[45] However, on 07 February 2016, Khaama Press reported the arrest of some ISI agents in Badakhshan province.[46]

On 29 March 2016, acting NDS Chief warned that Pakistani intelligence agency (ISI) was trying to expand the war beyond Afghanistan. Mr. Massoud Andrabi told Afghan parliament that Pakistan army controlled some parts of Afghanistan. The issue of ethnic and sectarian loyalties within the NDS was a matter of great concern for the Afghan government and the United States as well.[47] The agency reported to various stakeholders including war criminals. Sectarian and political loyalties divided the NDS between different funding parties. However, the NDS was unable to provide security to Afghan army commanders in the war zones due to the high number of defections of its agents to the Taliban.[48]

In 2015, Mullah Mansour Dadullah, former Taliban commander, released a video addressing his complaints about the Taliban and Pakistan's intelligence service to Afghan Islamic Press on Sept. 5. The Dadullah's interview was recorded on 02 September 2015, just days after his followers and the Taliban clashed in Zabul province.[49] Dadullah, in his videotape, accused the Taliban leadership of being "lecherous, rakish and malicious" and described "intelligence networks," which presumably included Pakistan's Inter-Services Intelligence Directorate, as "dirty and disgraced," according to a translation of the Afghan Islamic Press article that was obtained by The Long War Journal. Additionally, he claimed that Mullah Omar, who died in April 2013, months before Dadullah was released, was murdered:

> We have tried from the very first moments of jihad to give control of the Islamic army to a religious, brave, independent and free Muslim. Ever since the relation between His Excellency Amir al-Momenin [Leader of the Faithful] Mullah Mohammad Omar Mujahid was disconnected and lecherous, rakish and malicious people had entered in the middle, we have raised our voice of truth. Now, the situation is very clear and you see that in the name of the new Amir al-Momenin [Mullah Mansour], the sincere Muslims and mujahedeen are being deceived again. The voice of truth, which the religious scholars raise, is prevented and dirty and disgraced intelligence networks once again dominate our faithful and Muslim nation. Thus, we openly made a decision once again

and in consultation with religious scholars, and we clearly declared our separation from those lying lecher people, who kept the killing of His Excellency Amir al-Momenin Mullah Mohammad Omar Mujahid for over two years from all the Muslims and who imposed their hated thoughts in the form of the decrees of the Leader Mullah [Omar] on all the Islamic world. We cannot accept Akhtar Mohammad Mansour as the new Amir based on consultation with and fatwa by the religious scholars. Dadullah said.[50]

On June 24 2015, Afghanistan's intelligence service said that a Pakistani intelligence officer helped the Taliban carry out an attack on parliament. Afghan intelligence services spokesman Hassib Sediqqi said that the officer in Inter-Services Intelligence helped the Haqqani network carrying out the attack outside parliament in Kabul, which killed two people and wounded more than 30 as lawmakers were meeting inside. The Chief of National Directorate of Security (NDS), Mr. Rahmatullah Nabil stepped down. His resignation was accepted by the government. Mr. Nabil won vote of confidence from the parliament with 154 votes in January 2015. Shortly after the Pak-Afghan leaders agreed to revive the controversial Afghan peace talks, Mr. Nabil issued a rare statement and said that innocent Afghan civilians were martyred and beheaded in Kandahar airfield, Khanshin district of Helmand, Takhar and Badakhshan while Nawaz Sharif was calling the enemy of Afghanistan as Pakistan's enemy.[51]

In parts of his message, Nabil criticized President Ghani for his remarks in Islamabad, saying: "At least 1,000 litres of blood of our innocent people spilled. "The colour of the blood was similar to the red carpet where we did a cat walk," he said. Frustrated with the growing interference of Pakistan in internal affairs of Afghanistan, and President Ghani's approach, Mr. Nabil questioned regarding the 5000-year-old history of Afghanistan saying it has kneeled to a 60-year-old history. Mr. Nabil also added that the Pakistani Taliban chief Mullah Fazlullah has been residing in Pakistan and ISI guesthouses during the past several months and years, insisting that Mullah Fazlullah is part of ISI projects. Mullah Akhtar Mansoor had been enjoying the escort and legion of ISI bodyguards in presence of Colonel Rana—his fake name "Rabbani". They were busy drawing future plans to kill our innocent people in Quetta's bypass area, Pakistan. And Sarajuddin Haqqani was enjoying a party of his son from his third wife in Hayatabad area of Peshawar Pakistan. Thank God I was not present there, Mr. Nabil said.[52]

Moreover, in an interview at his office in Kabul, Mr. Massoud said the confidence expressed by Ghani and Abdullah, in Afghanistan's unity government, does not reflect political and military realities. Citing U.S. military figures, the U.S. Special Inspector for Afghanistan Reconstruction, a watchdog, reported that the Afghan government controlled just 72% of the country's 407 districts, believed to be the lowest figure in years.[53] Taliban insurgents continued fighting government forces through a bloody winter, defying the usual lull in violence that comes in Afghanistan's colder months and prompting U.S. military officials to reconsider reducing the U.S. troop presence the White House planned. The Interior Minister, Mr. Noor-ul-Haq Olomi, also resigned due to some pressures from foreign intelligence agencies operating in Afghanistan. "Look at the current state of the nation: the economy is weak, people continue to suffer from joblessness, there are still social problems, there is still political infighting even at the highest level," Massoud said.[54]

Chapter - 8

Decoding Afghan Security Forces' Failures and Fixing Afghanistan's Struggling Security Forces

Ghulam Farooq Mujaddidi

What went wrong with the NDS?

The May 31 deadly terror attack in the heart of Kabul that killed and wounded hundreds of ordinary Afghans was not the first one in such a highly important area, nor was it the first time that the Afghan National Defense and Security Forces (ANDSF) have failed to safeguard their own perimeters – not to mention their repeated failures to protect key civilian institutions, peaceful gatherings, and diplomatic missions in the country over the years. A month before the deadly Kabul attack, a Taliban suicide squad stormed the Afghan National Army's (ANA) main base in the north of the country, leaving carnage behind – 150 Afghan soldiers were killed and another 100-plus were injured.

Over the past several months, militants were able to breach security parameters and hit key ANDSF institutions deep inside the Afghan capital, Kabul. Among the targets were the largest Afghan Military Hospital, cadets of the Afghan National Police (ANP), the Afghan Ministry of Defense, and the Directorate of VIP Protection and Security – an elite agency responsible for protecting high-ranking Afghan government officials and prominent leaders. Although Pakistani "safe haven and support" for the insurgent groups along with insurgents' resilience and adaptability are notable factors in carrying out such deadly assaults, the main reasons why ANDSF consistently fails to foil high-profile attacks are inattention to Afghanistan's main intelligence agency, known as the National Directorate of Security (NDS), and political interference and appointments in ANDSF institutions.

Right after toppling the Taliban regime in late 2001 for refusing to handover Osama bin Laden – the perpetrator of the 9/11 attacks – the U.S.-led international community embarked on a state-building mission in Afghanistan. Part of their mission was – and still is – to build the ANDSF. Although their intention was noble and realistic, their approach has been misguided and wrong. Rather than prioritizing the ANDSF brain, the NDS, they have concentrated their efforts on building the ANDSF's body parts, namely the Afghan National Army (ANA) and the Afghan National Police (ANP).

Due to this historical mistake, NDS – the main organ of the ANDSF – remains highly under-resourced and ill-equipped to tackle the challenges emanating from terrorist groups, as well as to counter unfriendly neighbouring countries' malicious intelligence interventions and activities inside the country. The number of high-profile attacks carried out since last year against hard ANDSF targets in the Afghan capital alone says it all about the status and competence of the NDS.

While high profile attacks against hard targets take months of planning, surveillance, and coordination, NDS is unable to detect and thwart these deadly attacks during any of the preparatory stages. But this is not the only problem; NDS seems to gravely suffer in the intelligence-gathering field as well, and thus misses important developments in the country – not to mention its failures to prevent new and/or root out existing Taliban infiltrators in ANDSF, who turn their guns on coalition troops. This has caused massive mistrust between foreign troops and Afghan security forces.

In 2016, an impostor was able to use ANA helicopters and armoured vehicles, travelling from province to province with

ANA transportation and protection after tricking an ANA corps commander along with several other high-ranking ANDSF officials with fake certificates of appreciation from the Presidential Palace. This wasn't his first time though; he had been engaging in such activities for more than a decade before his arrest. Nor was he the first person to do so. Before him, a "shopkeeper" disguised as a prominent Taliban leader and negotiator made it to the Presidential Palace and met with the former Afghan president, and another man posing as a "peace messenger" severely injured the former head of the NDS itself, to name some high profile cases.

Furthermore, NDS is still disastrously dependent on pen and paper, not because of security and/or reliability issues, but simply because computers, email, and secure intranet connectivity are alien ideas for a lot of people serving in the agency. Therefore, not only is NDS not in a position to form a coherent front to respond to the psychological warfare and social media conspiracies crippling the very foundations of the new democratic Afghan regime, but it has even failed to regulate a social media policy for the agency itself to control the rising Facebook craze among its own employees, whose immature posts and social media engagements are often contrary to the spirit and main objectives of the NDS itself.

Revitalizing the Neglected NDS

Equally important is NDS revitalization and reform. Overwhelmed with the need for local fighting force in their "war on terror" campaign in Afghanistan, the Bush and the Obama administrations overlooked the importance of the indigenous intelligence agency – the NDS – and hedged their bets on building the Afghan army and police force. History has proven that ignoring NDS was a deadly mistake. Not only have ordinary Afghans and ANDSF been bleeding largely due to intelligence failures, but also insurgents' surprise assaults and deadly suicide attacks have been badly hurting the popularity of an already struggling Afghan government.

To mitigate threats and prevent further damages and losses, NDS reform and capacity building must be a key component of the new American policy for Afghanistan. The United States and its NATO allies need a vigilant, proactive, and formidable Afghan intelligence force to minimize ANDSF's vulnerabilities and to thwart insurgents' deadly suicide attacks against soft and hard targets in Afghanistan. The following measures would help revitalize the forgotten NDS.

First of all, to upgrade, diversify, and depoliticize the agency's human capital, NDS needs a transparent, systematic and open to all – online – recruitment policy and procedure. Right now, due to a highly flawed and restrictive recruitment method, it is almost impossible to join NDS without an affiliation, no matter how highly educated and or talented one is. The agency is haunted by the practice of closely guarding its job application forms. Only individuals with links to influential people or current NDS officials can get one, which provides opportunities for nepotism, ethnic favouritism, and preferential treatments.

Second, illiterate and unqualified individuals from the rank and file of the NDS should be removed through an impartial audit and merit-based requalification tests. To fill the gap, minimize the agency's drastic dependence on pen and paper as the primary means of communication and exchange, and boost its capacity with a highly educated new generation who knows the language and technologies of the modern world, a nationwide campaign should be launched to indiscriminately recruit the young Afghan Fulbrighters, Chevening scholars, and recipients of various other scholarships from different countries around the globe, as well as top local graduates.

Third, the United States and NATO allies must also help with the latest training, modern equipment, and structural reform. A structural overhaul to replace the old Soviet era arrangements of the NDS, which the agency has inherited from its predecessor, is a must to make the agency compatible with the modern world and ready to address threats emanating from highly adaptable terrorist organizations and foreign adversaries. Fourth, pay reform; in its current range, an NDS salary is almost a starvation wage, making employees prone to favours and corruption. Right now, the average NDS salary is a tiny fraction of what international organizations, NGOs, foreign embassies, and the private sector pay to their employees in Afghanistan. In addition to minimizing embezzlement pretexts, pay raise would also help attract highly competent applicants.

And last, to further decrease the probability of insider attacks against RS personnel working with the ANDSF, the authority of the NDS should be extended to oversee ANA and ANP recruitment and to establish a permanent presence in all ANDSF units deployed across the country. In addition to minimizing the possibility of enemy infiltration in the armed forces, doing so would also help in monitoring and reporting misuse of resources and all sorts of abuses to the leadership of the Afghan government. Depoliticizing ANDSF institutions and revitalizing the neglected NDS are the only viable options to strategically turn the tide of the battle in the Afghan war theatre, save American treasure and Afghan blood, and convince Pakistan that its terror proxies cannot overthrow the democratic Afghan regime. Otherwise, no matter how many extra coalition troops the United States and its NATO allies pour into Afghanistan, it will only achieve short-term tactical advantages that would once again evaporate with the drawdown of foreign forces.

The May 31 2018 deadly terror attack in the heart of Kabul that killed and wounded hundreds of ordinary Afghans was not the first one in such a highly important area, nor was it the first time that the Afghan National Defence and Security Forces (ANDSF) have failed to safeguard their own perimeters – not to mention their repeated failures to protect key civilian institutions, peaceful gatherings, and diplomatic missions in the country over the years. A month before the deadly Kabul attack, a Taliban suicide squad stormed the Afghan National Army's (ANA) main base in the north of the country, leaving carnage behind – 150 Afghan soldiers were killed and another 100-plus were injured.

Over the past several months, militants were able to breach security parameters and hit key ANDSF institutions deep inside the Afghan capital, Kabul. Among the targets were the largest Afghan Military Hospital, cadets of the Afghan National Police

(ANP), the Afghan Ministry of Defense, and the Directorate of VIP Protection and Security – an elite agency responsible for protecting high-ranking Afghan government officials and prominent leaders.

Although Pakistani "safe haven and support" for the insurgent groups along with insurgents' resilience and adaptability are notable factors in carrying out such deadly assaults, the main reasons why ANDSF consistently fails to foil high-profile attacks are inattention to Afghanistan's main intelligence agency, known as the National Directorate of Security (NDS), and political interference and appointments in ANDSF institutions.

Toxic Political Interference and Appointments

Political interference and appointments in ANDSF institutions and affairs is another culprit behind the deteriorating ANA, ANP, and NDS capabilities. From government officials and parliamentarians to the so-called opposition leaders, almost every influential Afghan figure intervenes or attempts to interfere in ANDSF institutions. Such interference is the root cause of many of ANDSF's problems. First of all, due to political meddling, political appointees have flooded ANDSF institutions and climbed the ladder to key positions, sometimes overnight – according to a former NDS chief, "over 90 percent" of key ANDSF positions were filled through "political and nepotistic" appointments.

While political intervention and appointments in other sectors might affect service deliveries or cause economic burdens, doing so in the security and defence sector costs lives. Afghan soldiers and ordinary citizens are paying for incompetent appointees with their blood. Meanwhile, people appointed through political patronage are more loyal to their patrons than to the institutions they are serving in or to the Afghan state in general.

Second, political interference has drastically affected rewards and punishments in ANDSF institutions. Not only are merit-based appointments and promotions eroding, but incompetent and/or corrupt individuals are less likely to be demoted or face other punishments due to their patrons' interventions. Often, security sector ministers cannot transfer or replace their subordinates because doing so would eventually cost them their own jobs. Afghan parliamentarians have played a significant role in worsening this situation; they have become self-centered power brokers at the cost of broader national interest.

This has, in turn, fuelled corruption in ADNSF institutions. There are multiple reports about embezzlement and misuse of ANDSF resources, but so far no one has bothered to explain why and how those serving in key ANDSF positions become so rich with salaries or less than $1,000 per month.

And finally, political interference has impeded reforming ANDSF institutions. Thus, most of these institutions are highly unprepared to face rising security challenges. Rather than being a proactive and aggressive force, ANDSF has been mostly defensive and reactive. Risk analysis and assessment, as well as contingency planning, are unfamiliar terms in most ANDSF institutions, and they are not adaptable learning organizations ready to keep pace with the evolving security environment.

Unprofessionalism and negligence of duty are at a peak in most ANDSF organizations. The Taliban were able to hit the elite protective agency last April simply because its leadership had allowed a public parking lot right next to the agency, without any oversight or precautionary measures. To provide another example, magnetic mines have become insurgents' new weapon of choice because reckless ANDSF members, who mostly leave government vehicles unattended, can be easily targeted with these mines.

Similarly, while the Taliban and other terrorist groups have been able to enforce nighttimes blackouts – forcing telecom providers to "shut down" their mobile phone networks after 5 pm in some major cities and provincial capitals–ANDSF has not pushed these same companies to stop selling unregistered and preregistered SIM cards, a dangerous tool allowing terrorists and criminals to get their messages through without being traced. They could simply use such SIM cards once and throw them away, making it impossible to trace them.

With such challenges in ANDSF institutions, preventing high-profile attacks in the Afghan capital and other large cities of Afghanistan is almost impossible, to say nothing of actually winning the Afghan war. Therefore, the Trump administration and the Afghan government must prioritize building NDS capabilities and work on depoliticizing all ANDSF institutions. Revitalizing NDS and depoliticizing ANDSF institutions are as important to securing Afghan cities and winning the Afghan war as making Pakistan stops aiding and abetting the terrorist groups fighting in Afghanistan. In order to prevent the increasingly damaging deadly suicide attacks in the Afghan capital and across the country, reduce the unsustainable battlefield casualties of the Afghan National Defence and Security Forces (ANDSF), and reverse insurgents' unprecedented territorial gains, Kabul and Washington must rethink their current strategy and address inherent problems in their approach to building the ANDSF.

Time has proven that restricting the U.S.-led foreign troops' role to training and advising in building a professional ANDSF has failed to produce the desired outcome, and ignoring the need to invest in and revitalize the Afghan intelligence agency – the National Directorate of Security (NDS) – has been a costly mistake. Therefore, rather than solely concentrating on short-term fixes, the Trump administrations and the Afghan government must look for lasting solutions and prioritize reforming the neglected NDS and jointly embark on depoliticizing the ANDSF.

Purging the ANDSF

Right now, due to deeply entrenched patronage networks, catastrophic but prevalent nepotism, and rampant ethnic favouritism, endemic corruption and poor leadership are haunting ANDSF institutions and ruining the Afghan forces' capabilities. Tales of commanders stealing fuel, food, and even weapons are widespread, as are the stories of incompetent commanders failing to lead or at least stay with their soldiers during hard times. Therefore, to prevent political meddling and clientelistic practices in ANDSF institutions, purge it of inept and corrupt elements, and make the ANDSF a professional, apolitical, and impartial national force, the Afghan government must once again allow its allies – as it did in the formation of the President Protective Service (PPS) – to handle ANDSF recruitment, promotions, and nominations for leadership positions.

The current condition of the ANDSF is not different from early days of the personal protection team of the Afghan president, now known as the PPS. Back in 2002, the American security advisers for Presidential Palace realized that unless they took charge of building the PPS, their training and advisory role in establishing a viable protective agency would not have the desired outcome. After reporting their concerns to the former Afghan president and receiving permission, they took control of recruiting, training, and structuring the PPS. That way, the Americans were able to make PPS a diverse, depoliticized and highly competitive protective agency where ordinary but talented Afghans were able to shine and occupy key positions.

The new U.S. administration and the Afghan government must once again agree on a similar arrangement and allow the NATO-led Resolute Support (RS) mission to fix the struggling ANDSF. Foreign troops are the best source for institutionalizing merit-based recruitment and promotion in the Afghan defence and security sector, and a viable option for depoliticizing the ANDSF. This, however, shouldn't sound odd to anyone; the coalition forces are not only already heavily involved in training, advising, and equipping the ANDSF, but also as experts with on-the-ground experience, they know very well the potential ANDSF leaders to fill the current void.

To successfully implement this, RS mentors and advisers must expand their presence and try to reach out to all Afghan National Army (ANA) and the Afghan National Police (ANP) units deployed across the country, and start interacting with the mid- and low-level officers as well as soldiers. The current approach of restricting themselves to the "ministerial and Army Corps level" has proven to be ineffective both in fighting corruption and in spotting incompetent commanders. Although such a move would increase the probability of insider attacks – incidents in which

Afghan soldiers or policemen turn their guns on coalition forces – making the visiting ANA and ANP unit commanders responsible for the safety and security of foreign troops should minimize the risk. If an ANDSF commander does not know about potential enemy infiltrators in his unit, he does not deserve to be leading a unit.

The American and NATO mentors must also encourage whistle blowing within the ANDSF and establish a mechanism to protect whistle-blowers from repercussions to fight corruption and other abusive practices. They need to also challenge and change a deeply embedded tradition in the Afghan armed forces' domestic training; under the guise of disciplining service members, Afghan officers traditionally pressure low-ranking members and soldiers to the extent of demoralization. That is why Afghan soldiers and police do not dare to question and are less likely to stop high-ranking official's vehicles or other cars similar to those of the top brass at the checkpoints – an unintended consequence of wrong training often exploited by the terrorist groups and criminal networks to easily pass through security checkpoints.

Meanwhile, the leadership of the Afghan government must also stand against political meddling in ANDSF institutions and strongly reject political recommendations for promotions or transfer of ANDSF officials. All such recommendations should be filed against the named ANDSF officials. The government leadership also needs to reassess their current approach of limiting their interactions to video conference calls with ANA and ANP's high-ranking officials and regional commanders, who are less likely to provide an honest assessment of the situation on the ground and or confess their own ineptness and embezzlements.

And finally, the Afghan government must make its high-ranking defence and security officials and commanders vulnerable and prone, as ordinary Afghans and soldiers are, to enemy attacks for two main reasons: to make them vigilant, and to prevent misuse of ANDSF resources. Right now, a considerable amount of highly scarce and much-needed ANDSF resources are wasted in the service and protection of those who are employed to protect the people and the country. Most of these officials and commanders have turned their houses and offices into small fortresses with reinforced concrete blast walls and guard towers.

While on the road, they have 360-degree protection inside their bulletproof vehicles and an added layer of safety provided by their artillery mounted pick-up trucks' escort – not to mention the number of security personnel and government vehicles serving and guarding their immediate family members. These fortresses and heavily armed motorcades inside the capital Kabul and other main cities not only haunt and torture ordinary Afghans psychologically, but also create lots of other problems such as traffic jams, road blockades, and other intimidating obstacles and practices that make daily life a misery for commoners. *(Courtesy: This article (Decoding Afghan Security Forces' Failures, and Fixing Afghanistan's Struggling Security Forces, Ghulam Farooq Mujaddidi, Diplomat June 23, and 24 2017), has been taken by a special permission of Senior Editors editor of Diplomat, Mr. Ankit Panda. The Diplomat is the premier international current-affairs magazine*

Chapter - 9

Torture, Illegal Detention and Sexual Harassment of Detainees in NDS Private Prisons

Afghanistan Independent Human Rights Commission (AIHRC) in its shadow report (2017) on realization and implementation of the UN Convention against torture and other cruel, inhuman or degrading treatment or punishment in Afghanistan has noted some aspects of the KHAD way of torture and inhuman treatment of detainees:

"Between 1978 and 1992, the agents of the ruling party, People's Democratic Party of Afghanistan (PDPA) arrested thousands of civilians, including elders, religious leaders, intellectuals, women, farmers, civil servants and shopkeepers. The PDPA subsequently tortured and killed a lot of these detainees. The ruling party (PDPA), specifically its intelligence agency, snatched people from streets and their houses during nights and made them disappeared without a trace and as a result, the fate of a lot of them is unknown to this day. In 2014, during the interrogation of a former Afghan intelligence officer residing in the Netherlands, who were allegedly involved in the crimes against humanity in Afghanistan between 1978 and 1979 accidentally, gave the name of a woman in Germany that had access to a list of people killed by the PDPA. This list contained the names of 4790 victims. The Embassy of The Netherlands in Kabul and the Afghanistan Independent Human Rights Commission officially published names of the victims in the list. Off course, this was only the name of a fraction of the people killed or disappeared by the PDPA, not an exclusive list by any means".[1]

Numerous reports published by international human rights organizations envisaged the torture tactics of Afghan intelligence agencies in their secret prisons. The NDS and KHAD have a notorious record of killing, torture and inhuman treatment of political opponents and terror suspects. In September 2014, in his short statement before the UNAMA research team, an NDS officer admitted that his agency tortures detainees in its private secret prisons:

> As a National Directorate of Security (NDS) human rights officer I do not have the necessary conditions to carry out my work. There is a general spirit of impunity for human rights violations. The NDS Director is not cooperative and the other colleagues shrug their shoulders and advise me to 'just leave it.' Nobody at NDS actively stops me from doing my work but there is passive resistance, inaction and denial of logistical support. My reports, which I send to my supervisors in Kabul, are not acted on.[2]

In Afghan constitution, torture has been defined as an illegal act. The 2003 constitution's penal-code (1) say that torture against detainees and everyone is illegal: "Torture is already illegal under the 2003 Constitution, the Penal Code (1) and the Convention against Torture which Afghanistan ratified in 1987. However, successive Afghan governments have honoured legal bans on torture almost entirely in the breach. In that sense, this new decree does not change the legal situation. However, if the president were to follow it through seriously, it could act as a wake-up call to the government itself and as an important, public signal of a change in what is expected and what will be tolerated in the behaviour of state officials".[3]

The research team of UNAMA found solid evidence of torture in the NDS secret prisons. According to the report, detainees receive ill-treatment in the NDS prisons, and they are not allowed to treat their wounds:

The 2011 and 2013 reports found sufficiently credible and reliable evidence that approximately half of the conflict-related detainees interviewed had experienced torture or ill-treatment during interrogation–mainly to obtain confessions or information–in detention facilities run by the NDS and ANP. UNAMA found that torture was used systematically within several NDS and ANP facilities and noted the Government of Afghanistan's position that torture and ill-treatment of detainees was not an institutional or Government policy. The reports noted measures taken by the International Security Assistance Force (ISAF) to address torture in Afghan custody including suspension of detainee transfers to ANP and NDS locations identified as practicing systematic torture and roll-out of a detention facility certification review process.[4]

Afghan constitution guarantees the right of life, and does not allow anyone to kill or torture detainees. The UK Home Office country report on prison conditions in Afghanistan has noted some and decisive points: "The 2004 Afghan Constitution, in article 23 asserts the right to life, envisaging at the same time the possibility of its deprivation by the provision of law. However, in accordance with Article 396 of Afghanistan's Constitution, a convict sentenced to death can appeal to two higher courts and article 129 of the Constitution establishes that "...All final decisions of the courts shall be enforced, except for capital punishment, which shall require presidential approval."[5]

The US Department of State (USSD) reported in its Human Rights report covering 2014 that: "The general directorate of prisons and detention centres (GDPDC), part of the Ministry of Interior, has responsibility for all civilian-run prisons (for both men and women) and civilian detention centres, including the large national prison at Pul-e-Charkhi. The Ministry of Justice's juvenile rehabilitation directorate (JRD) is responsible for all juvenile rehabilitation centres. The ANP [Afghan National Police], which is under the Ministry of Interior and the NDS [national directorate of security] also run short-term detention facilities at the provincial and district levels, usually collocated with their headquarters facilities. The Ministry of Defence runs the Afghan National Detention Facilities at Parwan and Pul-e-Charkhi".[6]

This issue has also been reported by the UN report (Update on the Treatment of Conflict-Related Detainees in Afghan Custody: Accountability and Implementation of Presidential Decree 129, United Nations Assistance Mission in Afghanistan Office of the United Nations High Commissioner for Human Rights, February 2015, Kabul, Afghanistan) with details:

> In Kabul, of the 112 detainees interviewed who had been held at one or more of three facilities, namely NDS Department 124, 40 and the NDS Kabul provincial facility, 36 detainees (32 per cent) experienced torture or ill-treatment with most incidents occurring in Department 124.40 Fewer incidents of torture were observed at NDS Department 4041 although of the 73 detainees interviewed, 29 were found to have experienced torture or ill-treatment in other NDS facilities prior to their transfer to Department 40. At the NDS Kabul provincial facility, nine of 33 detainees interviewed (27 per cent) were subjected to torture or ill-treatment.[7]

The legal prohibition against using evidence gained through torture as the basis for prosecution or conviction at trial and a detainee's right to mandatory access to defence counsel were found to be routinely violated by judges and prosecutors. 'The government of Afghanistan has shown it is serious about addressing torture and ill-treatment through Presidential Decree 129 and other measures. Further efforts are needed to fully end and prevent its use, reinforce the prohibition of torture and improve accountability".

Amnesty International (2015/2016) expressed deep concern about the power abuse of NDS officers who illegally torture and abuse detainees in their secret prisons. The NDS authorities detained Afghans for acts that were not terror related acts under the Afghan law.[7] According to the detailed report of the American University Washington College of Law-2014) on inhuman treatment and torture of detainees by the NDS authorities:

Prisoners report being beaten with several kinds of instruments and abused in a variety of ways. Many prisoners reported being deprived of sleep and required to stand for prolonged periods.... In other cases, too, such treatment was exacerbated by prisoners being exposed to sun or forced to stand in water or snow.... Some prisoners reported being only threatened with electric shock torture, but many others reported being subjected to it, apparently quite routinely at an early stage as well as later stages of their interrogation. The most common electric shock torture device is referred to as the "telephone": a small machine that looks like an old-fashioned telephone with wires that are attached to the victim's body and a handle which is turned or pulled to apply the current. Other prisoners simply referred to a small box with wires coming out of it.... Several other forms of serious physical abuse were reported. These included prisoners having a bottle or in one case a heated wire thrust into the rectum, having fingernails pulled out or needles inserted under them, being cut with a knife, having a chair placed on the stomach or hands and sat upon, being burnt with cigarettes, being scalded with very hot water, and having hair torn out.[8]

The UNAMA investigative researchers have noted in their report (2015) some important facts about the torture and investigation mechanism of the National Directorate of Security (NDS). In January 2014, in Shindand district a prisoners no 24 explained his inhuman treatment by the agency investigators:

The NDS punched me in the stomach and hit me with a cable on my back as I was sitting on the floor. One of the two also grabbed my hair and slapped me on the face twice. It was terrible. Then, I was told to sit outside near a wall in the semi-dark. I do not know how long I was out there, but I was called to go in the same room again. I was terrified and completely lost. At one point, they made me lie on my back and raise my feet up with one of them holding them firmly and the other hitting on the sole of my feet. I was screaming. Then, I had to give a confession and say that I am an IED planter and was involved in the IED explosion. Only then they stopped beating me. They showed me a paper and forced me to thumbprint it twice. [9]

However, in December 2014, detainee No 376 in the NDS department 124 also told the UNAMA team about his torture story: "On Saturday three people came to my cell and one of them told me: 'Tell us the full truth and do not force us to beat you up.' They took me from my cell to the upper floor, to a small office. There were three persons. When I entered the room, before even questioning me, one person hit me with a plastic pipe on my legs, back and my hands. My nails turned black [from the beatings]. With some pauses, the beating continued for three hours. They demanded that I confess being a Taliban member, and I did because I couldn't take it anymore. Then they asked me to tell them who else was with me. I gave them the name of my cousin. After that they left me. On the second day, nobody interrogated me. On the third day in the morning at 9 o'clock they came and hung me on a wall near the bathroom of the cell block for two hours. I had already confessed, but they still hung me."[1] Another detainee No-161 in the same department explained his cruel treatment by NDS in these words:

> "I was taken to NDS Department 124. They started beating me. They kicked me with their boots and they punched me on the first day. On the second day, they also beat me but this time with a water pipe for about two hours. On the third day, they used a machine on my sexual organs. It was like a clip or pliers and they used it to squeeze my sexual parts till I cried. After this, I made a confession I was a Talib. I was scared because they threatened they would destroy my sexual organs. I just said anything and they wrote it down and I put my thumb prints on the papers. I thought I might die if they destroyed my sexual organs."[10]

Moreover, in Kandahar and Takhar provinces, the UNAMA recorded two more torture stories of detainees in the secret prisons of NDS: "I was arrested by NDS Spin Boldak and was slapped repeatedly while in the NDS vehicle. I was taken to NDS Takhtapul (halfway between Spin Boldak and Kandahar) and there three

NDS used a cable to beat me on my back, waist and feet. They also tried to choke me by forcing a piece of cloth in my mouth and at the same time clasping my neck. They wanted me to confess I was a Talib and after this, I did confess, verbally, to whatever they wanted."[11]

"I was arrested and taken to NDS HQ detention facility in Taloqan city. I was there for 12 days. I was interrogated four times. I told the interrogator everything but he didn't agree with me. Due to that, he started beating me with several electric cables which were about one meter long and about one inch thick. Three times the interrogator who was a tall man together with two other hooded me and laid me down. Two of them held my arms and the third one started beating me on my feet. The interrogator told me if I didn't confess that I learned making IEDs in Pakistan, was involved in terrorist activities and planting IEDs especially in the election sites, he would beat me more and give me electric shocks. I was scared and agreed and he stopped beating me."[12]

In October 2011, a human right department was established in the NDS headquarters to monitor all detention facilities and human rights violations. In January 2012 it was named the "Human Rights Monitoring Sub-Directorate" with a plan to have a permanent presence in 16 provinces with officers responsible for training NDS officials on human rights issues. In 2013 NDS merged the Human Rights Monitoring Sub-Directorate with other NDS 'policy-related' units into its Department 47 responsible for Foreign Affairs, Protocol, Human Rights, Gender and Women Affairs.

Postscript

The United States and its NATO allies killed innocent women and children, bombed important military and civilian installations, buildings, and national critical infrastructure in Afghanistan. Under the Bilateral Security Agreement (BSA), the US maintained nine military bases at strategic locations across Afghanistan including those bordering Iran, Pakistan and Central Asia.[1] The emergence of Russia with the reinvention of its strongest intelligence infrastructure in Afghanistan and Central Asia is a biggest challenge for the United States in its so-called war on terrorism. Russia returned to Afghanistan with an offensive strategy to expel NATO and the US from the country. China and Russia share an interest in checking and containing US strategic power in the region. That was on full display in September 2018 when Russia staged its biggest military exercise in decades in the country's far eastern region.[2]

Political and military alliance of these two states and their relationship with Central Asian, South Asian and South East Asian states was a positive sign that after the balance of power in the region, the United States is no more the sole super power. Asia Nikkei commentator, Hiroyuki Akita (July 11, 2018) devised the alliance basic motive to undermine UD domination in Asia:

"Now, China and Russia are forging a similar strategic partnership to undermine American supremacy. The two countries are forming their own "axis," seeking to break up the U.S.-dominated world order and create a multipolar world. On the face of it, China and Russia appear solidly united in their goal of undermining U.S. dominance. Beijing and Moscow came together to rebuke U.S. attacks in Syria, and its withdrawal from

Iran's nuclear deal. The duo also seeks to undercut U.S. leadership in negotiations with North Korea. During a June 8 meeting with Chinese President Xi Jinping in Beijing, Russian President Vladimir Putin lauded the relationship between the two countries, saying bilateral cooperation "has reached an unprecedented level." The two leaders signed a statement aimed at putting diplomatic pressure on the U.S."[3]

To that end, Alliance between the two states will teach a lesson to the United States in Asia and Africa. In their article published in the American Interest (11 September 2018) Brian Fonseca and David J. Kramer have spotlighted forces driving Russia and China closer together: "Several forces driving China and Russia closer together include: U.S. primacy and the desire in Beijing and Moscow to challenge that primacy; increasing American rhetoric projecting China and Russia as threats; China's rise and need to mitigate U.S. efforts to contain or confront it; and Russia's limited economic, political, and military power combined with its desire to remain a great power. Furthermore, both China and Russia have a common desire to undermine the allure of democracy relative to authoritarian models".[4]

Russia's diplomatic overtures in various parts of Asia, with all the differences in their specifics, have several important common features, forming what we can call Moscow's Asia-policy model. Creating a Moscow-Beijing-New Delhi triangle has been Russia's diplomatic dream since the late 1990s. Mr. Andrey Afanasyev (21 May 2018) highlighted the ISIS full scale offensive against Russia and China through Chinese and Russian Central Asia:

Sources in Russian military and intelligence agencies, say that the preparation of a full-scale offensive operation against Russia through Tajikistan and Uzbekistan is in the final phase. Citing data from closed communication channels with defense ministries of China, Pakistan and Afghanistan, they say that Afghanistan is the cornerstone issue in this plan. Similar messages have been received earlier; in particular, this was mentioned at a recent security conference held in Uzbek capital Tashkent. Then the Tajik Foreign Minister Sirodzhiddin Aslov openly announced the activation of terrorists in the region: "We see the activation of terrorist groups, their advancement to the northern regions of Afghanistan, especially in the territories bordering with Tajikistan, the increase in the number of ISIS supporters, and the participation of a certain number of citizens of the post-Soviet republics in the terrorist groups and movements present in Afghanistan ... this causes our serious concern". Russian intelligence sources say there will two routes for IS offensive. One will lead to Tajikistan through Nuristan and Badakhshan provinces; another will go through Farakh, Ghor, Sari-Pul and Faryab to Turkmenistan".[5]

Besides its close military relations with both China and India, Russia is increasingly building good relations with Bangladesh, Indonesia, Malaysia, Myanmar, Pakistan, the Philippines and Thailand. Moscow is in contact with Taliban to counter the ISIS terrorist groups that killed innocent women and children in Iraq, Syria and Afghanistan, and continues to expand its geographical matrix to Central Asia. Sources in the Afghan Defence Ministry confirmed Russian military support to Taliban. Said Sabir Ibrahimi (November 02, 2018) has painted this picture with different perspective and noted Russian concern on the exponentially growing ISIS strength in Afghanistan:

"Moscow's contact with the Taliban is not new and there have been contacts since 2005. Russia has allegedly shared intelligence with the Taliban, and there has been much speculation that Moscow has even armed them. Whether these claims are true or false, Russia's contact with the Taliban has given the group a degree of legitimacy and recognition at a time when the Afghan government could use some of that legitimacy and recognition itself. Russia has also been in contact with some Afghan warlords in the north. To add to the confusion, since 2016, Russia has been conducting annual joint military drills with Pakistan along the Afghan border. Some Afghans are concerned that Afghanistan once again may become a geopolitical battlefield between the two great powers, this time the United States and Russia. This could take Afghanistan to a different and more dangerous level of turmoil than even the current conflict. Moscow's main concerns in Afghanistan are linked to the expansion of the Islamic State's regional iteration, the Islamic State Khorasan Province (ISKP), and the flow of narcotics northward. These are legitimate concerns. Russia has said its contact with the Taliban is for the safety of its citizens present in Afghanistan and to end the Afghan conflict".[6]

Eighteen years after the US and NATO ousted the Taliban government, Afghanistan still remains one of the worse place for journalist, NGOs, Doctors, businessmen and women. The John Kerry government (Unity Government) hardly control 30% percent territory of the state, while Daesh and Taliban pose bigger challenge to the ANA and its associated private militias. After two decades of its withdrawal from Afghanistan, Moscow returned to the country with a strong Taliban group, GRU and an incarnated KGB (MGB) network to intercept the US and NATO expansion towards Central Asia, and eliminate the ISIS terrorist organization.[7]

Russia wants to apply the Syrian strategy in Afghanistan, and deploy strong intelligence units along the Afghan-Tajik, and, Pak-Afghan borders. However, China also wants to ensure the security of its borders by deploying security and intelligence unites along the Afghan and Pakistan's borders to intercept the infiltration of Uyghur separatists inside the country. Beijing and Moscow fear that there are serious grounds to expect that security situation in Afghanistan may rapidly deteriorate as the Unity Government's legitimacy is in spike.[8]

Now, with the emergence of Russia with a strong military might more than fifty nations and their intelligence agencies in Afghanistan have failed to effectively counter Russian and Chinese secret agencies? The Putin administration has invested heavily in Afghanistan and continues to reduce the political and military space of the United States and its NATO allies who neither stabilized the war torn country, nor established a strong army. This inattention of international community resulted in the resentment of Afghan population towards their presence. China helped the United States in its war against the Soviet Union, but now helps Russia in its war against the United States. However, Pakistan and Russia are moving towards an embrace, but looking at each other with suspicion. Pakistan faces isolation and dependent on Chinese economic support. Chinese involvement in Afghanistan is growing, and it has established good contacts with Afghan and Pakistani extremist organizations. However, in 2014, China introduced its own special envoy to Afghanistan and Pakistan.[9]

The recent Pentagon China-phobia policy, its containment of China, the emergence of new military and intelligence alliance among China, Pakistan and Russia, has become a hot debate in electronic and print media in South Asia. The increasing Chinese influence in Pakistan, Afghanistan and Central Asia and its strong presence in European and African market together with the aggrandizement of Russian economy and military industry have caused an unending torment for the United States and its European allies. The Pentagon authorities didn't sleep a wink since the commencement of recent joint Russia-China-Pakistan rapprochement. The recent establishment of a new military intelligence agency, 'Defence Clandestine Intelligence Service' (DCIS) and its focus on China raised many questions about the US presence in Afghanistan. The emergence of China as an economic and military power is no doubt irksome for Pentagon that wants to contain and confine both China and Russia to specific regions.[10]

For Russia and China, one of the leading security challenges is the aggravation of war in Afghanistan where crisis phenomena continue to grow. The most violent threat is posed by the exponentially growing influence of ISIS Khorasan group in the country that controls more than 70 districts where it trains and equips fighters from Chinese and Russian Central Asia. These political and strategic developments forced Russia and China to reactivate their policies towards Afghanistan in the political and military spheres. Moscow and Beijing are trying to deploy more intelligence units from Badakhshan to swat region, and from Gilgit-Baltistan to Tajikistan to intercept the infiltration of the ISIS terrorists into Central Asia.[11]

However, the altercation of Afghanistan and the rise of Daesh group is a part of Russia's relations with the United States where competition between the two powers has been accompanied by partial cooperation. Having realised security threat from the ISIS and the expansion of NATO eastwards, President Putin organised an Afghan Taliban group — funded and adorned with modern weapons on the one hand, and reincarnated KGB, and merged all domestic and foreign intelligence agencies into one agency (MGB) on the other. This process was named the reorganisation and reinvention of intelligence infrastructure.[12]

On 26 January 2019, the US and Taliban made "significant progress" in negotiations aimed at ending the country's destructive 18-year war in Afghanistan, Zalmay Khalilzai said. "Meetings here were more productive than they have been in the past," he tweeted, without providing further details. In December 2018, and January 2019, the US Special Envoy Dr. Zalmay Khalilzad resumed talks with the concerned parties and reached at Doha capital of Qatar. Beside Qatar, Zalmay Khalilzad travelled to Pakistan, Afghanistan, and Russia. Mr. Khalilzad met with President Ghani, Chief Executive Abdullah, and other Afghan stakeholders to coordinate closely on efforts to bring the Taliban to the negotiating table with the Afghan government.[13]

Trust-building between Kabul and Islamabad was of high significance for regional peace and prosperity. In his interview with a Chinese monthly magazine, Pakistani Ambassador to China Masood Khalid commented on the first China-Afghanistan-Pakistan Foreign Minister's dialogue very positively. "The trilateral forum will contribute to the greater connectivity, economic prosperity and peace and development of the three countries and the region."[14]

The Bonn Agreement of 2001 was a power-sharing agreement, while the International Community on several occasions, conferences and seminars strived to bring the warring factions and Afghan governments to dialogue. On 28 February 2010, international conference was held in London to highlight peace efforts in Afghanistan. The One-day conference was meant to chart a new mechanism for political settlement in the country. After this gathering, on 05 September 2010, former Afghan President Hamid Karzai announced the establishment of High Peace Council

(HPC), but on 20 September 2011, Burhanuddin Rabbani, head of High Peace Council was killed by a suicide bomber. This act of Taliban widened the gap between their leadership and the Afghan government.[16]

In November 2012, Pakistan released some Taliban leaders to expedite peace talks but Taliban refused to talk with the Afghan government. In December 2012, peace talks between Taliban and the Afghan government recommenced in France, On 18 June 2013, Taliban officially opened up office in Qatar. The Taliban criticized the United States for its flawed approach to peace and stability in Afghanistan. On 28 August 2013, Afghan President visited Islamabad to motivate Pakistani leadership on supporting Afghan peace initiatives, but, Mr. Karzai came back empty hands due to the country's miltablishment's intransigence to support peace process in Afghanistan.[17]

On 30 November 2013, former Pakistani Prime Minister Nawaz Sharif visited Kabul to showcase his resolve to help the Afghan government in political settlement. On 09 January 2015, President Ghani offered Taliban a share in government, but Taliban rejected the offer. On 02 May 2015, Taliban launched series of meeting with the Afghan government in Qatar to expedite the process of political settlement in Afghanistan. In May 2015, talks between Afghanistan and Taliban leaders were facilitated by China and Pakistan in Urumqi, and in June 2015, Taliban and Afghan female delegation discussed peace process in Oslo, Norway. However, in July 2015, Afghan representatives held talks with Taliban leadership in Murree, Pakistan, in which Chinese and US officials also participated.[18]

In December 2015, in Asia Ministerial Conference in Herat was clutched between Pakistan, Afghanistan, US and China regarding peace and stabilization process in the country. On 29 January 2016, Taliban showed willingness to continue talks with the Ghani administration, while President Ghani speech in Parliament on 25 April 2016 generated some hopes of political settlement. In February 2016, China, US, Pakistan, and Afghanistan tried to open new chapter of peace process in their fourth times meeting, but the killing of Taliban leader Mullah Mansoor on 21 May 2016, vanished a hope of reconciliation. Mullah Mansoor was killed by the US drone and said Mullah Mansoor was a threat to peace in Afghanistan.[19]

In 2016, there were different national security and counterterrorism approaches, priorities and mechanism in Afghanistan that contradicted each other. Majority of people in the northern parts of Afghanistan perceived the Taliban as a terrorist organisation while the Unity government in Kabul perceived the Taliban groups as a political opposition. Interestingly, those who fought against the Taliban in northern, eastern and southern provinces were removed from their services by the Unity government in 2015 and 2016. However, Special Advisor to President, Ahmad Zia Massoud and Dr Abdullah were against the Taliban, while the national security advisor supported the Taliban and ISIS groups. General Dostum termed the Taliban as a terrorist group, while the other group perceived them as political opposition. In Helmand, Arozgan and Kunar provinces, government ordered Afghan army commanders to leave their military posts to the Taliban. In Mazar-e-Sharif, Kunduz, Baghlan and Badakhshan provinces fight against the Taliban intensified.[20]

On 29 September 2016, peace deal between Gulbuddin Hekmatyar group and the Afghan government was praised by experts said it was a step towards political settlement. In January 2016, Quadrilateral Coordination Group (QCG) once again tried to revive peace process in Afghanistan, however, on 27 December 2016, Russia, China and Pakistan held Trilateral Dialogue on Afghanistan. They adopted flexible measures to remove names of Taliban leaders from the sanction list. In April 2017, Russia, Afghanistan, Pakistan, China, India, Iran and Central Asian states held talks in Moscow to revive peace process, while on 07 June 2017, the Kabul peace process held between Afghanistan and 20 states including India, China and Saudi Arabia, but result of these efforts was antipathetic.

All the above cited peace initiatives in Afghanistan could not succeed to settle long war, but gave courage to Taliban, regional states and Afghanistan to proceed with strong resolve. The root of failure of all the above mentioned peace efforts can often be found in the lack of coordination, intransigence of regional powers, and privatization of war in Afghanistan. The agenda of regional powers is crystal clear. India, Iran and Pakistan are pursuing their own agendas, and purveying arms to their proxies. India wants to confine Pakistan to its own challenges, and wants to teach Pakistan a lesson by establishing networks of Baloch insurgence in Afghanistan. Pakistan's role vis-a-vis India has been contentious.

As per its tribal structure and ethnic composition, the country has never built up a professional army as it has been dependent on tribal, private and criminal militias for decades. As a failed, broken and polarised state, the country has been embroiled in intense ethnic and sectarian violence and unable to deliver good governance to its citizens. The government of President Hamid Karzai has lost its legitimacy. To elucidate the main causes of state failure in Afghanistan, I want to quote prominent author Robert I Rotberg's valuable ideas about a failed state:

"Weak states include a broad continuum of states that are: inherently weak because of geographical, physical, or fundamental economic constraints; basically strong, but temporarily or situationally weak because of internal antagonism, management flaws, greed, despotism, or external attacks; and a mixture of the two. Weak states typically harbour ethnic, religious, linguistic, or other inter-communal tensions that have not yet, or not yet thoroughly, become overtly violent. Failed states are tense, deeply conflicted, dangerous, and contested bitterly by warring factions."

In the case of Afghanistan, the state failure is characterised by weak and corrupt governance, lawlessness, unprofessional approach to the affairs of the state, drug and arms trafficking and the Taliban insurgency. As mentioned earlier, civil wars that characterise failed states like Afghanistan usually stem from or have roots in ethnicity, factionalism and sectarianism. According to Rotberg's recent analysis, in most failed states, regimes prey on their own constituents. Most experts understand that criminal violence is also a contributing factor to the causes of a failed state.

Appendix 1

Security and Defence Cooperation Agreement between the Islamic Republic of Afghanistan and the United States of America

Preamble

The Islamic Republic of Afghanistan (hereinafter, "Afghanistan") and the United States of America (hereinafter, "the United States"), referred to collectively as "the Parties" and singularly as a "Party;"

Recognizing the Enduring Strategic Partnership Agreement between the Islamic Republic of Afghanistan and the United States of America, signed May 2, 2012, (the "Strategic Partnership Agreement") and reaffirming that, as recognized in that Agreement, the Parties are committed to strengthen long-term strategic cooperation in areas of mutual interest, including: advancing peace, security, and stability; strengthening state institutions; supporting Afghanistan's long-term economic and social development; and encouraging regional cooperation;

Confirming the recognition in the Strategic Partnership Agreement that cooperation between the Parties is based on mutual respect and shared interests;

Emphasizing also the Strategic Partnership Agreement's recognition that the Parties will go forward in partnership with confidence because they are committed to seeking a future of justice, peace, security, and opportunity for the Afghan people, as well as the reaffirmation of the Parties' strong commitment to the sovereignty, independence, territorial integrity, and national unity of Afghanistan;

Recognizing the enduring partnership between Afghanistan and the United States, and affirming the mutual intent of the Parties to expand, mature, promote and further elevate their security and defence cooperation based on this Agreement;

Desiring to continue to foster close cooperation concerning defence and security arrangements in order to strengthen security and stability in Afghanistan, contribute to regional and international peace and stability, combat terrorism, achieve a region which is no longer a safe haven for al-Qaida and its affiliates, and enhance the ability of Afghanistan to deter threats against its sovereignty, security, and territorial integrity; and noting that the United States does not seek permanent military facilities in Afghanistan, or a presence that is a threat to Afghanistan's neighbours, and has pledged not to use Afghan territory or facilities as a launching point for attacks against other countries;

Recalling the Chicago Summit Declaration on Afghanistan, issued on May 21, 2012, by the Heads of State and Government of Afghanistan and Nations Contributing to the North Atlantic Treaty Organization (NATO)-led International Security Assistance Force (ISAF), and specifically, the participants' renewed firm commitment to a sovereign, secure, and democratic Afghanistan and acknowledgment that ISAF's mission will be concluded by the end of 2014 and that their close partnership will continue beyond the end of the transition period including through NATO and Afghanistan's mutual commitment to work to establish a new NATO-led Mission to train, advise, and assist the Afghan National Defence and Security Forces (ANDSF), and noting here that such a mission will also need to be provided with the necessary authorities, status arrangements, and legal basis;

Reaffirming the continued support of the Parties for regional cooperation and coordination mechanisms, with a goal of increasing security and stability by reducing tensions, uncertainty, and misunderstanding;

Recalling the 2013 Consultative Loya Jirga's recognition that this Security and Defence Cooperation Agreement between Afghanistan and the United States is important for the security of Afghanistan;

Desiring to develop further the means of defence and security cooperation between the Parties, based on the principles of full respect for the independence, sovereignty, and integrity of their territories, and non-interference in the domestic affairs of each other, in order to promote security and stability in the region, and to combat terrorism;

Agreeing on the importance of cooperative relationships between Afghanistan and its neighbours conducted on the basis of mutual respect, non-interference, and equality and calling on all nations to respect Afghanistan's sovereignty and territorial integrity, and to refrain from interfering in Afghanistan's internal affairs and democratic processes; and

Affirming also that the Parties' cooperation is based on full respect for the sovereignty of each Party, the purposes of the United Nations Charter, and a shared desire to provide a framework for defence and security cooperation between the Parties; and reaffirming their strong commitment to the sovereignty, independence, territorial integrity, and national unity of Afghanistan, as well as respect for Afghan laws, customs, and traditions;

Have agreed as follows:

Article 1

Definition

1. "United States forces" means the entity comprising the members of the force and of the civilian component, and all property, equipment, and materiel of the United States Armed Forces present in the territory of Afghanistan.

2. "Member of the force" means any person belonging to the land, sea, or air services of the United States Armed Forces.

3. "Member of the civilian component" means any person employed by the United States Department of Defence (DoD) who is not a member of the force. However, "member of the civilian component" does not mean persons who are permanently resident in Afghanistan or Afghan nationals who normally reside in Afghanistan.

4. "Executive Agent" means Ministry of Defence (MoD) for Afghanistan and DoD for the United States. The Executive Agent

serves as the principal contact for its respective Party for the implementation of this Agreement.

5. "United States contractors" means persons and legal entities that are supplying goods and services in Afghanistan to or on behalf of United States forces under a contract or subcontract with or in support of United States forces.

6. "United States contractor employees" mean the employees of United States contractors.

7. "Agreed facilities and areas" means the facilities and areas in the territory of Afghanistan provided by Afghanistan at the locations listed in Annex A, and such other facilities and areas in the territory of Afghanistan as may be provided by Afghanistan in the future, to which United States forces, United States contractors, United States contractor employees, and others as mutually agreed, shall have the right to access and use pursuant to this Agreement.

8. "Afghan National Defence and Security Forces" or "ANDSF" means the entity comprising the members of the security forces under the Ministry of Interior and the MoD of Afghanistan and, as appropriate, the National Directorate of Security, and other entities as mutually agreed.

9. "Taxes" means all taxes, duties (including customs duties), fees, and similar or related charges of whatever kind, imposed by the Government of Afghanistan which, for the purposes of this Agreement, means by governmental authorities of Afghanistan at any level, including provincial and district levels, and by the agencies of such governmental authorities.

ARTICLE 2

Purpose and Scope

1. The Parties shall continue to foster close cooperation to strengthen security and stability in Afghanistan, counter terrorism, contribute to regional and international peace and stability, and enhance the ability of Afghanistan to deter internal and external threats against its sovereignty, security, territorial integrity, national unity, and its

constitutional order. Unless otherwise mutually agreed, United States forces shall not conduct combat operations in Afghanistan.

2. To that end, the United States shall undertake supporting activities, as may be agreed, in close cooperation and coordination with Afghanistan, to assist ANDSF in developing capabilities required to provide security for all Afghans, including as may be mutually agreed: advising, training, equipping, supporting, and sustaining ANDSF, including in field engineering, countering improvised explosive devices, and explosive ordnance disposal; establishing and upgrading ANDSF transportation and logistics systems; developing intelligence sharing capabilities; strengthening Afghanistan's Air Force capabilities; conducting combined military exercises; and other activities as may be agreed. The Parties will continue to work on the details of ANDSF development as set forth in the Afghan Program of Record, adopted at the Chicago Summit in 2012, and in the context of the Afghanistan-United States Bilateral Security Consultative Forum.

3. The Parties recognize that ANDSF are responsible for securing the people and territory of Afghanistan. The Parties shall work to enhance ANDSF's ability to deter and respond to internal and external threats. Upon request, the United States shall urgently determine support it is prepared to provide ANDSF in order to respond to threats to Afghanistan's security.

4. The Parties acknowledge that U.S. military operations to defeat al-Qaida and its affiliates may be appropriate in the common fight against terrorism. The Parties agree to continue their close cooperation and coordination toward those ends, with the intention of protecting U.S. and Afghan national interests without unilateral U.S. military counter-terrorism operations. U.S. military counter-terrorism operations are intended to complement and support ANDSF's counter-terrorism operations, with the goal of maintaining ANDSF lead, and with full respect for Afghan sovereignty and full regard for the safety and security of the Afghan people, including in their homes.

5. In furtherance of the activities and operations referred to in this Article and for other purposes and missions as may be mutually

agreed, and consistent with the authorizations as detailed in this Agreement, United States forces may undertake transit, support, and related activities, including as may be necessary to support themselves while they are present in Afghanistan under the terms of this Agreement, and such other activities as detailed in this Agreement, or as may be mutually agreed.

6. This Agreement, including any Annexes and any Implementing Agreements or Arrangements, provides the necessary authorizations for the presence and activities of United States forces in Afghanistan and defines the terms and conditions that describe that presence, and in the specific situations indicated herein, the presence and activities of United States contractors and United States contractor employees in Afghanistan.

ARTICLE 3

Laws

1. It is the duty of members of the force and of the civilian component to respect the Constitution and laws of Afghanistan and to abstain from any activity inconsistent with the spirit of this Agreement and, in particular, from any political activity in the territory of Afghanistan. It is the duty of United States forces authorities to take necessary measures to that end.

2. The Parties' respective obligations under this Agreement, and any subsequent arrangements, are without prejudice to Afghan sovereignty over its territory, and each Party's right of self-defence, consistent with international law. Cooperation and activities relating to implementation of this Agreement shall be consistent with the Parties' respective commitments and obligations under international law.

3. United States forces shall not enter Afghan homes for the purpose of military operations and searches except under extraordinary circumstances involving the urgent risk to life and limb of U.S. nationals. United States forces shall not arrest or imprison Afghan nationals, nor maintain or operate detention facilities in Afghanistan.

ARTICLE 4

Developing and Sustaining Afghanistan's Defence and Security Capabilities

1. With full respect for Afghanistan's sovereignty, the Parties recognize Afghanistan's current requirement for continued international security assistance, and share the goal of Afghanistan taking increasing and, ultimately full, responsibility for funding its defence and security needs and sustaining ANDSF.

2. Afghanistan shall make, consistent with its political and economic stability and its general economic condition, the full contribution permitted by its manpower, resources, and facilities to the development and sustainment of its own defence and security forces. Afghanistan shall take all necessary measures to develop and sustain its defence and security capacities.

3. So long as the Strategic Partnership Agreement so provides, and guided by the pledges set forth at the Chicago Summit in 2012, the United States shall have an obligation to seek funds on a yearly basis to support the training, equipping, advising, and sustaining of ANDSF, so that Afghanistan can independently secure and defend itself against internal and external threats, and help ensure that terrorists never again encroach on Afghan soil and threaten Afghanistan, the region, and the world. The United States shall consult with Afghanistan regarding the amount of funding needed to accomplish the purposes of this Agreement, keeping in mind pledges made in Chicago, and shall take the results of those consultations into consideration in executing this obligation. Taking into account Afghanistan's annual priorities, the United States shall direct appropriate funds through Afghan Government budgetary mechanisms, to be managed by relevant Afghan institutions implementing financial management standards of transparency and accountability and procurement, audit, and regulatory oversight in accordance with international best practices.

4. The Parties recognize the importance of ANDSF having the necessary equipment and materiel to secure Afghanistan. To that

end, the United States shall continue to cooperate with Afghanistan on providing equipment and materiel for ANDSF.

5. Afghanistan and the United States may cooperate and coordinate with other countries to strengthen ANDSF, as may be mutually agreed, including on equipping ANDSF.

6. In order to contribute effectively to the security of Afghanistan and the region, the United States agrees to cooperate with Afghanistan to continue the development of ANDSF capabilities consistent with Afghanistan's status as a Major Non-NATO Ally.

7. The Parties recognize the benefits for Afghanistan's defence and security to be derived from developing defence capabilities and systems that are consistent with NATO standards and that promote interoperability with NATO. The Parties shall coordinate in the development of Afghanistan's defence and security forces, equipment, materiel, facilities, operational doctrine, and institutions to achieve standardization and interoperability with NATO, in order to promote further the effective utilization and maintenance of defence and security assistance provided to Afghanistan, and to maximize the benefits of cooperation between ANDSF and United States forces. This coordination shall not preclude Afghanistan from procuring independently equipment and materiel for ANDSF from non-NATO countries with its own resources.

ARTICLE 5

Defence and Security Cooperation Mechanisms

1. The Parties agree to direct the Afghanistan - United States Working Group on Defence and Security Cooperation, established under the Strategic Partnership Agreement, to:

a. Develop appropriate measures of effectiveness for the analysis and strengthening of Afghanistan's use of available defence and security resources, consistent with the purpose and scope of this Agreement;

b. Complete semi-annual assessments of actual performance against these measures to inform the Parties' respective resource allocation decisions and their cooperation in developing and sustaining Afghanistan's defence capabilities;

c. Develop a process consistent with the purpose and scope of this Agreement, for making timely, accurate, and effective cooperative assessments of internal and external threats to Afghanistan; and

d. Make specific recommendations on enhancing information and intelligence sharing and evaluation.

2. The Parties share the objective of continuing to improve their ability to consult on such threats, including considering how to establish secure or dedicated channels of communication.

ARTICLE 6

External Aggression

1. Afghanistan has been subject to aggression and other uses of force inconsistent with the United Nations Charter by foreign states and externally based or supported armed groups. In the context of this Agreement, the Parties strongly oppose such uses of armed force or threats thereof against the territorial integrity or political independence of Afghanistan, including in this regard provision to armed groups of support, such as sanctuary or arms, by any state or other armed groups. The Parties agree to cooperate to strengthen Afghanistan's defences against such threats to its territorial integrity, sovereignty or political independence.

2. The United States shall regard with grave concern any external aggression or threat of external aggression against the sovereignty, independence, and territorial integrity of Afghanistan, recognizing that such aggression may threaten the Parties' shared interests in Afghanistan's stability and regional and international peace and stability.

3. On a regular basis, the Parties shall consult on potential political, diplomatic, military, and economic measures that could form part of an appropriate response in the event of such external

aggression or the threat of external aggression against Afghanistan. Consultations shall seek to develop a list of political, diplomatic, military, and economic measures.

4. In the event of external aggression or the threat of external aggression against Afghanistan, the Parties shall hold consultations on an urgent basis to develop and implement an appropriate response, including, as may be mutually determined, consideration of available political, diplomatic, military, and economic measures on the list developed pursuant to paragraph 3, in accordance with their respective constitutional procedures.

5. The Parties shall develop comprehensive procedures to promote the effective accomplishment of such regular and urgent consultations.

a. Such comprehensive procedures shall recognize consultations involving the participation of the Afghanistan Foreign Minister and the United States Secretary of State, the Afghanistan Defence Minister and the United States Secretary of Defence, and respective Ambassadors in Kabul and Washington, D.C., as primary channels to initiate urgent consultations in the event of external aggression, or threat of external aggression.

b. Such comprehensive procedures shall not, however, limit or prejudice the Parties' ability to consult each other in other channels or through other mechanisms, as urgency or exigency may require.

6. The Parties agree to direct the Afghanistan - United States Working Group on Defence and Security Cooperation to promote the effective implementation of this Article, including development of such comprehensive procedures, and review on a regular basis the list of measures developed pursuant to paragraph 3.

ARTICLE 7

Use of Agreed Facilities and Areas

1. Afghanistan hereby provides access to and use of the agreed facilities and areas, as defined in paragraph 7 of Article 1, solely to implement the purpose and scope of this Agreement, taking into

account locations of ANDSF and the local Afghan population. Access to and use of such agreed facilities and areas for other purposes shall be as mutually agreed by the Parties.

2. Under this Agreement, Afghanistan hereby authorizes United States forces to exercise all rights and authorities within the agreed facilities and areas that are necessary for their use, operation, defence, or control, including the right to undertake new construction works. United States forces may carry out such construction works with members of the force and the civilian component or by contract.

3. Afghanistan hereby authorizes United States forces to control entry to agreed facilities and areas that have been provided for United States forces' exclusive use, and to coordinate entry with Afghan authorities at joint-use agreed facilities and areas, for the purposes of safety and security. Upon request, the United States shall provide to relevant authorities of Afghanistan access to any agreed facility or area that has been provided for United States forces' exclusive use. The Parties shall establish mutually agreed procedures regarding Afghan authorities' access to any agreed facility or area that has been provided for United States forces' exclusive use. Such procedures and access shall be established with due respect for United States forces operations and security requirements. Acknowledging that United States forces may conduct force protection activities at and in the vicinity of agreed facilities and agreed areas as are necessary, the Parties agree to coordinate and integrate their respective plans for force protection to ensure the safety of United States forces, with full respect for Afghan sovereignty and with full regard for the safety and security of the Afghan people. In furtherance of this objective, United States forces shall not target Afghan civilians, including in their homes, consistent with Afghan law and United States forces' rules of engagement.

4. In pursuit of the purpose and scope of this Agreement, in particular United States efforts to train, equip, advice, and sustain ANDSF; Afghanistan shall provide all agreed facilities and areas without charge to United States forces.

5. United States forces shall be responsible for the construction, development, operations, and maintenance costs for agreed facilities and areas provided for their exclusive use, unless otherwise agreed by the Parties. Construction, development, operations, and maintenance costs for agreed facilities and areas provided for joint use, or otherwise used jointly by United States forces and ANDSF or other entities, shall be shared on the basis of proportionate use, unless otherwise agreed.

6. The United States confirms its commitment to respect relevant Afghan environmental and health and safety laws, regulations, and standards in the execution of its policies. United States forces operations and activities on agreed facilities and areas shall be conducted with due regard for the protection of the natural environment and human health and safety, with due respect for applicable Afghan laws and regulations, and in accordance with applicable United States laws and regulations and applicable international agreements.

7. United States forces operations and activities on agreed facilities and areas shall be conducted with full respect for Afghan laws and regulations for the protection of sites or artefacts of historic and cultural heritage. United States forces shall notify and consult immediately with appropriate Afghan authorities through the Joint Commission when sites or artefacts of historic and cultural heritage are discovered on an agreed facility or area.

ARTICLE 8

Property Ownership

1-United States forces shall return to Afghanistan any agreed facility or area, or any portion thereof, including buildings, non-relocatable structures, and assemblies connected to the soil, including those constructed, altered, or improved by United States forces, when no longer needed for United States forces' use. United States forces shall keep the requirement for such agreed facilities and areas under periodic reassessment with a view toward such return. The Parties or their Executive Agents shall consult regarding the terms of return of any agreed facility or area.

The Parties agree to pursue a preventative rather than reactive approach to environmental protection and human health and safety. The Parties recognize that the policies and practices of the United States are designed to avoid such damage and endangerment and to apply the more protective of either Afghan or United States standards. In accordance with United States forces policy, United States forces shall take prompt action to address a substantial impact to human health and safety due to environmental entity comprising the members of the security forces under the Ministry of Interior and the MoD of Afghanistan and, as appropriate, the National Directorate of Security, and other entities as mutually agreed.

Environmental contamination that is caused by activities of United States forces and is located on an agreed facility or area.

2. All buildings, non-relocatable structures, and assemblies connected to the soil at the agreed facilities and areas, including those constructed, used, altered, or improved by United States forces, are for the exclusive use of United States forces, United States contractors, and United States contractor employees, and for others as mutually agreed. All such buildings, non-relocatable structures, and assemblies connected to the soil built by United States forces or provided to United States forces for their access and use may be modified by United States forces, and United States forces may use them exclusively until they are no longer required by United States forces.

3. United States forces and United States contractors shall retain title to all equipment, materiel, supplies, relocatable structures, and other movable property they have installed in, imported into, or acquired within the territory of Afghanistan in connection with the presence of United States forces and United States contractors in Afghanistan. The Parties shall consult regarding the possible transfer to or purchase by Afghanistan of equipment determined to be excess, as may be authorized by United States laws and regulations.

ARTICLE 9

Positioning and Storage of Equipment and Materiel

1. Afghanistan authorizes United States forces to position the equipment, supplies, and materiel of United States forces within agreed facilities and areas, and at other locations as mutually agreed. United States forces shall maintain title to and control over the use and disposition of such equipment, supplies, and materiel that are stored in the territory of Afghanistan and shall have the right to remove such items from the territory of Afghanistan.

2. The United States confirms its commitment to respect relevant Afghan safety laws, regulations, and standards. United States forces shall take all necessary measures to protect and safely store equipment, supplies, and materiel of United States forces that are of a hazardous nature in accordance with applicable United States laws and regulations. In accordance with United States forces policy, United States forces shall take prompt action (1) to clean up spills located on an agreed facility or area; and, (2) to address a substantial impact to human health and safety due to environmental contamination that is caused by activities of United States forces and is located on an agreed facility or area.

3. The United States, taking into account its obligations under the Convention on the Prohibition of the Development, Production, Stockpiling and Use of Chemical Weapons and on their Destruction, done at Paris on January 13, 1993, and the Convention on the Prohibition of the Development, Production and Stockpiling of Bacteriological (Biological) and Toxin Weapons and on their Destruction done at Washington, London, and Moscow on April 10, 1972, agrees that chemical and biological weapons shall not be stored in the territory of Afghanistan. The Parties affirm that the United States will not position or store nuclear weapons in the territory of Afghanistan.

ARTICLE 10

Movement of Vehicles, Vessels, and Aircraft

1. Afghanistan has full sovereignty over its airspace, territory, and waters. Management of Afghanistan's airspace and transportation shall be exercised through relevant Afghan authorities.

2. With full respect for Afghan sovereignty and consistent with the purpose and scope of this Agreement, Afghanistan authorizes United States government aircraft and civil aircraft that are operated by or exclusively for United States forces to enter, exit, overfly, land, take off, conduct aerial refuelling, and move within the territory of Afghanistan. United States government aircraft and civil aircraft that are operated by or exclusively for United States forces shall not be subject to payment of over flight or navigation fees, or landing or parking fees at government-owned airfields, or other charges. United States government aircraft shall be operated with full respect for the relevant rules of safety and movement in Afghanistan, including notification requirements. Civil aircraft being operated by or exclusively for United States forces are subject to notification requirements regarding their entry into and exit from the territory of Afghanistan as required by the civil aviation authorities of Afghanistan.

3. With full respect for Afghan sovereignty and consistent with the purpose and scope of this Agreement, Afghanistan authorizes United States government vessels and vehicles and other vessels and vehicles that are operated by or exclusively for United States forces, to enter, exit, and move within the territory of Afghanistan. All such vessels and vehicles shall be operated with full respect for the relevant rules of safety and movement in Afghanistan. Members of the force and of the civilian component have a duty to respect Afghan motor vehicle regulations when operating official vehicles.

4. United States government aircraft, vessels and vehicles shall be free from boarding without the consent of United States forces authorities. United States government aircraft, vessels, and vehicles shall be free from inspection, regulation, or registration requirements within Afghanistan, except as otherwise provided in this Agreement or as otherwise agreed by the Joint Commission.

5. United States forces shall pay reasonable charges for services requested and received for United States government aircraft, vehicles, and vessels, free of taxes or similar charges.

6. The Parties agree to establish procedures to implement this Article. The Parties shall review and update, as appropriate, such procedures, and shall address any issues immediately through the Joint Commission that may arise regarding such procedures.

ARTICLE 11

Contracting Procedures

1. United States forces, in accordance with United States laws, may enter into contracts for the acquisition of articles and services, including construction, in the territory of Afghanistan. Afghanistan recognizes that United States forces are bound by the laws and regulations of the United States in the solicitation, award, and administration of such contracts. United States forces shall strive to utilize Afghan suppliers of goods, products, and services to the greatest extent practicable, in accordance with United States laws and regulations.

2. United States contractors are subject to registration in Afghanistan, via an expedited process that shall include issuance of a business registration license valid for three years and payment of a reasonable, standard, one-time service charge to the Afghanistan Investment Support Agency as required by the laws and regulations of Afghanistan. United States contractors shall otherwise be exempt from all other Afghan licenses and similar requirements in relation to their entry into or execution of contracts and subcontracts with or on behalf of United States forces.

3. Recognizing the importance of transparency, including through the sharing of information and consultations as may be mutually agreed, United States forces shall give due consideration to concerns and disputes expressed by Afghan authorities regarding United States contractors. The Parties will work together to improve transparency, accountability, and effectiveness of contracting

processes in Afghanistan with a view to preventing misuse and bad contracting practices.

4. Upon the request of either Party, the Parties shall consult immediately through the Joint Commission concerning any issues, including issues concerning the activities of United States contractors and United States contractor employees that may arise regarding implementation of this Article.

ARTICLE 12

Utilities and Communications

1. United States forces may produce and provide services including but not limited to water, electricity, and other utilities for agreed facilities and areas and for other locations as mutually agreed. The production and provision of such services shall be notified to and coordinated with the Joint Commission on a periodic basis. United States forces and United States contractors may use Afghan public water, electricity, and other Afghan public utilities on terms and conditions, including rates or charges, no less favourable than those paid by ANDSF, less taxes or similar or related charges, unless otherwise mutually agreed. United States forces' or United States contractors' costs shall be equal to their proportionate use of such public utilities.

2. Afghanistan recognizes that United States forces shall use the radio spectrum. The Afghan side shall allocate Afghan owned frequencies based on relevant Afghan regulations. The United States shall be allowed to operate its own telecommunications systems (as telecommunication is defined in the 1992 Constitution of the International Telecommunication Union), including the use of such means and services as required to ensure full ability to operate telecommunications systems, and the use of radio spectrum allocated by appropriate Afghan authorities for this purpose. Use of radio spectrum shall be free of cost to the United States.

3. United States forces, in recognition of Afghan ownership and allocation of frequencies within Afghanistan and in the interest

of avoiding mutually disruptive interference, shall coordinate with appropriate Afghan authorities for the allocation of frequencies for United States forces present in Afghanistan. United States forces shall respect frequencies in use by or reserved for local operators.

4. Use of telecommunications by United States forces shall be done in a manner that avoids interference with use of radio spectrum or other telecommunication equipment operated by the Afghan government and other organizations the Afghan government has granted permission to use radio spectrum and/or telecommunications equipment.

ARTICLE 13

Status of Personnel

1. Afghanistan, while retaining its sovereignty, recognizes the particular importance of disciplinary control, including judicial and non-judicial measures, by United States forces authorities over members of the force and of the civilian component. Afghanistan therefore agrees that the United States shall have the exclusive right to exercise jurisdiction over such persons in respect of any criminal or civil offenses committed in the territory of Afghanistan. Afghanistan authorizes the United States to hold trial in such cases, or take other disciplinary action, as appropriate, in the territory of Afghanistan.

2. If requested by Afghanistan, the United States shall inform Afghanistan of the status of any criminal proceedings regarding offenses allegedly committed in Afghanistan by the members of the force or of the civilian component involving Afghan nationals, including the final disposition of the investigations or prosecution. If so requested, the United States shall also undertake efforts to permit and facilitate the attendance and observation of such proceedings by representatives of Afghanistan.

3. In the interests of justice, the Parties shall assist each other in investigation of incidents, including the collection of evidence. In investigating offenses, United States authorities shall take into account any report of investigations by Afghan authorities.

4. The United States recognizes the critical role that Afghan law enforcement officials play in the enforcement of Afghan law and order and the protection of the Afghan people. Relevant Afghan authorities shall immediately notify United States forces authorities if they suspect a member of the force or of the civilian component is engaged in the commission of a crime so that United States forces authorities can take immediate action. Members of the force and of the civilian component shall not be arrested or detained by Afghan authorities. Members of the force and of the civilian component arrested or detained by Afghan authorities for any reason, including by Afghan law enforcement authorities, shall be immediately handed over to United States forces authorities.

5. Afghanistan and the United States agree that members of the force and of the civilian component may not be surrendered to, or otherwise transferred to, the custody of an international tribunal or any other entity or state without the express consent of the United States.

6. Afghanistan maintains the right to exercise jurisdiction over United States contractors and United States contractor employees.

ARTICLE 14

Bearing of Arms and Wearing of Uniforms

1. When present in Afghanistan under this Agreement, members of the force and of the civilian component may possess and carry arms in Afghanistan as required for the performance of their duties and as authorized by their orders. When issuing such orders, United States forces authorities shall consider relevant Afghan officials' views regarding appropriate locations for the presence of arms, including considerations of public safety. In consideration of such views, United States forces shall not, for military operations, enter mosques or other sites of religious significance being used for religious purposes. Members of the force may wear uniforms while in Afghanistan. United States forces authorities shall take appropriate measures to ensure that members of the force and of the civilian component are mindful of their presence in public areas, including in the carrying of weapons.

2. The Parties agree that United States contractors and United States contractor employees are not permitted to wear military uniforms and may only carry weapons in accordance with Afghan laws and regulations.

3. United States contractors performing security services in Afghanistan are subject to all relevant requirements of Afghan laws and regulations.

4. Upon the request of either Party, the Parties shall consult immediately through the Joint Commission concerning any issues that may arise regarding implementation of this Article.

ARTICLE 15

Entry and Exit

1. Members of the force and members of the civilian component may enter and exit Afghanistan at agreed facilities and areas at locations listed in Annex A, at official points of embarkation and debarkation as listed in Annex B, and at other areas as mutually agreed, with identification cards issued by the United States, and either collective or individual movement orders. Passports and visas shall not be required. Such personnel shall be exempt from Afghan law and regulations on registration and control of foreign nationals.

2. United States contractors and United States contractor employees may enter and exit Afghanistan at the places of entry and exit described in paragraph 1 of this Article. Passports and visas shall be required in accordance with Afghan law. If a visa is required, and requested by a United States contractor or a United States contractor employee, it shall provide for multiple entries and exits and shall be valid for a period of not less than one year. The appropriate Afghan authorities may issue or decline to issue required visas expeditiously. In the event Afghanistan declines to issue such visa, the appropriate Afghan authorities shall notify the person concerned and United States forces authorities. For exceptional situations as may be agreed through the Joint Commission, Afghanistan shall seek to put in place and make

available to United States contractor employees a process for the issuance of visas upon their arrival in Afghanistan.

3. The United States recognizes the sovereign right of Afghanistan to request the removal of any member of the force or member of the civilian component from Afghanistan. United States forces authorities shall take appropriate measures to remove expeditiously such persons from Afghanistan upon request by proper Afghan authorities.

4. The Parties agree to establish procedures to implement this Article. The Joint Commission shall periodically review and update procedures for appropriate Afghan authorities to process members of the force and of the civilian component who arrive at or depart from the places of entry and exit described in paragraph 1 of this Article, including coordination and inspection of documentation. Afghan authorities may develop lists of members of the force and of the civilian component entering and exiting Afghan territory at the agreed facilities and areas, as necessary.

ARTICLE 16

Importation and Exportation

1. United States forces and United States contractors may import into, export out of, re-export out of and transport and use in Afghanistan any equipment, supplies, materiel, technology, training, or services. The authorizations in this paragraph do not cover the activities of United States contractors that are not related to the presence of United States forces in Afghanistan. Identifying documents shall be provided to indicate that such equipment, supplies, materiel, technology, training, or services being imported by United States contractors are for United States forces' purposes and not for any private commercial purposes.

2. Members of the force and of the civilian component, United States contractors, and those United States contractor employees who are not Afghan nationals, may import into, export out of, re-export out of and transport and use in Afghanistan personal effects. The imported quantities shall be reasonable and proportionate to

personal use. The property referred to in this paragraph may not be sold or otherwise transferred in Afghanistan to persons who are not entitled to import such items duty free unless such transfer is in accordance with agreed procedures, including on payment of any taxes or fees due as a result of such transaction, established by the Joint Commission.

3. United States forces authorities, working with relevant Afghan authorities, shall take appropriate measures to ensure that no items or material of cultural or historic significance to Afghanistan are being exported and that, as provided in United States Central Command General Order Number 1, no alcohol, pornography, illegal narcotics, or privately owned firearms, or other contraband or items as may be mutually agreed, are being imported using the authorizations provided in paragraphs 1 and 2 of this Article.

4. The importation, exportation, re-exportation, transportation, and use of any articles brought into Afghanistan pursuant to paragraphs 1 and 2 of this Article shall not be subject to restrictions, such as licensing, inspection, or verification, except as provided in this Article, or taxes and customs duties or other charges assessed by government authorities in Afghanistan within the territory of Afghanistan. If Afghan authorities suspect the abuse of the privileges granted in paragraph 2 of this Article to United States contractors and United States contractor employees, then relevant Afghan authorities reserve the right of inspection of such personal effects when arriving or departing from civilian airports in Afghanistan or in personal vehicles at border crossings.

5. The relevant Afghan authorities reserve the right of verification of any container imported by United States contractors and United States contractor employees containing items for United States forces' purposes in Afghanistan or for personal use, as authorized in paragraphs 1 and 2 of this Article. Without causing undue delay, and upon presentation by the relevant Afghan authorities of information to United States forces authorities that a United States contractor is abusing the authority granted in paragraphs 1 or 2 of this Article, United States forces authorities shall open and verify suspected shipments or containers intended for import

in the presence of the Afghan authorities. Afghan authorities shall consent to the security requirements of United States forces and upon request by United States forces authorities permit such verifications to take place within agreed facilities and areas or other areas as mutually agreed.

6. Sharing the common goal with Afghanistan of preventing the improper entry into Afghan markets of items imported into Afghanistan under the terms of this Agreement, United States forces authorities shall take measures to prevent abuse of the authorizations in paragraphs 1 and 2 of this Article, and shall conduct inquiries and assist the relevant Afghan authorities in the conduct of inquiries and the collection of evidence relating to the suspected improper importation, exportation, re-exportation, transfer, or disposition of goods by members of the force, members of the civilian component, United States contractors, and United States contractor employees.

7. Items imported into Afghanistan or purchased in Afghanistan pursuant to this Article may be disposed of in Afghanistan with due respect for Afghan laws and regulations.

8. Upon the request of either Party, the Parties shall review and consult immediately through the Joint Commission concerning any issues that may arise regarding implementation of this Article.

ARTICLE 17

Taxation

1. The acquisition in Afghanistan of articles and services by or on behalf of United States forces shall not be subject to any taxes or similar or related charges assessed within the territory of Afghanistan.

2. United States forces, including members of the force and of the civilian component, shall not be liable to pay any tax or similar or related charges assessed by the Government of Afghanistan within the territory of Afghanistan.

3. United States contractors shall not be liable to pay any tax or similar or related charges assessed by the Government of Afghanistan within the territory of Afghanistan on their activities, and associated income, relating to or on behalf of United States forces under a contract or subcontract with or in support of United States forces. However, United States contractors that are Afghan legal entities shall not be exempt from corporate profits tax that may be assessed by the Government of Afghanistan within the territory of Afghanistan on income received due to their status as United States contractors.

4. United States contractors are subject to Afghan requirements regarding employer withholding of personal income tax from United States contractor employees who normally reside in Afghanistan and from United States contractor employees who are Afghan nationals for payment to Afghanistan as required by the laws and regulations of Afghanistan.

5. United States contractor employees who do not normally reside in Afghanistan and United States contractor employees who are not Afghan nationals shall not be liable to pay any tax or similar or related charges assessed by the Government of Afghanistan within the territory of Afghanistan on their activities, and associated income, relating to a contract or subcontract with or in support of United States forces.

6. United States contractors and United States contractor employees are not exempt under this Agreement from paying taxes assessed by the Government of Afghanistan within the territory of Afghanistan on their activities in Afghanistan that are not associated with supplying goods and services in Afghanistan to or on behalf of United States forces under a contract or subcontract with or in support of United States forces.

ARTICLE 18

Driving and Professional Licenses

1. Afghanistan agrees to accept as valid, without a driving test or fee, driving licenses or permits issued by United States authorities

to members of the force or of the civilian component, United States contractors, and United States contractor employees for operation of vehicles, vessels, aircraft, or other equipment by or for United States forces within the territory of Afghanistan.

2. Afghanistan agrees to accept as valid all professional licenses issued by United States authorities to members of the force or of the civilian component and United States contractors or United States contractor employees in relation to the provision of services as part of their official or contractual duties.

3. United States forces authorities shall endeavour to ensure that members of the force or of the civilian component, United States contractors, and United States contractor employees have current, valid driving licenses and permits for operation of vehicles, vessels, aircraft, or other equipment by or for United States forces within the territory of Afghanistan. The Joint Commission shall establish mechanisms to exchange information on United States licenses and permits. In response to requests from Afghan authorities, the United States shall seek to verify the validity of such licenses.

ARTICLE 19

Motor Vehicles

Afghanistan agrees to accept as valid the registration and licensing by United States forces authorities of the official vehicles of United States forces. Upon the request of United States forces authorities, Afghan authorities shall issue, without charge, license plates for United States forces' official, non-tactical vehicles. United States forces' official, non-tactical vehicles shall display official Afghan license plates that are indistinguishable from other Afghan license plates, upon their provision by Afghanistan.

ARTICLE 20

Service Support Activities

1. United States forces may directly or through contract establish and operate at agreed facilities and areas service support activities, including military post offices, banking services,

military service exchanges, commissaries, recreational service areas, and telecommunications services, including broadcast services. It is not the United States' intention for broadcasting, media, and entertainment services to reach beyond the scope of the agreed facilities and areas. Taking into consideration Afghan laws, traditions, and customs, United States forces may continue to make available television and radio broadcast services such as media and entertainment programming for the purposes of morale, welfare, and recreation of United States forces and other authorized recipients located on agreed facilities and areas.

2. United States forces shall take appropriate measures to limit broadcasting, television programs, media, and entertainment services to authorized recipients and to agreed facilities and areas.

3. Access to service support activities shall be in accordance with United States regulations. United States forces authorities shall adopt appropriate measures to prevent the abuse of such service support activities and the sale or resale of goods or services to persons who are not authorized to patronize such service support activities or providers.

4. No license, permit, or inspection shall be required by Afghanistan for activities connected with such service support activities.

5. The activities, and any organizations undertaking the activities referred to in this Article, are integral parts of United States forces and shall be accorded the same fiscal and customs exemptions granted to United States forces, including those provided in Articles 16 and 17 of this Agreement. Such organizations and activities shall be maintained and operated in accordance with applicable United States regulations. Such activities shall not be required to collect or pay taxes or to pay other fees related to their operations. Access to these service support activities shall be restricted to members of the force, members of the civilian component, United States contractors and United States contractor employees, and others as may be authorized.

6. Mail shipped within the United States Military Postal Service transportation system shall be exempt from inspection, search, or seizure by Afghan authorities.

7. The Joint Commission shall periodically review the service support activities and resolve by mutual agreement questions arising in the course of implementation of this Article.

ARTICLE 21

Currency and Exchange

The Parties agree to establish procedures regarding currency and exchange. The Parties shall review and update, as appropriate, such procedures and shall address any issues immediately through the Joint Commission that may arise regarding such procedures.

ARTICLE 22

Claims

1. Each Party waives any and all claims (other than contractual claims) against the other for damage to, loss of, or destruction of its property or injury or death to members of ANDSF or United States forces, and their respective civilian components, arising out of the performance of their official duties in Afghanistan.

2. For claims not excluded under paragraph 1 of this Article, United States forces authorities shall pay just and reasonable compensation in settlement of meritorious third party claims arising out of acts or omissions of members of the force and of the civilian component done in the performance of their official duties and incident to the non-combat activities of United States forces. Such claims shall be expeditiously processed and settled by United States forces authorities in accordance with the laws and regulations of the United States and seriously considering the laws, customs, and traditions of Afghanistan.

3. In settling third party claims, United States forces authorities shall take into account any report of investigation or opinion provided to them by Afghan authorities regarding liability or amount of damages.

4. The settlement or adjudication of contract claims shall be carried out in accordance with the terms of the contracts.

5. Upon the request of either Party, the Parties shall consult immediately through the Joint Commission concerning any issues that may arise regarding implementation of this Article.

ARTICLE 23

Annexes

Any Annex appended to this Agreement shall form an integral part of this Agreement, and may be amended by written agreement of the Parties.

ARTICLE 24

Disputes and Implementation

1. Any divergence in views or dispute regarding the interpretation or application of this Agreement shall be resolved through consultations between the Parties and shall not be referred to any national or international court, tribunal or other similar body, or any third party for settlement.

2. The Parties, or their Executive Agents including through the Joint Commission, may enter into Implementing Arrangements and procedures to carry out the provisions of this Agreement.

3. Cooperation under this Agreement is subject to the relevant laws and regulations of the respective Parties, including applicable appropriations laws. 4. United States forces authorities shall pay reasonable, fair market charges, minus any taxes, for goods or services they request and receive.

ARTICLE 25

Joint Commission

1. The Parties hereby establish a Joint Commission to oversee implementation of this Agreement. The Joint Commission shall be co-chaired by representatives of the Executive Agents. The Joint

Commission may include other governmental representatives requested by the Executive Agents and appointed by the Parties.

2. The Joint Commission shall determine its own procedures and arrange for such auxiliary organs, including the establishment of Working Groups and administrative services, as may be considered appropriate. Each Executive Agent shall bear the costs of its participation in the Joint Commission.

3. The Joint Commission shall coordinate and exchange information, as appropriate, with the Afghanistan - United States Working Group on Defence and Security Cooperation established under the Strategic Partnership Agreement.

ARTICLE 26

Entry into Force, Amendment, and Termination

1. This Agreement shall enter into force on January 1, 2015, after the Parties notify one another through diplomatic channels of the completion of their respective internal legal requirements necessary for the entry into force of this Agreement. It shall remain in force until the end of 2024 and beyond, unless terminated pursuant to paragraph 4 of this Article.

2. This Agreement, upon its entry into force, shall supersede the exchange of notes dated September 26, 2002, December 12, 2002, and May 28, 2003, regarding the status of United States forces in Afghanistan. This Agreement shall also supersede any prior agreements and understandings which the Parties mutually determine, through a subsequent exchange of diplomatic notes, to be contrary to the provisions of this Agreement.

3. This Agreement may be amended by written agreement of the Parties through the exchange of diplomatic notes.

4. This Agreement may be terminated by mutual written agreement or by either Party upon two years' written notice to the other Party through diplomatic channels. Termination of any Annex to or Implementing Arrangement under this Agreement does not result in termination of this Agreement. Termination of this Agreement in

accordance with this paragraph shall, without further action, result in termination of all Annexes and Implementing Arrangements.

IN WITNESS WHEREOF, the undersigned, being duly authorized by their respective Governments, have signed this Agreement.

DONE at Kabul, the 30th day of September 2014 in duplicate, in the Pashto, Dari, and English languages, each text being equally authentic. FOR THE ISLAMIC REPUBLIC OF AFGHANISTAN:

H.E. Mohammed Haneef Atmar

National Security Advisor of the Islamic Republic of Afghanistan FOR THE UNITED STATES OF AMERICA:

H.E. James B. Cunningham

Ambassador of the

United States of America

ANNEX A

List of Locations in Afghanistan of Afghan Facilities and Areas Provided by Afghanistan for United States Forces Access and Use ("Agreed Facilities and Areas")

Kabul

Bagram

Mazar-e-Sharif

Herat

Kandahar

Shorab (Helmand)

Gardez

Jalalabad

Shindand

Agreed facilities and areas also include other facilities and areas, if any, of which United States forces have the use as of the effective date of this Agreement and other facilities and areas at other locations in Afghanistan as may be agreed and authorized by the Minister of Defence.

ANNEX B

Official Points of Embarkation and Debarkation

Bagram Airbase

Kabul International Airport

Kandahar Airbase

Shindand Airbase

Herat International Airport

Mazar-e-Sharif Airport

Shorab (Helmand)

Land Ports:

Toorkham, Nangarhar Province

Spinboldak, Kandahar Province

Toorghundi, Herat Province

Hairatan, Balkh Province

Sherkhan Bandar, Kunduz Province

Other official points of embarkation and debarkation as may be mutually agreed.

Notes to Chapters

Introduction

1. It's time to end America's war in Afghanistan: As the country's longest war continues, it is sapping resources and focus while the list of far more serious national security threats continues to grow. Michael H Fuchs. The Guardian, 19 August 2018.

2. Ibid

3. When, If Ever, May States Deploy Military Force Without Prior Security Council Authorization? Thomas M. Franck, Washington Post, 08 November 2018

4. NBC News, 07 December 2018

5. Ibid

6. Ibid

7. 21 August 2017, President Trump speech

8. The Guardian, 04 February 2012

9. The Afghan Intel War, pp, 46

10. Ibid

11. The BBC News, 20 December 2018

12. Jang New (Urdu), 20 September 2010

13. The Afghan Intel War-Introduction pages

14. Ibid

15. Whose Army, Jalalzai, pp, 67

16. General Flynn Paper, 2010

17. Daily Outlook, 2010

18. Global Research in 25 November, 2018 published revelations of Afghan writer, analyst, and representative of Revolutionary Association of the Women of Afghanistan (RAWA) on the intentional killings of US and NATO forces in Afghanistan.

19. On 14 November 2013, Global Research in its report documented some aspects of US army war crimes in Afghanistan

20. The CIA torture report prepared by Senator Diane Feinstein (D-CA)

21. Journalist claims US used dogs to rape-Afghans as torture technique, Latest.com, 29 December 2014, Ian Welsh, 29 December 2014

22. September 2018, Voice of America News reported the United States discountenance to cooperate with the International Criminal Court (ICC) if it carried out investigation into the US army war crimes in Afghanistan.

23. Ibid

24. Ibid

25. Daily Outlook, December 2018

26. Ibid

27. The Bensouda-2016-report, The Prosecutor of the International Criminal Court, Fatou Bensouda, issued her annual Report on Preliminary Examination Activities (2016). The International Criminal Court (ICC) investigates and, where warranted, tries individuals charged with the gravest crimes of concern to the international community: genocide, war crimes, crimes against humanity and the crime of aggression. https://www.icc-cpi.int/pages/item.aspx?name=pr1252. 14 November 2016.

28. Intelligence in Vex, Jalalzai, 2018

29. The Afghan Intel Crisis, Jalalzai, 2017

30. How the heroin trade explains the US-UK failure in Afghanistan: After 16 years and $1tn spent, there is no end to the fighting – but western intervention has resulted in Afghanistan becoming the world's first true narco-state. Alfred W McCoy, the Guardian, 09 January 2018.

31. The Afghan Intel Crisis, Jalalzai, 2017

32. Ibid

33. Ibid

34. Ibid

35. Ibid

36. Pakistan: Living with a nuclear monkey, Jalalzai, 2018

37. Ibid

38. Ibid

39. The Guardian, 21 October 2015

40. China and Russia sought a bigger role by supporting Taliban insurgents, and Pakistan. They received Taliban delegations in 2017 and 2018. No easy escape from Afghan war for Trump Russia, China and Iran now backing Taliban and stymieing US peace efforts, Brahma Chellaney, Nikki Asian Review, 02 October 2018.

41. Ibid

42. Ibid

43. Strengthening Afghanistan's National Directorate of Security (NDS): Is it equipped to counter 'emerging' threats? Anant Mishra, 27 February, 2018, Modern Diplomacy.

44. Ibid

45. Daily Times, 21 December 2015

46. Ibid

47. Ibid

48. Ibid

49. Why the NDS matters: The emergence of the Afghan intelligence agency after 9/11, Diva Patang Wardak, The Journal of Intelligence and Terrorism Studies, 29 January 2017. https://www.veruscript.com/JITS/publications/afghan-intelligence-agency/

50. The Afghan Intel Crisis, Jalalzai, 2017

51. Ibid

52. Manish Rai, has criticized ethnic composition and incompetency of the Afghan intelligence (NDS) in his article, and argued that this type of composition poses challenges to the ability of the agency; Afghans should fix their home first. Rather than just focusing on responding to terror attacks, the Afghan military strategists should chalk out a proactive strategy which engages the enemy in their stronghold. Manish Rai, Daily Times, 10 September 2018.

53. Afghan intelligence chief warns Iran and Russia against aiding Taliban, Ahmad Majidyar, 05 February, 2018, Middle East Institute.

54. Ibid

55. The Afghan Intel Crisis, Jalalzai, 2017

56. Ibid

57. Ibid

58. Ibid

59. Afghan spy chief resigns after rows with president: Rahmatullah Nabil, outgoing head of NDS, strongly opposed Ashraf Ghani's moves towards rapprochement with Pakistan, Reuter, 10 December 2015.

60. The Afghan Intel Crisis, Jalalzai, 2017

61. Ibid

62. Ibid

63. Ibid

64. Why the NDS matters: The emergence of the Afghan intelligence agency after 9/11, Diva Patang Wardak. The Journal of Intelligence and Terrorism Studies, 29 January 2017. https://www.veruscript. com/JITS/publications/afghan-intelligence-agency/

65. Ibid

66. The Afghan Intel Crisis, Jalalzai, 2017

67. Ibid

68. Ibid

69. Ibid

70. Pakistan: living with a Nuclear Monkey, Musa Khan Jalalzai, 2018, Vij Book, India

71. Ibid

72. Ibid

73. Fixing Intel paper, Mike Flynn Report, 2010

74. Ibid

75. Ibid

76. Research scholar Matt Waldman described the flawed policies of the US and its allies in a recent article. The Prospect of Nuclear Jihad in South Asia: Pakistan's Army, Extra-judicial Killings, and the Forceful Disappearance of Pashtuns and Balochs, Musa Khan Jalalzai, Algora Publishing, 1 Oct 2015.

77. New York Times, 23 June 2010

78. The Guardian, 24 November 2013

79. ibid

80. The Washington Post 02 March 2014

81. Ibid

82. On 16 October 2017, Tolonews quoted the report of Times of London, which noted Russian involvement in Afghanistan.

83. Ibid

84. The Times of London, 16 October 2017

85. Ibid

86. Geopolitica Russia, 21 May 2018

87. On 02 August 2018, an article of analyst Mr. Nicholas Trickett in Diplomat Magazine article highlighted Russian involvement in Afghanistan.

88. Reuters, 10 June 2018

89. Reuters, 14 May 2018

90. Ibid

91. Astute News, in 27 May 2018 report, and Off Guardian News in its 20 May 2018 commentary explained the role of warlord Gulab Mengal in strengthening the ISIS terrorist group in Jalalabad province. Special Service's Agent: Attack On Russia is Being Prepared, World news Daily, Andrey Afanasyev. http://www.informationclearinghouse. info/49471.htm

92. Ibid

93. Ibid

94. Ibid

95. Ibid

Chapter-1

The Intelligence War in Afghanistan: Regional and International Intelligence Agencies Play the Tom & Jerry Endless Game on the Local Chessboard

1. Global Witness Research Report for 2016

2. Ibid

3. Ibid

4. The War is Worth Waging": Afghanistan's Vast Reserves of Minerals and Natural Gas: The War on Afghanistan is a Profit driven "Resource War". Prof Michel Chossudovsky, Global Research, 28 September, 2018, Afghanistan Times 26 October 2018

5. New Cold War: NATO Washes the Car, 25.October 2018

6. On 23 March 2018, the US commander told BBC that Russia was arming Taliban

7. Russia Returns to Afghanistan, the National Interest, 12 January 2017, Arif Rafiq

8. On 06 October 2018, ToloNews

9. What's Behind China's Growing Security Presence in Afghanistan?, Andrew Small Tuesday, World Politics Review, 21 March, 2017

10. Foreign Affairs, 02 January 2018

11. Ibid

12. Intelligence Theory: Key Questions and Debates, Peter Gill, Stephen Marrin and Mark Phythian, Studies in Intelligence series, Routledge, 2009

13. On 02 April, BBC spotlighted some aspects of Russian involvement in Afghanistan

14. On 21 May 2018, analyst Andrey Afanasyev's commentary on the ISIS operation and Russian fear spotlighted some important aspects of the geographical expansion of the group.

15. ISIS starting invasion of Central Asia, supported by US: Russian & Chinese sources fear?: Russian Analyst citing sources in Russian & Chinese Intelligence argues that an Islamist group (ISIS) may launch full-scale operations in Russian territories through Central Asia using its bases in Afghanistan. Andret Afasanev, Global Village Space, 18 May, 2018. Russian, Chinese intelligence: ISIS heading for Central Asia with US cover, Operatives of the crumbling Islamic State in Syria and Iraq (ISIS) are moving to new battlegrounds near the Russian border, intelligence sources have revealed. Free West Media, 22 May 2018,

16. The Guardian newspaper on 22 October 2017 published a news story, in which concerns of the Afghan government were accentuated.

17. Ibid

18. On 05 February 2018, analyst Ahmad Majidyar in his paper noted frustration of Afghan intelligence chief about the involvement of Russian intelligence in Afghanistan.

19. ISIS heading for Central Asia with US cover, Operatives of the crumbling Islamic State in Syria and Iraq (ISIS) are moving to new battlegrounds near the Russian border, intelligence sources have revealed. Free West Media, 22 May 2018.

20. Privacy International, Policy Briefing – UK Intelligence Sharing Arrangements 04 April 2018 A new Privacy International report based on an international collaborative investigation carried out by 40 NGOs in 42 countries has found alarming weaknesses in the oversight arrangements that are supposed to govern the sharing of intelligence between state intelligence agencies, including in the UK. Privacy International urges governments to enact urgent reforms and improve public understanding about the scope of intelligence sharing and the safeguards and oversight currently in place.

21. Ibid

22. Ibid

23. Ibid

24. Intelligence in an Insecure World, Peter Gill and Mark Phythian, Polity Press UK 2006

25. Intelligence Elsewhere: Spies and Espionage Outside the Anglosphere, Philip H. J Davies and Kristian C. Gustafson, Georgetown University Press, Washington, USA, 2013, and Intelligence Cycle, Intelligence Branch, Federal Bureau of Investigation (FBI), https://www.fbi.gov/about-us/intelligence/intelligence-cycle

26. AFP, 21 December 2018-12-28

27. CNN, 22 December 2018-12-28

28. Ibid

29. Anant Mishra article

30. Ibid

31. Afghanistan Times 26 October 2018

32. Ibid

33. Anant Mishra

Chapter 2

National Directorate of Security (NDS), Taliban, and the Islamic State of Khorasan

1. Endless Endgame: Whither Russia-West Confrontation? Elkhan Nuriyev. Russia in Global Affairs, 6 April 2018

2. Afghanistan Presents Risk of Confrontation between the US and Russia, Alexei Fenenko Valdai Discussion Club--17.05.2017

3. Russia in Global Affairs Magazine, No 3 July/September 2018, https://eng.globalaffairs.ru/

4. Ibid

5. The Major Flaws in Afghanistan's Intelligence War: The United States needs an honest reassessment of Afghanistan's defence capabilities

as it ramps up its combat-training role. Javid Ahmad, the National Interests, 12 February, 2018

6. Ministers of Defence and Interior Should Overhaul Afghan Defence and Security Institutions to Match Defeat Existing Security Challenges. Mohammed Gul Sahibbzada. Daily Outlook Afghanistan, 01 January, 2019. http://outlookafghanistan.net.

7. Inside the CIA's secret war in Afghanistan, Michael Krepon, Herald, 19 Apr, 2018, On 12 January 2015, CBS News reported potential gains of the Taliban in Helmand and ISIS in Jalalabad, Kunar and Nuristan provinces

8. Reforming Afghan intelligence agencies, Musa Khan Jalalzai, Daily Times, 23 December 2014

9. Security Services in Communist Afghanistan (1978-1992): AGSA, KAM, KHAD and WAD, Council of European Union, Brussels, 2001.

10. Taliban tighten grip on Afghan City of Kunduz, BBC, 30 September 2015, http://www.bbc.co.uk/news/world-asia-34398371, The Guardian 28 September 2015

11. On 12 January 2015, CBS News reported potential gains of the Taliban in Helmand and ISIS in Jalalabad, Kunar and Nuristan provinces, the capture of Kunduz, Sangin and parts of Badakhshan provinces, kidnapping for ransom, and the emergence of a new anti-Pakistan Taliban group in Paktika province, all raised serious questions over the credibility of NDS.

12. ToloNews, 14 March 2016

13. Strengthening Afghanistan's National Directorate of Security: Is it Equipped to Counter 'Emerging' Threats? Anant Mishra, modern diplomacy, February 27, 2018

14. On 23 April 2018, Al Jazeera reported the killing of 57 people in a suicide attack on a voter registration centre in the city.

15. Strengthening Afghanistan's National Directorate of Security (NDS): Is it equipped to counter emerging' threats? Anant Mishra, Modern Diplomacy, 27, February 2018

16. In January 2017, the Marine Corps Times reported Taliban's spring attacks and noted that the US army was going to deploy a task force

of 300 personnel (known as Task Force Southwest) for nine months to South-Western Afghanistan

17. On 12 February 2017, Daily Huffington Post reported US aircraft conducting around 30 air strikes in Helmand Province

18. On 23 July 2017, following heavy clashes in Ghor province, Taywara district collapsed to the Taliban. Public order police commander in Ghor said the Taliban stormed the district centre. ToloNews Afghanistan

19. Ibid

20. Marine Corps Times, January 2017

21. Stenographic Transcript Before the Committee of Armed Forces, United States Senate Hearing to Receive Testimony on the Situation in Afghanistan, Thursday, February 9, 2017, Washington, D.C. https://www.armed-services.senate.gov. U.S. General Seeks 'a Few Thousand' More Troops in Afghanistan, By Michael R. Gordon, New York Times, 09 February 2017.

22. 18 April 2017, in his New York Times book Review

23. Govt. Failed to Identify Spies Within The System: Critics. Saleh lashed out at government says there are spies in their administration who report to other nations. 29 January 2018.

24. 23 April 2017, CNN reported Taliban's deadly attack on a northern army base that killed or wounded more than 100 people.

25. On 29 January 2018, ToloNews reported Mohammad Hashim Alokozai, head of Senate's Defence Committee criticized United Government's failure to identify elements inside the administration. Former Chief NDS, Mr Amrullah Saleh said government knew a number of spies within the government institutions. Mr. Saleh claimed that one of the deputies of the National Security Council (NSC) was a Pakistan spy.

26. Ibid

27. Govt Divides Kabul into Four Security Zones. ToloNews, 08 September 2018

28. Ariana News, 06 September 2018

29. On 25 December 2018, ToloNews reported President Ashraf Ghani's decree that nominated Amrullah Saleh as Minister of Interior and Assadullah Khalid as Minister of Defense. Saleh and Khalid served as head of the National Directorate of Security (NDS) during former President Hamid Karzai's government.

30. Ibid

31. The Nation, 24 December 2018

32. Afghanistan Times, 24 December 2018

33. Ibid

34. Ibid

35. 11 August 2018, ToloNews

36. Will the New Scheme Improve the Security Condition in Kabul? Mohammad Zahir Akbari, Daily Outlook Afghanistan, 10 September 2018.

37. Voice of America (VoA), 11 February 2018

38. Ibid

39. Pakistani fighters in Ghazni, Afghanistan Times, August 2018

40. ToloNews, 27 January 2018

41. Ibid

42. Security Sector Reform: Long Overdue in Afghanistan: Afghanistan's failure to bring reform to its security apparatus is long overdue for a fix. By Samim Arif, Diplomat, 25 January, 2017

43. Ibid

44. Human Costs of War for Afghanistan and Pakistan, 2001 to mid-2016, Neta C.Crawford, Boston University, August 2016. https://watson.brown.edu/costsofwar/files/cow/imce/papers.

45. International Rescue Committee in its report. 2016

46. On 26 November 2016, ToloNews reported dozen of displaced Afghan families living in tents in the Capital of Afghanistan, Kabul.

47. The Guardian, 04 March 2016

48. July 2016, the UK Home Office Country Information Report

49. 26 November 2016, ToloNew reported dozen of displaced Afghan families living in tents in the Capital of Afghanistan, Kabul

50. 18 April 2015, Daily Outlook Afghanistan

51. 24 November 2016, Pajhwok News

52. 23 July 2016, Associated Press

53. Ibid

54. 22 November 2016, ToloNews TV reported the ISIS suicide attack on a Kabul mosque, in which 50 people were killed and 50 injured.

55. 03 May 2017, Sayed Masood Sadat, Asia Foundation 52-16 June 2017, the Guardian Newspaper, London

56. June 2017, the US Congress report

57. General Assembly Seventy-first session Agenda item 36. The situation in Afghanistan. Security Council,, Seventy-second year. The situation in Afghanistan and its implications for international peace and security. Report of the Secretary-General, 2017. More violent, more widespread: Trends in Afghan security. Thomas Ruttig, Afghanistan Analysis Networks, 29 January 2018.

58. UN mission in Afghanistan reports 'worrying' rise in child casualties, 19 October 2016, https://news.un.org/en/story/2016/10/543132-un-mission-afghanistan-reports-worrying-rise-child-casualtie.

59. The US Special Inspector General for Afghanistan Reconstruction (SIGAR) in its report in 30 April 2017

60. 15 May 2018, ToloNews

61. Joseph Fitsanakis, 2018

62. Ibid.

63. ToloNews, 14 January 2019

64. Regional states muscle in to seek a bigger 'say' in Afghan conflict: Pakistan, Russia, China and Iran are joining forces against terrorist group the Islamic State Khorasan Province in Afghanistan, Asia times M.K. Bhadrakumar, Asia Times, 19 July, 2018

65. Geopolitical Rivalries and Afghanistan's Open-Ended War. China Extends its Influence to the Detriment of America. Shifting Geopolitical Reality in Afghanistan: Threat to US Hegemony? Fraidoon Amel. Global Research, January 29, 2018

66. Afghanistan's Security: A Victim of Regional Rivalries. Sajjad Ashraf, NUS, 6 July 2017

67. Islamic State Khorasan: Impact on Prospect for Peace and Security in Afghanistan. Geopolitical Insight, 30 August, 2018

68. 16 January 2019, ToloNews

69. Geopolitical Rivalries and Afghanistan's Open-Ended War. China Extends its Influence to the Detriment of America. Shifting Geopolitical Reality in Afghanistan: Threat to US Hegemony? Fraidoon Amel. Global Research, January 29, 2018

70. Afghanistan Times, 22 January 2019

Chapter-3

Why the NDS Matters: The Emergence of the Afghan Intelligence Agency after 9/11. Dr. Diva Patang Wardak

1. Philip H. J. Davies and Kristian C. Gustafson, Intelligence Elsewhere: Spies and Espionage Outside the Anglo Sphere. Washington, USA: Georgetown University Press, 2013 and Intelligence Cycle, Intelligence Branch, Federal Bureau of Investigation (FBI), https://www.fbi.gov/about-us/intelligence.

2. Abdul Zuhir Qayomi, "Fall of Kunduz city: Nabil apologizes to nation, tells lawmakers intelligence reports were overlooked," Afghanistan Times, 30 September 2016, http://afghanistantimes. af/fall-of-kunduz-city-nabil-apologizes-to-nation-tells-lawmakers-intelligence-reports-were-overlooked/.

3. Country Reports on Terrorism 2015, "United States Department of State Publication," Released 2 June 2016. 228, http://www.state. gov/documents/organization/258249

4. Musa Khan Jalalzai, The Prospect of Nuclear Jihad in Pakistan, New York, USA: Algora Publishing, 2015, PP 7.

5. Jon Boone, Musharraf: Pakistan and India's backing for 'proxies' in Afghanistan must stop, The Guardian, 12 February 2015, http://

www.theguardian.com/world/2015/feb/13/pervez-musharraf-pakistan-india-proxies-afghanistan-ghani-taliban.

6. Sudhakar Rajee, Pakistan's Intelligence, New Delhi, India: Manas Publications, 2012.

5. Maloy Krishna Dhar, Fulcrum of EvilISI-CIA-Al-Qaeda, NewDelhi, India: ManasPublications,2015, 252.

6. Jon Boone, "Musharraf: Pakistan and India's backing for 'proxies' in Afghanistan must stop," The Guardian, 12 February 2015, http://www.theguardian.com/world/2015/feb/13/pervez-musharraf-pakistan-india-proxies-afghanistan-ghani-taliban.

7. Jeffrey Goldberg, Ex-Pakistani ambassador: My country supports terrorism, Bloomberg View, 22 October 2013, Retrieved 16 September 2016,1.

8. Anisha Shaheed, Ex-Afghan spy boss leaks documents, calls on world to designate Pakistan state-sponsor of terrorism, Tolo News, 14 July 2016,

9. Rosanne Klass, Afghanistan: The Great Game Revisited. New York, USA: Freedom House, 1987

10. bram N. Shulsky and Gary James Schmitt, Silent Warfare: Understanding the World of Intelligence, Lincoln, USA: Potomac Books, Inc., 2002.

11. Peter Gill, Stephen Marrin and Mark Phythian, Intelligence Theory: Key Questions and Debates, Studies in Intelligence series, New York: Routledge, 2009.

12. Peter Gill and Mark Phythian, Intelligence in an Insecure World Cambridge, UK: Polity PressUK, 2006.

13. Afghanistan. The World Fact book. CIA. 16 September, 2016.

14. Ibid, 4.

15. Panagiotis Dimitrakis, the Secret War in Afghanistan: The Soviet Union, China and Anglo-American Intelligence in the Afghan War, London, UK: I.B. Tauris, 2013.

16. Security Services in Communist Afghanistan (1978–1992): AGSA, KAM, KhAD and WAD, Council of European Union, Brussels, 2001.

17. Robin R. Barnett, the Fragmentation of Afghanistan, London, UK: Yale University Press, 2002, 114.

18. Security Services in Communist Afghanistan (1978–1992): AGSA, KAM, KhAD and WAD, Council of European Union, Brussels, 2001. Before 1978 the Afghan police have been aided by West Germany. KhAD was organized and assisted by the KGB and, apparently, the EastGermanStasi. TheGRUmayhavebeenmorecloselyinvolvedwithAGSAandKAM.

19. Ibid,4.

20. Barnett, the Fragmentation of Afghanistan, 133.

21. Rajee, Pakistan's Intelligence, 25.

22. Barnett, The Fragmentation of Afghanistan, 122.

23. Rosanne Klass, Afghanistan: The Great Game Revisited 147.

24. Security Services in Communist Afghanistan (1978–1992):AGSA,K AM,KhADandWAD,Council of EuropeanUnion,Brussels,2001,4

25. Rosanne Klass, Afghanistan: The Great Game Revisited, Freedom House; 2nd revised edition, 7 Sept. 1990

26. Ibid

27. Ibid

28. Cornelius Van H. Engert, "A Report on Afghanistan," U.S. Department of State, Division of Publications, Series C., No. 53, Afghanistan No. 1, 1924.

29. U.S.NationalArchives,NEAMemorandumofconversation,file89 0H.00/122,1930

30. Klass, Afghanistan: The Great Game Revisited, Freedom House; 2nd revised edition, 7 Sept. 1990

31. The Helmand Valley Project in Afghanistan A.I.D. Evaluation Special Study No. 18 C Clapp-Wicek & E Baldwn, U.S. Agency for International Development, published December 1983.

32. The Helmand Valley Project in Afghanistan A.I.D. Evaluation Special Study No. 18 C Clapp-Wicek & E Baldwn, U.S. Agency for International Development, published December 1983.

33. Rosanne Klass, Afghanistan: The Great Game Revisited Freedom House; 2nd revised edition, 7 Sept. 1990

34. Ibid, 46.

35. Ibid, 46.

36. Ibid, 46.

37. Musa Khan Jalalzai, Whose Army? Afghanistan's Future and the Blueprint for Civil War New York, USA: Algora Publishing, 2014.

38. Dimitrakis, the Secret War in Afghanistan, 2013.

39. Amnesty International, "Afghanistan: Reports of torture and long-term detention without trial, "March 1991

40. Interview with former president of Afghanistan, Hamid Karzai, London, 20 April 2016.

41. Security Services in Communist Afghanistan (1978–1992): AGSA, KAM, KhAD and WAD, Council of European Union, Brussels, 2001.

42. Ronny Kristofferson, "Breeding for the village: Success and failure in the hands of the local power brokers," June 2007, https:// globalecco. org/en_GB/ctx-v1n2/bleeding-for-the-village-success-or-failure-in-the-hands-of-the-local-powerbrokers.

43. Interview with the former Afghan Army Chief, Sher Muhammad Karimi, March 2016.

44. Musa Khan Jalalzai, "Afghanistan: Indo-Pak proxy war," Daily Times, 26 January 2016, http://dailytimes.com.pk/opinion/26-Jan-16/ afghanistan-indo-pak-proxy-war.

45. Interview with the former Afghan Army Chief, Sher Muhammad Karimi, March2016.

46. Interview with the former Afghan Army Chief, Sher Muhammad Karimi, March2016.

47. Sylvana Q. Sinha, "National Directorate of Security Prison Visit, May 2011," World Justice Project, 10 December 2012, http:// worldjusticeproject.org/blog/national-directorate-security-prison-visit-may-2011-0.

48. General Campbell, "Opening Remarks," hearing on "Situation on Afghanistan," before the U.S. Senate Committee on the Armed Services, 4 February 2016, 6–7.

49. Ibid, 6–7.

50. Musa Khan Jalalzai, "Reforming Afghan intelligence agencies," Daily Times, 23 December 2014.

51. Hamid Karzai interview, RT, 27April 2016.

52. James R. Clapper, "Worldwide Threat Assessment of the U.S. Intelligence Community," statement for the record, U.S. Senate Select Committee on Intelligence, hearing on "Worldwide Threats," 9 February2016.

53. Jessica Donati and Margherita Stancati, "Intelligence gap fuels extremist rise in Afghanistan," The Wall Street Journal, 2015,

54. Hamid Karzai interview, RT, 27 April 2016.

55. United States Department of State Publication, Country Reports on Terrorism 2015, Released 2 June 2016, 233, http://www.state.gov/documents/organization/258249.pdf. 56 Ibid, 230.

57. AmyBelasco, "The Cost of Iraq, Afghanistan, and Other Global War on Terror Operations Since 9/11,"Congressional Research Service, 8 December 2014,

58. SIGAR, "Quarterly Report," 30 April 2015, 91. OSD, "Department of Defence Budget, Fiscal Year 2017, Justification for FY 2017 Overseas Contingency Operations (OCO) Afghanistan Security Forces Fund (ASFF)," February2016.

59. President Barack Obama, "Remarks by the President in Address to the National on the Way Forward in Afghanistan and Pakistan," West Point, N.Y., 1 December 2009.

60. SIGAR, "Quarterly Report," 30 April 2015, 13.

61. President Barack Obama, "Remarks by the President in Address to the National on the Way Forward in Afghanistan and Pakistan," West Point, N.Y., 1 December 2009.

62. SIGAR, "Quarterly Report," 30 April 2015, 13.

63. Ibid, 13.

Chapter 4

National Directorate of Intelligence (NDS), GRU, CIA, Taliban, and the ISIS Terror Group

1   Chinese troops appear to be operating in Afghanistan, and the Pentagon is OK with it, Shawn Snow, Military Times, 05 March, 2017

2. Russia's Afghan Policy, in the Regional and Russia-West Context. Ekaterina Stepanova, Russia/NIS Centre, May 2018

3. The Guardian, 22 October 2017

4. BBC, 02 April 2018

5. 06 July 2018, ToloNews reported members of Helmand Peace Convoy protest outside Russian embassy in Kabul.

6. The West on the Brink of Failure In Afghanistan, Zabihullah Noori, ToloNews, 25 JULY 2017

7. We Can't Win in Afghanistan Because We Don't Know Why We're There, Steve Coll, Jan. 26, 2018, New York Times

8. Ibid

9. Thomas Joscelyn, long War Journal, 30 May 2018

10. Challenging the ISK Brand in Afghanistan-Pakistan: Rivalries and Divided Loyalties, Amira Jadoon, Nakissa Jahanbani , and Charmaine Willis, Combating Terrorism Centre, Vol 11 Issue 4, April 2018.

11. Ghulam Farooq Mujaddidi, Diplomat, 2017

12. ToloNews, 11 March 2017

13. The Major Flaws in Afghanistan's Intelligence War: The United States needs an honest reassessment of Afghanistan's defence capabilities as it ramps up its combat-training role. Javid Ahmad, National Interests, 12 February 2018

14. Afghans should fix their home first: Rather than just focusing on responding to terror attacks, the Afghan military strategists should chalk out a proactive strategy which engages the enemy in their

stronghold. Manish Rai, Dawn, 10 September 2018, Times of Israel, 12 September 2018.

15. US plan to improve Afghan intelligence operations branded a $457m failure: Pentagon's use of taxpayers' money under scrutiny after special watchdog finds contracts to train and mentor Afghan soldiers fell short of stated objectives. Karen McVeigh. The Guardian, 02 August 2017

16. Afghan security sector in dire need of reform, Ihsanullah Omarkhail, Asia Times, 21 May 2018

17. Decoding Afghan Security Forces' Failures: Afghanistan's woefully unprepared intelligence and security agencies are as much of a problem as cross-border terrorism. Ghulam Farooq Mujaddidi, The Diplomat, 23 June 2017.

18. Strengthening Afghanistan's National Directorate of Security: Is it Equipped to Counter 'Emerging' Threats?, Anant Mishra. Small War Journal

19. War against the Taliban: Why It All Went Wrong in Afghanistan. Sandy Gall, 17 Jan 2013

20. Musa Khan Jalalzai. The Afghan Intel Crisis, 2017

21. Dawn, 24 June 2015

22. The Guardian, 30 April 2013

23. Ibid

24. Express Tribune, 25 June 2015

25. Dawn, 13 February 2015

Chapter-5

Pakistan's Deep State, Democratic Forces, Tug-of-War, and Afghanistan

1. Jalalzai Musa Khan, Pakistan: Living with a Nuclear Monkey, PP-1, 2, 3, introduction

2. Ibid

3. An Economic Crisis in Pakistan again: What is different this Time? Daniel F. Runde and Ambassador Richard Olson, Centre for Strategic

and International Studies, 31 October, 2018. https://www.csis.org/analysis/economic-crisis-pakistan-again-whats-different-time.

4. Ibid

5. Jalalzai Musa Khan, Pakistan: Living with a Nuclear Monkey, PP-5

6. The Corrosive Influence of Pakistan's Deep State. Imad Zafar, Asia Times, 28 March 2018

7. Reform of Pakistan's Intelligence Services, Hassan Abbas, Belfer Center for Science and International Affairs, 15 March 2008. https://www.belfercenter.org/publication/reform-pakistans-intelligence-services.

8. Pakistan: Reorganization of Intelligence infrastructure. Musa Khan Jalalzai, Daily Times, 24 March 2014, https://dailytimes.com.pk/writer/musa-khan-jalalzai/page/9/

9. Pakistan: Fixing the Intelligence Machine. Musa Khan Jalalzai, Daily Times, 14 April 2014, https://dailytimes.com.pk/writer/musa-khan-jalalzai/page/9/

10. Reform of Pakistan's Intelligence Services, Hasan Abbas, Belfer Centre for Science and International Affairs, 15 March 2008. https://www.belfercenter.org/publication/reform-pakistans-intelligence-services.

11. Pakistan: Reorganization of Intelligence infrastructure. Jalalzai Musa Khan, Daily Times, 24 March 2014, https://dailytimes.com.pk/writer/musa-khan-jalalzai/page/9/

12. Jalalzai Musa Khan, Pakistan: Living with a Nuclear Monkey, chapter-12, PP, 172-173

13. Ibid, Chapter-11, PP-161

14. Government Report Highlights Scale Of Enforced Disappearances Across Pakistan. Abubakar Siddique, 10 June 2018, Gandhara

15. Press TV 18 July 2018

16. Pakistan: Reorganization of Intelligence infrastructure. Jalalzai Musa Khan, Daily Times, 24 March 2014, https://dailytimes.com.pk/writer/musa-khan-jalalzai/page/9/

17. Ibid

18. Jalalzai Musa Khan, Pakistan: Living with a Nuclear Monkey, PP-174

19. Pakistan: Living with a nuclear monkey, Musa Khan Jalalzai, 2018, India.

20. Ibid

21. The Prospect of Nuclear Jihad in Pakistan, Musa Khan Jalalzai, 2015, New York

22. On February 25, 2014, former Prime Minister Nawaz Sharif approved and published the National Internal Security Policy (2014-2018) and introduced a new mechanism to counter internal and external threats.

23. Ibid

24. Daily Times, 14 April 2014

25. Ibid

26. The growing 'tug-of-war' between Pakistan's spy agencies: Conflict between the civilian Intelligence Bureau (IB) and the military's Inter-Services Intelligence (ISI) is at boiling point, with the former accused of overstepping constitutional bounds, F.M. Shakil. Asia Times, 04 October 2017. http://www.atimes.com/article/growing-tug-war-pakistans-spy-agencies/

27. Ibid

28. Ibid

29. The growing 'tug of war' between Pakistan's Spy Agencies: The growing 'tug-of-war' between Pakistan's spy agencies: F.M. Shakil, Asia Times, 04 October 2017. http://www.atimes.com/article/growing-tug-war-pakistans-spy-agencies/

30. Reform of Pakistan's Intelligence Services, Hasan Abbas, Belfer Center for Science and International Affairs, 15 March 2008. https://www.belfercenter.org/publication/reform-pakistans-intelligence-services.

31. Jalalzai Musa Khan, Pakistan: Living with a Nuclear Monkey, PP-165-167

32. Imad Zafar, Dawn Leaks: A Tweet that Underscored the State within State, 01 May 2017, https://nation.com.pk/01-May-2017/dawn-leaks-a-tweet-that-underscored-the-state-within-a-state

33. The Afghan Intel crisis, PP: 133

34. Jalalzai Musa Khan, Pakistan: Living with a Nuclear Monkey, Chapter, 10, PP-130-131

35. Ibid

36. Why Pakistan supports terrorist Groups. Vanda Felbab-Brown, Brookings, 05 January 2018. https://www.brookings.edu/blog/order-from-chaos/2018/01/05/why-pakistan-supports-terrorist-groups-and-why-the-us-finds-it-so-hard-to-induce-change/

37. Robert D. Kaplan, the Revenge of Geography: What the Map Tell us about Coming Conflicts and the Battle against Fate. Random House International, 01 November 2012.

38. Marketing Terrorism and Fear, Daily Times, 24 April 2016

39. Dawn, 28 February 2018

40. Jalalzai Musa Khan, Pakistan: Living with a Nuclear Monkey, Chapter-1, PP-4

41. The Guardian, 02 November 2017

42. Dawn, On 25 September 2018

43. Mainstreaming Jihad: Why Now? Pervez Hoodbhoy, Dawn, 16 December 2017. https://www.dawn.com/news/1376805.

44. Pakistan to become Singapore or Syria-the Choice is Starker, Jan Muhammad Achakzai, Global Village Space, 25 December 2018

45. BBC, 23 November 2016

46. Ibid

47. Pakistan unprepared' for refugees fleeing operation against Taliban, Jon Boone. The Guardian, 26 Jun 2014

48. Nuclear Jihad in South Asia, Algora, 2015, New York

49. Lt General Aslam resigns after being superseded, Pakistan Today, 28 November 2013, and Lt General Aslam resigns after he fails to become Pakistan Army Chief, The Economic Times,28 Nov, 2013,

50. Military-Intelligence-Militant Nexus in Pakistan: Fighting a War of Asymmetry against India. Sanjeeb Kumar Mohanty and Jinendra Nath Mahanty.

51. Pakistan's Armed Forces: Impact on the Stability of the State. Dhruv C Katoch, Journal of Defence Studies, Vol. 5 No. 4 October 2011

52. Fault Lines in Pakistan's Armed Forces: Impact on the Stability of the State. Dhruv C Katoch. Journal of Defence Studies. Vol. 5 No. 4 October 2011

53. The Menace That Is Lashkar-e-Taiba, Ashley J. Tellis. March 2012

54. Radicalisation of Pakistani Armed Forces. Alok Bansal, CLAWS, June 28, 2011

55. Pakistan's Internal and External Enemies. Yunis Khushi, International Relations Department, Lahore Garrison University, Pakistan, Submission: March 26, 2018; Published: September 05, 2018

56. Pakistan's Enduring Challenges. C. Christine Fair and Sarah J. Watson, University of Pennsylvania Press. 18 February 2015

57. India TV, 28 October 2015

58. Today Magazine, 11 Feb 2016

59. Pakistan Army: Coping with Internal Security Challenges, Brig Gurmeet Kanwal, CLAWS, August 24, 2013, http://www.claws.in/1066/pakistan-army-coping-with-internal-security-challenges-brig-gurmeet-kanwal.html. Pakistan's Internal Security Challenges: Will the Military Cope? 01 August, 2013-Issue Brief. http://www.ipcs.org/issue_select.php?recNo=526.

60. The Prospect of Nuclear Jihad in South Asia: Pakistan's Army, Extra-judicial Killings, and the Forceful Disappearance of Pashtuns and Balochs, Musa Khan Jalalzai, Algora Publishing, 01 Oct 2015.

61. Lashkar-e-Taiba: Evolving Into A Hybrid Entity? Brigadier Kuldip Singh, CLAWS, May 2017, http://www.claws.in/images/publication_pdf/2047051809_16_Lashkar-e-Taiba_Evolving_Into_A_Hybrid_Entity.pdf

62. Whose Army? Afghanistan's Future and the Blueprint for Civil War, Musa Khan Jalalzai, Algora Publishing, 01 Mar 2014

63 The Prospect of Nuclear Jihad in South Asia: Pakistan's Army, Extrajudicial Killings, and the Forceful Disappearance of Pashtuns and Balochs, Musa Khan Jalalzai, Algora Publishing, 01 Oct 2015.

Chapter 6

Pakistan Army, Forced Disappearance and Terrorism in Afghanistan

1. Pakistan's Internal Security Challenges: Will Military Cope? Issue Brief, The Institute of Peace and conflict Studies (IPCS), 06 August 2013

2. Defenders of human rights in Balochistan in need of defence, Angelika Pathak, August 2011, http://reliefweb.int/sites/reliefweb.int/files/resources/AHRC-PRL-035-2011-01.pdf

3. Dawn, 25 September 2017

4. The missing debate, I.A. Rehman, Dawn, September 10, 2017 1 Comment.

5. The United Nations counter-terrorism Complex: Bureaucracy, political Influence and Civil Liberties, United Nations, 23 February, 2017

6. Dawn, On 25 September 2017

7. Ibid

8. Indian Express 14 January, 2017

9. Amnesty international in its report of 2016/2017 noted serious violation of human rights in all provinces of Pakistan

10. Indian Express 14 January, 2017

11. The Guardian Tue 29 Mar 2011

12. Charles Pierson, Wall Street Journal, Counterpunch, 31 March, 2014

13. 12 December 2012 Amnesty International report

14. 1-Debating military courts: There is a disturbing nexus between military courts and enforced disappearances, Farhatullah Babar,

The Friday Times. 25 Jan 2019. https://www.thefridaytimes.com/tft/debating-military-courts/, and also SouthAsia Oneworld net, 28 December 2016

15. Country Reports on Human Rights Practices for 2011

16. Dawn, 28 August 2017

17. Ibid

18. The News International, 10 Sep 2017, Mr. Sher Ali Khalti noted important facts of missing persons in Baluchistan and Khyber Pakhtunkhwa provinces.

19. India Today 02 September 2016

20. Dawn, 25 August 2016

21. Samar Abbas, Enforced disappearances continue in Pakistan, International Press Agency, 16.July 2017

22. 30 August 2017, World Sindh Congress and Asian Human Rights Commission (AHRC), Voice of Baloch Missing Persons (VBMP) and Rights now joint report.

23. Dawn, 30 July 2017

24. Ibid

25. Enforced Disappearances and Extrajudicial killings of Workers in Pakistan, The Indian Panorama, 04 August 2017, https://www.theindianpanorama.news/unitedstates/enforced-disappearances-extra-judicial-killings-workers-pakistan/

26. The News, 30 July 2017, Amnesty International, 06 November 2017

27. Human Rights Commission of Pakistan Report, 2009

28. Ibid, and also US Department of State, 2009 Country Reports on Human Rights Practices, Report, 11 March 2010

29. The mass graves of Baluchistan, Malik Siraj Akbar, Huffpost, https://www.huffingtonpost.com/malik-siraj-akbar/the-mass-graves-of-baloch_b_5696642.html

30. Ibid

31. Ibid

32. Assassinations Decimate Pakistan's Tribal Leadership, May 06, 2014, https://gandhara.rferl.org/a/assassinations-decimate-pakistans-tribal-leadership/25374570.html, and also reported by; Foreign Affairs, How War Altered Pakistan's Tribal Areas: Cultural Change Comes to FATA, Umar Farooq, 06 October, 2017, https://www.foreignaffairs.com/articles/pakistan/2017-10-06/how-war-altered-pakistans-tribal-areas

33. November 2017, Dawn report

34. Ibid

35. Ibid

38. Dawn, 25 September 2016

37. Involvement of Pakistani Intelligence Agencies and the Army Generals in Extrajudicial Killings, Forced Disappearances and Terrorist Attacks in India and Afghanistan

38. Major Challenges For Pak Army 29 December, 2014, Manish Rai, The Times of Israel, http://blogs.timesofisrael.com/major-challenges-for-pak-army/

39. Musa Khan Jalalzai, The Afghan Intel crisis, 2017, New York

40. National Action Plan: Implementation Gaps & Successes, Shakeel Ahmed Ramay, Sustainable Development Policy Studies, October 2016).

42. Is Pakistan's National Action Plan Actually Working? Two years after Pakistan unveiled its strategy for fighting terrorism, the results are mixed. Zeeshan Salahuddin, the Diplomat, December 24, 2016.

43. Ibid

44. Pakistan's National Security Adviser on Counterterrorism: Lt. Gen. Janjua speaks about his strategy and his views on current progress in Pakistan's fight on terror. Zeeshan Salahuddin, April 07, 2017

45. Ibid

46. Pervez Musharraf forms 'Grand Alliance' of 23 political parties. The grand alliance named Pakistan Awami Ittehad (PAI) will be headed by 74-year-old Musharraf, while Iqbal Dar has been appointed as Secretary-General, 11 November 2017. http://www.freepressjournal.in/world/pervez-musharraf-forms-grand-alliance-of-23-political-

parties/1168747.Also, Countering Violent Extremism: Evaluating Pakistan's Counter Radicalization and De-radicalization Initiatives, Abdul Basit, IPRI Journal XV, no. 2. 2015

47. Security experts view these counter-measures as flawed and brutal for the reason that this unprofessional security approach cannot restore the confidence of minorities, ethnicities and political parties. The Afghan Intelligence crisis, Musa Khan Jalalzai, Algora, New York, 2017

48. The prospect of Nuclear Jihad in Pakistan, PP; 143

49. Ibid

50. Ibid

51. Pakistan's military is waging a quiet war on journalists: As activists and journalists are kidnapped, entire regions of the country are going silent. Kiran Nazish, 27 March 2018

52. The Afghan Intelligence Crisis, Musa Khan Jalalzai, New York, 2017

53. Ibid

54. Ibid

55. Role of Pakistan Police in Counterinsurgency, Hassan Abbas, Research Fellow, Belfer Centre, Harvard University, Brookings Counterinsurgency and Pakistan Paper Series, No. 5 Terrorism & Political Islam: Origin, Ideology, and Methods. A Counterterrorism Textbook, 2nd Edition, Erich Iviarquartd, and Christopher Heffelfinger https://www.aclu.org/files/fbimappingfoia/20111019/ACLURM000540.pdf

56. The Afghan Intel Crisis, Musa Khan Jalalzai

57. A Bullet has been chosen for you: Attacks on journalist in Pakistan. Amnesty International 2014, https://www.amnesty.org.uk/files/pakistan_journalists_300414.pdf

58. Agha Khaild, 29 August 2013, the News International Pakistan

59. The News International, 26 August 2013

60. Agency men found involved in kidnapping of traders. The News International, 29 August 2013, Pakistan. https://www.thenews.

com.pk/archive/print/632694-agency-men-found-involved-in-kidnapping-of-traders

61. Dawn, 01 April 2018

62. I.A Rehman, Dawn, 16 March 2017

63. Ibid

64. Dawn, 06 January 2017

65. Dawn, 12 October 2017

66. Ibid

67. Outlook India, 30 October 2017

68. The Unrepresented Nations and People Organization (UNPO), and the Frontline Defenders organizations condemned their disappearance, Pakhtunkhawa Times, 02 November 2017; Jalazai's book also reported it (The Prospect of Nuclear Jihad in Pakistan, Musa Khan Jalalzai, Algora Publishing, New York.

69. UNPO Strongly Condemns the Enforced Disappearance of Baloch Activists' Families. 02 Nov, 2017. The Unrepresented Nations and People Organization (UNPO) is an international, nonviolent and democratic membership organisation. American Friends of Baluchistan (AFB) statement on attacks on Baloch and Pashtun students on Punjab University campus, Lahore, 24 January 2018

70. South Asia Terrorism Portal, March 2017

71. Baloch leader claims abduction of women, children part of Pak propaganda, Hyrbyair Marri also said both China and Pakistan were trying to annihilate the Baloch nation to strengthen their grip on its soil. Deccan Chronicle, Nov 2, 2017, https://www.deccanchronicle.com/world/europe/021117/baloch-leader-claims-abduction-of-women-children-part-of-pak-propaganda.html. Baloch women, children abduction part of Pak's campaign of enforced-disappearances. Business Standard, November 2, 2017, http://www.business-standard.com/article/news-ani/baloch-women-children-abduction-part-of-pak-s-campaign-of-enforced-disappearances-117110200501_1.html

72. Ibid

73. States must put an end to widespread practice of enforced disappearances, International justice, 30 August 2017.

74. The Afghan Intelligence Crisis, Musa Khan Jalalzai, 2017, New York

75. Ibid

76. -Did Pakistani security agents kidnap bloggers to make a point? Pamela Constable Washington Post 14, 2017, https://www.washingtonpost.com/world/asia_pacific/did-pakistani-security-agents-kidnap-bloggers-to-make-a-point/2017/02/12/3f672d72-ed66-11e6-a100-fdaaf400369a_story.html?utm_term=.f1745c9c2267. Abducting social activists, Dr. Pervez, Hoodbhoy, Dawn 14 January, 2017, https://www.dawn.com/news/1308254

77. Indian Express, 10 September 2017

78. Dawn, 26 January 2018

79. Tribune India, 02 February 2018

80. Dawn, 26 January 2018

81. The News International, 26 January 2018

82. Ibid

83. Afghanistan Times Editorial: Pashtun Long March—soon to bear result 13 February, 2018

84. Dawn Investigation: Rao Anwar and the killing fields of Karachi: What kind of law-enforcement system accommodates and protects cops like the former Malir SSP? Fahim Zaman | Naziha Syed AliU, February 18, 2018

85. Daily Times, 19 February 2018

86. The Inter Services Intelligence (ISI) and Intelligence Bureau (IB) Support Terrorist Organizations in India, Afghanistan and Central Asia

87. Dawn, 14 August 2015

88. Ibid

89. Ibid

90. Dunya News, 14 August 2015

91. 26 September 2017, Dawn report

92. NDTV 26 September 2017

93. The news International, 26 September 2017

94. The Nation, 26 September 2017

95. Ibid

Chapter-7

Tongue-Lashing of Intelligence Sharing between the NDS and Pakistani Intelligence (ISI)

1. Vanda Felbab Brown article, Brooking, 5, 01 2018

2. The Diplomat, Samuel Ramani, December 22, 2018

3. Dawn, Shah Mahmood Statement, December 28, 12, 2018

4. The News International, 24 December 2018, Chief of Army Staff (COAS) General Qamar Javed Bajwa said that Pakistan supports Afghan-led peace plan to help bring lasting peace in the neighbouring state. On 05 January 2016, Abdul Manan Bhat also criticized nexus of Pakistan and Saudi Arabi and their role in promoting Salafist-Wahabi ideology

6. Dawn, Shah Mahmood Statement, December 28, 12, 2018

7. The Revenge of Geography: What the Map Tells Us about Coming Conflicts and the Battle Against Fate, Robert D. Kaplan, Tantor Media, Inc; Unabridged, 29 Oct. 2012

8. Robert Cassidy, 31 January, 2018, Modern Institute

9. Daily Times, 20 December 2018

10. Dawn, 26 December 2018

11. India Today Magazine, 18 October 2018

12. Ibid

13. Policy Analysis No. 849: Double Game: Why Pakistan Supports Militants and Resists U.S. Pressure to Stop, Sahar Khan, CATO Institute, 20 September, 2018,

14. Ibid

15. VOA, 16 10, 2018

16. The Battle for Ghazni: A Wake-Up Call? Ankit Panda. Diplomat, August 14, 2018

17. Daily Times, 25, December, 2018

18. The Afghan Intel Crisis, Musa Khan Jalalzai, New York 2017, Daily Outlook Afghanistan, May 2015, and Silent Warfare: Understanding the World of Intelligence, Abram N. Shulsky, Gary James Schmitt, Potomac Books, Inc, 2002.

19. Dawn, 19 May 2015

20. ToloNew, 24 May 2015

21. Diplomatic sources in Islamabad admitted that the issue was highlighted in talks between Lieutenant Gen Rizwan Akhtar, the Director General of the Inter-Services Intelligence (ISI), and Masud Andrabi, the Director General of Afghanistan's National Directorate of Security (NDS). ToloNews, 08 February 2016.

22. On 15 January 2018, NDS arrested a government employee in the western province of Herat for alleged spying for Iran. Jilani Farhad, the spokesman for Herat's governor, told RFE/RL that the man, identified as Assadullah Rezai, was detained and sent to Kabul for further investigation. ToloNews.

23. Iran's game plan in Afghanistan, Hassan Dai, Al Arabia, 17 January 2017

24. On 31 January 2018, Geonews reported Afghan Interior Minister, Intelligence Chief visited Islamabad for further cooperation between the two states.

25. 30 April 2018, the Guardian

26. Pakistan, Afghan military officials agree to work on roadmap for reconciliation in Afghanistan, Xinhua, 28 May, 2018

27. Sky News, 31 May 2017

28. Daily Pakistan, 11 July 2018

29. Afghanistan and Its Neighbors an Ever Dangerous Neighborhood, Professor Marvin G. Weinbaum, United States Institute of Peace, June 2006

30. On 18 August 2018, Pajhwok Afghan News reported NDS officials blamed ISI for its involvement in Ghazni City attack

31. Ibid

32. Ibid

33. The Guardian, 15 February 2015

34. Daily Times, 25 May 2015

35. Ibid

36. On May 23, 2015, Mr. Doval said that the memorandum was based on a faulty assumption: "What Pakistan wanted was to get an assurance and put pressure on Afghanistan so that it will not allow its territory to be used for any security related work by India.

37. Khaama Press 24 May 2015

38. Pakistan Today 27 June 2015

39. Hindustan Times, 19 May 2015

40. ToloNews, 18 May 2015

41. Hindustan Times, 19 May 2015

42. Dawn, 19 May 2015

43. Dawn, 04 February 2016

44. On 08 August 2015, a truck bomb killed 400 civilians in Kabul due the NDS failure to intercept a monition laden truck on the border, ToloNews

45. 01 February 2016, Pajhwok News

46. 07 February 2016, Khaama Press

47. ToloNews, 29 March 2016

48. Ibid

49. VoA News, 11 November 2016

50. Long War Journal, 07 September 2015

51. Khaama Press, 10 December 2015

52. Ibid

53. Loss Angeles Times, 18 February 2016

54. Ibid

Chapter-8

Decoding Afghan Security Forces' Failures and Fixing Afghanistan's Struggling Security Forces, By:Ghulam Farooq Mujaddidi.

Chapter-9

Torture, Illegal Detention and Sexual Harassment of Detainees in NDS Private Prisons

1. Clark, Kate: Torture, Illegal Armed Groups: Signs of Possible Afghan Government Action?, 22. February 2013.

2. United Nations Assistance Mission in Afghanistan Office of the United Nations High Commissioner for Human Rights February 2015 Kabul, Afghanistan

3. The UK Home Office Country Information and Guidance Afghanistan: Prison conditions Version 1.0 September 2015

4. US Department of State, Country Report on Human Rights Practices 2014, Afghanistan, 26 June 2015, Section 1c. Prison and Detention Centre Conditions

5. United Nations Assistance Mission in Afghanistan Office of the United Nations High Commissioner for Human Rights February 2015 Kabul, Afghanistan

6. he UNAMA report on the treatment of conflict-related detainees in Afghan Custody: Accountability and Implementation of Presidential Decree 129. Afghanistan Annual Report 2014, Protection of Civilians in Armed Conflict', 25 February 2015.

7. Amnesty International Report, 2015-2016

8. Finding Patterns through Documentation: Reconstructing the History of Torture and Cruel, Inhuman and Degrading Treatment of Detainees in Afghanistan, Patricia Gossman, War Crimes Research

Office, March 2014, American University Washington College of Law.

9. UNAMA, Detainee 394, NDS Spin Boldak, December 2013 and Detainee No-202, April 2014

10. Ibid

11. Ibid

12. Ibid

Postscript

1. Global Research, 28 January 2018

2. A resurgent Russia sets its sights on Asia: Moscow is regaining much of what it lost in Asia, a new drive for power that overtly targets the US while delicately cutting into China's position and interests, Bertil Lintner Chiang Mai, Asia Times, 26 Janaury, 2019

3. China and Russia build anti-US 'axis,' but Moscow has concerns: The relationship between the two powers has huge implications for the world, Asia Nikkei, Hiroyuki Akita, July 11, 2018

4. A Strategic Alliance in the Making? The American Interest, 11 September 2018, Brian Fonseca and DavidJ.Kramer,https://www. the-american-interest.com/2018/09/11/a-strategic-alliance-in-the-making/.

5. Russian, Chines Intelligence: IS Starting Invasion to Central Asia. Andrey Afanasyev, 21 May 2018, Geopolitical Russia, https://www. geopolitica.ru/en/article/russian-chinese-intelligence-starting-invasion-central-asia-covered-us

6. Can Russia Help Bring Peace to Afghanistan? Sabir Ibrahimi, Centre on International cooperation, November 02, 2018, https://cic.nyu. edu/news/Can-Russia-Help-Bring-Peace-to-Afghanistan.

7. Daily Times, 17 January 2017

8. Ibid

9. Ibid

10. The Afghan Intel Crisis, Musa Khan Jalalzai, 2017

11. Ibid

12. Ibid

13. ToloNews, 26 January 2019

14. Taliban's Unreasonable Bargain is an Obstacle before Fruitful Talks, Hujjatullah Zia, 20 December 2018, http://outlookafghanistan.net/topics.php?post_id=22498

15. Ibid

16. Ibid

17. Daily Times, 28 August 2913

18. Outlook, July 2015

19. Daily Times, December 2015

20. Daily Times, October 2016

Bibliography

Adams, Mark and Mark Bradbury, 1995, Conflict and Development: Organisational Adaptation in Conflict Situations; An Oxfam working Paper, Oxford.

Afghan people dialogue on peace: building and foundations for an Inclusive Peace Process. Local Roadmap for Peace.10 June 2014 UNAMA Office Kabul, Afghanistan

Ahmad Javid. 2018. The Major Flaws in Afghanistan's Intelligence War: The United States needs an honest reassessment of Afghanistan's defence capabilities as it ramps up its combat-training role. National Interests

Afghan people dialogue on peace: building and foundations for an Inclusive Peace Process. Local Roadmap for Peace.10 June 2014 UNAMA Office Kabul, Afghanistan

Agha H. Amen. David J. Ossineke Paul Andre Deterges. 2010. The Development of Taliban Factions in Afghanistan and Pakistan: A Geographical Account. Edwin Millen

Agfa H. Amen. David J. Ossineke Paul Andre Deterges. 2010. The Development of Taliban Factions in Afghanistan and Pakistan: A Geographical Account. Edwin Millen

Ball, Nicole and Tammy Halevy 1996, Making Peace Work: The Role of International Development Community; Overseas Development Council USA.

Barakat, Sultan and Arne Strand 1995, Rehabilitation and Reconstruction of Afghanistan: A Challenge Afghans, NGOs and the UN Disaster Prevention and Management; Volume 4 No.1 MCB University Press UK.

Barakat, Sultan, Mohammed Ehsan and Arne Strand 1995, NGOs and Peace Building in Afghanistan; Workshop Report University of York UK.

Brian Glyn William. 2011. Afghanistan Declassified: A Guide to America's Longest War, University of Pennsylvania Press.

Brown Wahid and Don Rasher. 2012. Fountain of Jihad: The Haqqani Nexus. 1973-2010. Hurst & Co. London

Beer, A. Francis 1990, The Reduction of War and The Creation of Peace A Reader In Peace Studies; Edited by Smoker, et al. Pergamon Press Oxford UK.

Bokhari, Imtiaz H.1995, Internal Negotiations among Many Actors: Afghanistan--Elusive Peace; Negotiating an End to Civil Wars; Edited by Zartman William I. The Brookings Institution.

Boyc, James K. 1999, Reflection: Comparative Peace Processes in Latin America; edited by Cynthia J.Aronson ; Woodrow Wilson Center Press USA.

Brown Wahid and Don Rasher. 2012. Fountain of Jihad: The Haqqani Nexus. 1973-2010. Hurst & Co. London

Bashir, Shahzad and Robert D. Crews. 2012. under the Drones: Modern Lives in the Afghanistan-Pakistan Borderlands. Harvard University Press

Barry, Michael. 2006. A History of Modern Afghanistan. Cambridge University Press

Bashir, Shahzad and Robert D. Crews. 2012. under the Drones: Modern Lives in the Afghanistan-Pakistan Borderlands. Harvard University Press

Rubin Barnett R. 2015. Afghanistan from the Cold War through the War on Terror, New York and Oxford University Press

Barry, Michael. 2006. A History of Modern Afghanistan. Cambridge University Press

Clark Kate. 2018. How to end the Afghan War? Afghanistan analysis Network, Kabul

Coll Steve. 2018. Directorate S: The C.I.A. and America's Secret Wars in Afghanistan and Pakistan New York: Penguin Press

Crews, Robert D. and Tarzi, Amin. 2008. The Taliban and the Crisis of Afghanistan. Harvard University Press

Collins Joseph J. 2016. Understanding war in Afghanistan, Create Space Independent Publishing Platform

Dimitrakis Panagiotis. 2013. The Secret War in Afghanistan: The Soviet Union, China and Anglo-American Intelligence in the Afghan War, I.B Tauris

Davis Anthony 1998, "How the Taliban Became A Military Force-Fundamentalism Reborn" in Afghanistan and the Taliban, edited by Maley William New York University Press USA.

Davies Philip H. J and Kristian C. Gustafson. 2013, Intelligence Elsewhere: Spies and Espionage Outside the Anglo-sphere, Georgetown University Press, Washington.

Emadi, Hafizullah. 2010. Dynamics of Political Development in Afghanistan: The British, Russian, and American Invasions. Palgrave Macmillan.

Ehrhart Hans Georg. 2012. Afghanistan in the Balance: Counterinsurgency, Comprehensive approach and Political Order. McGill-Queen's University Press

Fraser David Major General, Brian Hanington, Mcclelland & Stewart 2018. Operation Medusa: The Furious Battle that Saved Afghanistan from the Taliban

Fair C. Christine. 2014. Fighting to the end: Pakistan's army Way of War Oxford University Press

Forsberg, Carl. 2009. "The Taliban's Campaign for Kandahar. Afghanistan Report, Institute for the Study of War

Gera Y K Maj General. 2010. Peace and stability in Afghanistan:

The Way Ahead, Vij books India

Giustozzi Antonio 2018. The Islamic State in Khorasan: Afghanistan, Pakistan and the New Central Asia

Gill Peter Stephen Marrin and Mark Phythian. 2009. Intelligence Theory: Key Questions and Debates, Studies in Intelligence series, Routledge, 2009

Gill Peter and Mark Phythian. 2006. Intelligence in an Insecure World, , Polity Press UK 2006

Giustozzi, Antonio. 2009. Empires of Mud: Wars and Warlords of Afghanistan, Hurst Publishers London

Gurr, Ted Robert 1993, Minorities at Risk: A Global View of Ethnopolical Conflicts; United States Institute of Peace Press, Washington D.C. USA.

Halliday, Fred 1990, Cold War: A Reader In Peace Studies; edited by Smoker et al. Pergamon Press Oxford UK.

Harpviken, Kristian. 2009. Social Networks and Migration in Wartime Afghanistan. Basingstoke: Palgrave Macmillan.

Hanifi Shah Mahmood. 2012. Power Hierarchies and Hegemony in Afghanistan: State Building, Ethnic Minorities and Identity in Central Asia. IB Tauris

Harpviken, Kristian Berg, 1997, Transcending Traditionalism: The Emergence of Non-State Military formations in Afghanistan, Journal of Peace Research Vol.34 No.3 Peace Research Institute Oslo and SAGE Publication UK.

Harpviken, Kristian Berg, 1999, Feature Review of Two titles on Afghanistan Third World Quarterly; Volume 20, No.4, CARFAX Publishing UK.

Ismail, Ahmed I. and Reginald Green Herbold 1999, Rehabilitation, Sustainable Peace and Development Towards Reconceptualisation, Third World Quarterly, Volume 20 No.1 CARFAX Publishing UK.

Ibrahimi, Niamatullah. 2009. 'Divide and Rule: State Penetration in Hazarajat from Monarchy to the Taliban. Working Paper No: 42, series 2.

Jadoon Amira Nakissa Jahanbani, and Charmaine Willis. 2018. Challenging the ISK Brand in Afghanistan-Pakistan: Rivalries and Divided Loyalties, Combating Terrorism Centre, Vol 11 Issue 4

Jackson Paul. 2003. 'Warlords as Alternative Forms of Governance. Small Wars & Insurgencies, Vol 14, No. 2

Jalalzai Musa Khan. 2014. Whose Army? Afghanistan's Future and the Blueprint for Civil War, Musa Khan Jalalzai, Algora Publishing New York, USA

Jowett. Adam.2018. No Way Out: The Searing True Story of Men under Siege. Sidgwick & Jackson Ltd

Johnson Thomas H. 2018. Taliban Narrative: The use and Power of Stories in the Afghanistan Conflict. Oxford University Press

Jack Fairweather. Jonathan Cape. 2014. The Good War: Why We Couldn't Win the War or the Peace in Afghanistan

Johnson, Thomas H. and Ahmad Waheed. 2011. 'Analyzing Taliban taranas (chants): an effective Afghan propaganda artefact', Small Wars & Insurgencies, Vol. 22, No.1.

Johnson, Thomas H. and M. Chris Mason. 2008. 'No sign until the Burst of Fire: Understanding the Pakistan-Afghanistan Frontiers. International Security, Vol. 32, No. 4.

Jalalzai Musa Khan, The Afghan Intel Crisis, New York, 2017

Khan, Riaz M. 2011. Afghanistan and Pakistan: Conflict, Extremism, and Resistance to Modernity. John Hopkins University Press

Kumar Radha and Dnyanada Palkar.2014. Afghanistan and its neighbours, Regional View. Delhi Policy Group Publication

Lieven Anatol. 2018. Peace in Afghanistan: The Duty of Afghanistan's Region. Russia in Global Affairs, Moscow Russia

Mujaddidi.Ghulam Farooq 23 June, 2017. Decoding Afghan Security Forces' Failures: Afghanistan's woefully unprepared intelligence and security agencies are as much of a problem as cross-border terrorism, The Diplomat.

Mishra Anant. 2018. Strengthening Afghanistan's National Directorate of Security: Is it Equipped to Counter 'Emerging' Threats?, Small War Journal, http://smallwarsjournal.com/jrnl/art/strengthening-afghanistans-national-directorate-security-it-equipped-counter-emerging.

McVeigh Karen. 02 August 2017. US plan to improve Afghan intelligence operations branded a $457m failure: Pentagon's use of taxpayers' money under scrutiny after special watchdog finds contracts to train and mentor Afghan soldiers fell short of stated objectives. The Guardian.

Nojumi, Neamatollah, Dyan Mazurana, Elizabeth Stites. 2008. After the Taliban: Life and Security in Rural Afghanistan. Rowman & Littlefield Publishers

Nojumi, Neamatollah. 2016. American State Building in Afghanistan and its Regional Consequences: Achieving Democratic stability and Balancing China's Influence, Lanham, MD: Rowman & Littlefield,

Nardin Terry 1998, The Comparative Ethics of War and Peace in The Ethics of War and Peace; Religious and Secular Perspectives edited by Terry Nardin; Princeton University Press USA.

Omarkhail Ihsanullah, 21 May 2018. Afghan security sector in dire need of reform, Asia Times,

O'Connell, James 1994, Can Peace Be Studied? A Lecture Delivered at the Annual Assembly of the Oxford Project for Peace Studies, Paper 37 UK.

O'Connell, James 1991, Teaching About Peace Concept: Peace Research Report No.27: Department of Peace Studies University of Bradford UK.

O'Connell, James 1989, Making The Future: Thinking and Acting About Peace in Contemporary Britain; Trentham Books UK.

Qassem, Ahmad Shayeq. 2009. Afghanistan's Political Stability: A Dream Unrealized. Ashgate Publisher London

Rais, Rasul Bakhsh. 2008. Recovering the Frontier Stage: War, Ethnicity, and State in Afghanistan. Lexington Books

Riecke Henning Riecke, Henning. 2012. Partner for Stability: Involving Neighbours in Afghanistan Reconstruction-Transatlantic Approaches. Nomos Publishers

Robert O'Neill, 2017. The Operator: Firing the Shots that Killed Osama Bin Laden and my years as a SEAL Team Warrior, Simon & Schuster

Saikal Amin.2011. The Afghanistan Conflict and Australia's Role, Melbourne University Press

Stepanova Ekaterina. 2018. Russia's Afghan Policy, in the Regional and Russia-West Context., Russia/NIS Centre

Sedra Mark. 12 Nov, 2013. China's Political Institutions and Leaders in Charts, Susan V. Lawrence, Congressional Research Service

Snow Shawn. 2017. Chinese troops appear to be operating in Afghanistan, and the Pentagon is OK with it, , Military Times

Seerat Rustam Ali. 2015. China's Role in Afghan-Taliban Peace Talks: Afghan Perspectives Research Intern, Institute of Chinese Studies

Shahrani. M. Nazif. 2018. Modern Afghanistan: The Impact of 40 years of War. Indiana University Press

Saikal Amin. 2016. Afghanistan and its Neighbours after the NATO Withdrawal (Contemporary Central Asia: Societies, Politic and Cultures), Lanham, MD: Lexington Books

Shahrani.M. Nazif. 2018 Modern Afghanistan: Impact of 40 Years War. Indiana University Press

Safi Khalilullah and Rutting Thomas. 27 June 2018. Understanding Hurdles to Afghan Peace Talks: Are the Taliban a Political Party? Afghanistan Analysts Network

Sultan Barakat and Zyck S.2010. 'Afghanistan's insurgency and the Viability of political Solution, Studies in Conflict and Terrorism, Vol. 33, No. 3.

T.Robert Fowler Dundurn. 2016. Combat Mission Kandahar: The Canadian Experience in Afghanistan. Dundurn

Theo Farrell. 2017. Unwinnable Britain's War in Afghanistan, 2001-2014, Bodley Head, Penguin Books Limited.

Theo Farrell. 2017. Unwinnable Brittan's War in Afghanistan. 2001-2014. Bodley Head Penguin Books Limited

Thomas Joscelyn. 30 May 2018. Long War Journal

Zabihullah Noori. 25 July 2017. The West on the Brink of Failure In Afghanistan, ToloNews

Zaeef Abdul Salam. 2010. My Life with Taliban. Edited by Alex Strick van Linschoten and Felix Kuehn, Hurst and Columbia University Press

Newspapers and Journals

Global Security Studies, spring 2013, Vol-4, Issue-2, University of North Carolina Wilmington, USA

Reforming Afghan intelligence agencies, Musa Khan Jalalzai, Daily Times, 23 December 2014

On 23 April 2012, The Christian Science Monitor

Musa Khan Jalalzai, Daily Times, 23 December 2014

Pajhwok Afghan News, 27 December 2015

Musa Khan Jalalzai, Daily Times, 26 January 2016

The Politics of Intelligence in Afghanistan, Daily Times, 06 January 2015

ToloNews, 25 March 2016

Intelligence Sharing, Musa Khan Jalalzai, Daily Times, 09 February 2016,

07 February 2016, Khaama Press reported the arrest of some ISI agents in Badakhshan province, ToloNews 01 February 2016

Intelligence Sharing, Musa Khan Jalalzai, Daily Times, 09 February 2016,

Musa Khan Jalalzai, Daily Times, 26 January, 2016

Weak Intelligence Capabilities Hinder Afghan Mission, Shawn Snow, January 28, 2016

Why the NDS Matters: The Emergence of the Afghan Intelligence Agency after 9/11. Diva Patang Wardak, Journal of Intelligence and Terrorism Studies, 2017

Mark Sedra. 12 Nov, 2013. China's Political Institutions and Leaders in Charts, Susan V. Lawrence, Congressional Research Service

Decoding Afghan Security Forces' Failures, Diplomat, Ghulam Farooq Mujaddidi, June 23, 2017

ToloNews, 11 March 2017.

The Major Flaws in Afghanistan's Intelligence War, Javid Ahmad, February 12, 2018

US plan to improve Afghan intelligence operations branded a $457m failure, Karen McVeigh, Guardian, 2 Aug 2017

Afghan security sector in dire need of reform, Ihsanullah Omar Khail, Asia Times, MAY 21, 2018

Decoding Afghan Security Forces' Failures, Diplomat, Ghulam Farooq Mujaddidi, June 23, 2017

Strengthening Afghanistan's National Directorate of Security (NDS): Is it equipped to counter 'emerging' threats? Anant

Mishra, Modern Diplomacy February 27, 2018

War Against the Taliban: Why It All Went Wrong in Afghanistan. Sandy Gall, Bloomsbury. 2013

The IRIN report, 27 February 2012

Dawn, 24 June 2015

The Guardian, 30 April 2013

The Role of MI6, ISI, CIA and Iran in Afghanistan and region crisis, Alhaj Ghulam Jilani Wahaj, Khaama Press, 19 March 2013

Afghanistan, War and Peace in Afghanistan: A Brief Survey of NATO's Intelligence Services in Afghanistan, Nikita Mendkovich, 03 January 2011

Express Tribune, 25 June 2015

Dawn, 13 February 2015

Index

U

United Nation Assistance Mission in Afghanistan (UNAMA) 11

Uzbekistan xviii, 2, 3, 6, 7, 25, 43, 149

V

Voice for the Baloch Missing Persons (VBMP) 75

Voice of America xi, 190

W

Wahhabi group 86

Wazarat-e-Amniat-e-Daulati (WAD) 43

Wolfowitz Doctrine 33, 36

Z

Zainabia Brigade 57

Zai-ul Haq 76

www.ingramcontent.com/pod-product-compliance
Lightning Source LLC
Chambersburg PA
CBHW031933090426
42811CB00002B/174